Following the Call

Following the Call

Living the Sermon on the Mount Together

Compiled and edited by

Charles E. Moore

PLOUGH PUBLISHING HOUSE

Published by Plough Publishing House
Walden, New York
Robertsbridge, England
Elsmore, Australia
www.plough.com

Plough produces books, a quarterly magazine, and Plough.com to encourage people and help them put their faith into action. We believe Jesus can transform the world and that his teachings and example apply to all aspects of life. At the same time, we seek common ground with all people regardless of their creed.

Plough is the publishing house of the Bruderhof, an international Christian community. The Bruderhof is a fellowship of families and singles practicing radical discipleship in the spirit of the first church in Jerusalem (Acts 2 and 4). Members devote their entire lives to serving God, one another, and their neighbors, renouncing private property and sharing everything. To learn more about the Bruderhof's faith, history, and daily life, see Bruderhof.com. (Views expressed by Plough authors are their own and do not necessarily reflect the position of the Bruderhof.)

ISBN: 978-1-63608-004-8

Front cover image by John M Lund Photography Inc/Getty Images

A catalog record for this book is available from the British Library.

Library of Congress Cataloging-in-Publication Data

Names: Moore, Charles E., 1956- editor.
Title: Following the call : living the Sermon on the mount together / compiled and edited by Charles E. Moore.
Description: Walden, New York : Plough Publishing House, [2021] | Includes bibliographical references and index. | Summary: "Fifty-two readings about The Sermon on the Mount designed to be read together with others, to discuss what it might look like to put these radical teachings into practice today"-- Provided by publisher.
Identifiers: LCCN 2021020622 (print) | LCCN 2021020623 (ebook) | ISBN 9781636080048 (paperback) | ISBN 9781636080055 (ebook)
Subjects: LCSH: Sermon on the mount--Criticism, interpretation, etc.
Classification: LCC BT380.3 .F65 2021 (print) | LCC BT380.3 (ebook) | DDC 241.5/3--dc23
LC record available at https://lccn.loc.gov/2021020622
LC ebook record available at https://lccn.loc.gov/2021020623

Nothing but the whole Christ, for the whole of life,
will change and renew everything.

EBERHARD ARNOLD
Salt and Light

CONTENTS

PART II

Kingdom Commands
(MATTHEW 5:17–48)

PART III

Kingdom Devotion
(MATTHEW 6:1–18)

Introduction

"WHEN CHRIST CALLS a man, he bids him come and die." These unforgettable words of the German martyr Dietrich Bonhoeffer express a fundamental truth: when Jesus calls us, our old life comes to an end and something new begins. That something, however, is not necessarily what we expect or what we want. Jesus' message is as unsettling as it is clear: "If anyone would come after me, he must deny himself and take up his cross daily and follow me." What does this entail? What does it mean to hear Jesus' voice and follow him?

There is no better place to start than to hear what Jesus says in the Sermon on the Mount. It is, as Harvey Cox states, "the most luminous, most quoted, most analyzed, most contested, and most influential moral and religious discourse in all of human history." The Sermon on the Mount includes many of the best-known scriptures in the Bible. Who isn't familiar with the Beatitudes? The Lord's Prayer? The Golden Rule? The command to love one's enemy? Or such vivid expressions as "Ask and it will be given to you, seek and you will find"?

The Sermon on the Mount possesses an irresistible, compelling quality. At the same time, who hasn't felt uneasy after reading Jesus' words? "By all means," Gandhi once wrote, "drink deep of the fountains that are given to you in the Sermon on the Mount, but then you will have to take sackcloth and ashes." Perhaps this is why Walter Kaufmann argues that Christianity is simply "the ever renewed effort to get around these sayings without repudiating Jesus." But the Sermon on the Mount is all but impossible to ignore. Jesus' words get to the root of the human condition. This is one reason why so much ink has been spilt over it, and why this collection exists.

This collection is unique in several respects. First, it consists of a range of voices from various traditions and time periods. In this way one can glean wisdom from outside one's own tradition. Second, this book is neither a commentary nor a devotional. Its thrust is prophetic, propelling readers toward putting Jesus' teachings into practice in their lives. Finally, this book is designed to be read slowly and carefully *with others*. The selections have been chosen to engage and inspire communities of faith. Toward that end there is a discussion guide at the back with reflection questions for each chapter. Jesus spoke to his disciples collectively, often responding to their questions. His aim was to form a band of followers who would put into practice what he said, and he painted a picture for them of such a community. Like the prophets, Jesus cast a vision of the coming age and exhorted his disciples to order their lives around its virtues.

The picture Jesus paints of God's kingdom community comes in the form of one long teaching, which has pride of place as the first of five major teaching discourses in the Gospel of Matthew. Matthew 5–7 is more than a collection of miscellaneous sayings. Though Jesus may not have delivered this sermon word for word in one sitting, it is the kind of talk he gave to those who had dropped everything to follow him and were wondering, "What next?"

In broad strokes, the Sermon consists of three sections. The first (5:3–16) comprises blessings and details the character of citizens of God's kingdom. The overarching theme of the second section (5:17–7:12) is the greater righteousness of the kingdom in relation to the Law of Moses, whether the subject is religious devotion or various social obligations. The Sermon is then rounded off by an epilogue (7:13–27) with warnings and a challenge to put these words into practice.

One thing that stands out throughout the Sermon is Jesus' use of language and images. The Sermon is masterfully poetical and also richly pictorial. Jesus refers to salt, light, a city on a hill, a splinter and a plank, two kinds of gates and two kinds of houses. He describes ordinary people and everyday life: a beggar on the roadside, a Roman official, a pious Pharisee, a local builder, a thief, a judge. The sights and sounds of nature – sun and rain, wind and flood, thistle and thorn, vine and figs, birds and moths, dogs and swine, sheep and wolves – help us visualize what life in the kingdom is like. Finally, Jesus' style is proverbial. He expresses truths and principles in a simple yet provocative way, often using vivid, hyperbolical language. He doesn't mean for us to literally cut off one of our hands if it causes us to sin, but he makes his point and uses startling language to ram it home.

The pictures and examples Jesus gives not only cast a vision of God's new kingdom of righteousness, peace, and love; they compel us to respond. When reading the Sermon on the Mount we can't just nod our heads. Jesus aims to jolt his listeners into a new frame of reference, a vision of life that radically alters everything. His followers have not always remembered this, falling into arguments over what he meant and diluting what he said with qualifying commentary.

During different periods of church history, the pendulum has swung back and forth between the belief that Jesus' teachings are fully realizable and the view that they are conditional and only partially realizable.

Are Jesus' teachings realistic, or possible to achieve, or relevant for today? How far can they be applied? What does it mean to live them out – personally, interpersonally, in various spheres of life and society? If we cannot take literally everything Jesus says, then is it better to just understand his words figuratively? Did Jesus bring a new law, more radical and far-reaching than the old, or was his focus mostly on the condition of the heart?

Part of the problem is that we live in the tension between two poles: the new order that God wants to bring about, which becomes possible in Christ, and the existing fallen order, of which we are still a part. All the more we should strive to grasp Jesus' original intention. The approach taken here views the Sermon on the Mount in terms of what life in the kingdom of God is like among those who have heeded the call to discipleship. Jesus intended his followers to put his words into practice individually and together, bearing witness to the in-breaking of his kingly rule here and now. The following three motifs, embedded in the Sermon itself, bear this out.

The Kingdom of God

THE HORIZON AND GOAL of the Sermon on the Mount is the kingdom of God – wholehearted, total, single devotion to the rulership of God. In Jesus' teachings, God's kingdom is not a place but the revolutionary effect of God reigning among his people here on earth. This kingdom is not an ethic or an ideal. Rather, it is a reality in which God's future breaks into our midst.

Jesus' words about a kingdom were inflammatory. One need only remember his execution and the reason given: "This is Jesus the King of the Jews." Announcing the arrival of another kingdom in a province governed by Rome was daring and provocative. There existed only one recognized political authority. The Romans tolerated no contender and were quick to squelch any rebellion or would-be messiah who might restore independence to the Jewish people.

Jesus' message also upended some of the Jews' expectations of who the Messiah would be and what he would do. In Jesus' kingdom, the poor and slaves are given dignity and all who pledge themselves to Jesus are brothers and sisters. It doesn't look much like a kingdom. It comes into being internally, hidden from sight in the lives of individuals. From there it flows out to others, binding them in relationship, but does not rest on power structures or any kind of top-down organization.

Jesus' message was more than a prophetic indictment of the existing order. It was ultimately good news. Matthew places accounts of Jesus' miracles right before and right after the Sermon. Jesus' words regarding God's reign are spoken against the backdrop of his works of healing. His commands belong to his gifts. The one who preached repentance is also the one through whom the power of evil and sin is broken. Jesus thus launches a new movement that both threatens and promises to change everything. His message is one of liberation, not so much from an empire or a religious system as from the bonds of sin, power, injustice, and death that give rise to exploitation and dehumanization.

A Contrast Community

THE SERMON ON THE MOUNT is neither an ethic for society in general nor an ideal of perfection for the individual. It makes no sense to view it as a universal code or pattern for all people to live by. When separated from Jesus, his teachings float in midair and can mean virtually anything. As Albert Schweitzer warns, expounding Jesus' words as though they were bound to win universal acceptance "is like trying to paint a wet wall with pretty colors. We first have to create a foundation for the understanding." Granted, the crowds were free to listen, but Jesus' focus was on his disciples. As John Stott writes in his book *Christian Counter-Culture*:

> The standards of the Sermon are neither readily attainable by every man, nor totally unattainable by any man. To put them beyond anybody's reach is to ignore the purpose of Christ's Sermon; to put them within everybody's is to ignore the reality of man's sin. They are attainable all right, but only by those who have experienced the new birth. . . . "Make the tree good, and its fruit will be good."

Jesus came to gather those who are ready to leave their old lives to join him on a new path. That he aims his remarks specifically at his disciples is shown by the fact that he calls them, in particular, "salt and light." His followers are different. They love their enemies, pray simply, give generously, and don't judge others. They know their need for God and are prepared to suffer for Jesus' sake.

These disciples, however, are not just a bunch of individuals. They are different because Jesus forms them into a distinct *community*. Plural pronouns are used throughout the Sermon on the Mount. The Lord's Prayer, for example, is a communal prayer, not a personal one. Jesus' warnings against wealth and worry presuppose practices of radical sharing, and his instructions about genuine worship presume unhindered brotherly and sisterly fellowship. When Jesus calls people to himself, a new kind of community is born. Life in God's kingdom means being a certain kind of people together. That is the essential mark and purpose of the church. The church's witness is the communal embodiment of the Sermon. It therefore serves as a contrast to society and does so by practicing righteousness and justice in every relationship and deed. Such a social witness is never established with the force of arms or won at the expense of bloodshed. Instead, Jesus gets at the root of what oppresses each person and what divides society in general. He confronts the destructive forces that break apart human relations: pride, anger, lust, envy, falsehood, retaliation, judgment, and unforgiveness. More importantly, he provides the antidote to these: a lowly way of love that leads to peace.

Jesus' disciples make up, in the words of the apostle Paul, a "new humanity," which includes people who by the world's standards should be mutually antagonistic but who are now reconciled and belong to one another (Eph. 2:11–22). Jews and Gentiles, for example, become comrades in a life together in which God's justice and peace are realized. This truly revolutionary order is the context in which to comprehend and live out the Sermon on the Mount.

A New Possibility

GOD'S NEW ORDER, however, is not some kind of alternative social blueprint. The Sermon on the Mount is not an

ideology. Jesus' message must be understood in the light of
who he is and why he came. Jesus himself *is* the in-breaking
of God's kingdom in person. As God's anointed one, he
is the king of the kingdom. Jesus himself is the content of
his sayings. He is not only the master teacher and the best
example of his own teaching, he demonstrates in his life
the very presence and power of God's future. Jesus' every
imperative – "Turn the other cheek," "Love your enemy," and
so forth – is rooted in his spirit-filled life. In heeding his call,
his followers are empowered by the same spirit to live out a
new possibility.

That new possibility involves matters of the heart as well as
the actions that follow. It is within the individual human heart
that the transformation begins. And yet deeds always follow.
Indeed, Jesus placed great emphasis on *doing* his word. Living
out his commands and the state of one's heart go hand in hand.
Jesus does not separate the outer and inner, the personal and
social. He is always concerned with the *whole* person.

Does this mean we can fully implement the Sermon on
the Mount? Yes, if we understand it against the horizon of
God's grace and his reign. No, if we treat it as some kind of
ethic we are obliged to live up to. The moment Jesus' words
are severed from his healing and invigorating power, they lose
their true significance. As Eberhard Arnold reminds us, the
Sermon on the Mount "is not a high-tension moralism" but
rather "the revelation of God's real power in human life. . . . It
is like a flame that shines, like the sap that pulses through a
tree. It is life." Jesus does not *impose* intolerable demands on us.
"If we take our surrender to God seriously," Arnold goes on,
"and allow him to enter our lives as light, as the only energy
which makes new life possible, then we will be able to live the

new life." Those who respond to Christ's call and willingly place themselves under his lordship will find in the Sermon on the Mount a priceless treasure full of wisdom, guidance, and assurance.

Though hard on the flesh, Jesus' words capture the qualities, actions, and attitudes of the citizens of God's new order. If a Roman soldier forces them to carry his pack one mile, they carry it two miles. Jesus calls us to turn every such situation around. Who knows what might happen? God's peace might just be advanced on earth.

The Sermon on the Mount can be as daunting as it is appealing, exciting but also sobering. In reading the following selections, we must remember that Jesus did not come to impose anything on us; he came to redeem, not condemn! Jesus does not call us to some "impossible possibility." No, he gives witness to the fact that God is able to meet our deepest longings for righteousness, mercy, peace, and love. Yes, Jesus calls us to pick up our cross daily, but in doing so we find life. "It is enough," Jesus says, "for the disciple to be like the teacher." By hearing Christ's call in his teaching, and then doing what he says in the strength of the promised Spirit, we will find our lives resting on solid rock and receive a foretaste of even greater things to come. ◆

Kingdom Character

The Beatitudes cannot be taken apart. They portray the heart of the people of the kingdom – a heart whose veins cannot be dissected and pulled to pieces. Because of this, the Beatitudes begin and end with the same promise of possessing the kingdom of heaven. Those who are blessed are characterized by their poverty and neediness, longing, hunger, and thirst. At the same time, they possess wealth in love, energy for peace, and victory over all resistance. . . . These are people of inner vision, who see the essential. They bear the world's suffering.

EBERHARD ARNOLD, *Salt and Light*

THE BEATITUDES are a summary of the entire Sermon, shorthand for what is to come. They describe Jesus himself, who is poor in spirit, a mourner, meek and lowly, hungry for righteousness, merciful, pure in heart, and a peacemaker who suffers for the right. And they depict the character of those who strive to follow Jesus. The Beatitudes show the effect God's kingdom has upon anyone who submits to Christ's rule.

With familiarity, the Beatitudes may have lost their original shock value. It's as if Jesus were to say to us today: blessed are the ugly, the deformed, the repulsive. Blessed are the dropouts, the losers, the abandoned, the incurably ill. And in a world that prizes a trouble-free life, Jesus tells his disciples to rejoice in their own persecution.

But is it not the rich who are blessed, the carefree who are happy, the assertive and aggressive who get ahead? Doesn't the "good life" consists of getting what you want? Not according to Jesus. To be meek, poor in spirit, merciful, and peace-loving is the key to happiness. Appearances to the contrary, the poor in spirit, those who mourn, those who thirst and hunger for righteousness are already experiencing God's kingdom. Through such people God can work and accomplish his will. They, not the religious elite or the powerful or the highly esteemed, play the decisive role in God's redemptive history.

Such a life will invariably look foolish. Nevertheless, the Beatitudes are a declaration that a certain way of being leads to human flourishing. Jesus assures us that following him, that living as citizens of God's kingdom, will not be in vain; his disciples are on the path that leads to life. ◆

I

Master Teacher

❖ ❖ ❖ ❖ ❖

Now when Jesus saw the crowds, he went up on a mountainside and sat down. His disciples came to him, and he began to teach them.

Matthew 5:1

E. Stanley Jones

THE SERMON ON THE MOUNT is practicable, for the man who first spoke these words practiced them, and the practicing of them produced a character so beautiful, so symmetrical, so compelling, so just what life ought to be, that he is as inescapable in the moral realm as the force of gravity is in the physical.

The words of the Sermon must be interpreted in the light of that face. Jesus puts a new content into old words by the illustration of his own life. In interpreting the Sermon on the Mount we have often applied methods of historical criticism and have taken words to mean what they meant in an Old Testament or in a contemporaneous setting. We may gain much for this method, but we may also entirely miss the point and reduce the whole to an echo of scattered sayings out of the past. His hearers did not feel that way about it, for they were struck with the utter newness of what he was saying: "They were astonished at his teaching: for he taught them as one having authority, and not as their scribes."

You may point to parallel sayings in the past, and yet when you do, you miss the central thing here, for the central thing was the aroma about the words, the contagion of his moral person, the sense of depth that came from the fact that he spoke them – and illustrated them. He was not presenting a new set of laws, but demanding a new loyalty to his person. The loyalty to his person was to be expressed in carrying out the things he embodied. He was the embodiment of the Sermon on the Mount, and to be loyal to him meant to be loyal to his way of life. . . .

There is a "beyondness" in the Sermon on the Mount that startles and appalls the legalistic mind. It sees no limit to duty – the first mile does not suffice, he will go two; the coat is not enough, he will give the cloak also; to love friends is not enough, he will love enemies as well. Come to that with the legalistic mind and it is impossible and absurd; come to it with the mind of the lover and nothing else is possible. The lover's attitude is not one of duty, but one of privilege. Here is the key to the Sermon on the Mount. We mistake it entirely if we look on it as the chart of the Christian's duty; rather, it is the charter of the Christian's liberty – his liberty to go beyond, to do the thing that love impels and not merely the thing that duty compels. The fact is that this is not a law at all, but a lyre, which we strike with the fingers of love in glad devotion. This glad, joyful piety is the expression of a love from within and not the compression of a dull law from without.

Put the Man who spoke these words into the background and look only at the sayings and they become as lofty as Himalayan peaks – and as impossible. But put the warm touch of his reinvigorating fellowship into it, and anything – everything – becomes possible. ◆

Henri J. M. Nouwen

THE WHOLE MESSAGE of the gospel is this: become like Jesus. We have his self-portrait. When we keep that in front of our eyes, we will soon learn what it means to follow Jesus and become like him.

Jesus, the Blessed One, is poor. The poverty of Jesus is much more than an economic or social poverty. Jesus is poor because he freely chose powerlessness over power, vulnerability over defensiveness, dependency over self-sufficiency. As the great "Song of Christ" so beautifully expresses: "[He] did not count equality with God something to be grasped. But he emptied himself . . . becoming as human beings are" (Phil. 2:6–7). This is the poverty of spirit that Jesus chose to live.

Jesus calls us who are blessed as he is to live our lives with that same poverty.

Jesus, the Blessed One, is gentle. Even though he speaks with great fervor and biting criticism against all forms of hypocrisy and is not afraid to attack deception, vanity, manipulation, and oppression, his heart is a gentle heart. He won't break the crushed reed or snuff the faltering wick. He responds to people's suffering, heals their wounds, and offers courage to the fainthearted. . . .

Jesus, the Blessed One, mourns. Jesus mourns when his friend Lazarus dies; he mourns when he overlooks the city of

Jerusalem, soon to be destroyed. Jesus mourns over all losses and devastations that fill the human heart with pain. He grieves with those who grieve and sheds tears with those who cry. The violence, greed, lust, and so many other evils that have distorted the face of the earth and its people cause the Beloved Son of God to mourn. We too must mourn if we hope to experience God's consolation.

Jesus, the Blessed Son of God, hungers and thirsts for uprightness. He abhors injustice. He resists those who try to gather wealth and influence by oppression and exploitation. His whole being yearns for people to treat one another as brothers and sisters, sons and daughters of the same God.

With fervor he proclaims that the way to the kingdom is not saying many prayers or offering many sacrifices but in feeding the hungry, clothing the naked, and visiting the sick and the prisoners. He longs for a just world. He want us to live with the same hunger and thirst.

Jesus, the Blessed Child of God, is merciful. Showing mercy is different from having pity. Pity connotes distance, even looking down upon. When a beggar asks for money and you give him something out of pity, you are not showing mercy. Mercy comes from a compassionate heart; it comes from a desire to be an equal. Jesus didn't want to look down on us. He wanted to become one of us and feel deeply with us. . . .

Jesus, the Beloved of God, has a pure heart. Having a pure heart means willing one thing. Jesus wanted only to do the will of his heavenly Father. Whatever Jesus did or said, he did and said it as the obedient Son of God: "What I say is what the Father has taught me; he who sent me is with me and has not left me to myself, for I always do what pleases him" (John 8:28–29). There are no divisions in Jesus' heart, no double motives or secret intentions. In Jesus there is complete inner unity because of his complete unity with God. Becoming like Jesus is growing into purity of heart. That purity is what gave Jesus and will give us true spiritual vision.

Jesus, the Blessed Child of the Father, is a peacemaker. His peace doesn't mean only absence of war. It is not simply harmony or equilibrium. His peace is the fullness of well-being, gratuitously given by God. Jesus says, "Peace I leave to you, my own peace I give you, a peace which the world cannot give, this is my gift to you" (John 14:27).

Peace is shalom – well-being of mind, heart, and body, individually and communally. It can exist in the midst of a war-torn world, even in the midst of unresolved problems and increasing human conflicts. Jesus made that peace by giving his life for his brothers and sisters. This is no easy peace, but it is everlasting and it comes from God. Are we willing to give our lives in the service of peace?

Jesus, the favorite Child of God, is persecuted. He who is poor, gentle, mourning; he who hungers and thirsts for uprightness; is merciful, pure of heart, and a peacemaker is not welcome in this world. The Blessed One of God is a threat to the established order and a source of constant irritation to those who consider themselves the rulers of this world. Without accusing anyone he is considered an accuser, without condemning anyone he makes people feel guilty and ashamed, without his judging anyone those who see him feel judged. In their eyes, he cannot be tolerated and needs to be destroyed, because letting him be seems like a confession of guilt.

When we want to become like Jesus, we cannot expect always to be liked and admired. We have to be prepared to be rejected. ◆

2

Good News

◆ ◆ ◆ ◆ ◆

Jesus went throughout Galilee, teaching in their synagogues,
proclaiming the good news of the kingdom, and healing every
disease and sickness among the people.

Matthew 4:23

Christoph Friedrich Blumhardt

JESUS SPOKE ABOUT the kingdom of heaven, and
he was filled with a mighty spirit, the spirit of the rule of
God. It raised a storm among his listeners when he said:
"Repent! Become quite a different person! Everything must
change. The kingdom of heaven is at hand!" That is, leave all
your preoccupations, give up all that has influenced you till
now, and give up every power that has gripped you. A new kind
of power is taking over. A new monarch is on the throne. A
new king has assumed his reign. You shall have a new lord over
you. The old is passing away and a new time is coming.

It must have been a powerful spirit in Jesus that made the
people shout, as with one voice, "What is that?" This spirit

made them believe him and trust themselves to the man from whom came the message for which many had been waiting. "That is he! That is the one through whom the almighty God is bringing in a new rulership, a new kingdom – that is he!" (John 6:14)

Although Christ spoke of human matters, what he said was not at all acceptable to the earthly authorities. What he said was natural enough, yet it was much more. His teaching was not against human nature, but it did bring something of the divine into human affairs, something heavenly into the natural world. Indeed, it was as if earth would become paradise. People ate bread in the wilderness, where there had been none, and in place of sickness, health was given. Even those who had died were given new life. Joy came in all its fullness where there had been suffering and mourning.

All this took place in the most commonplace experiences of human life. No thrones were demolished, no special parties formed, no statues were erected – everyone continued in his own house and his own place. But everyone, especially the poorest, had access now to something quite other, something from heaven, from God himself. When the kingdom of heaven comes close to us we experience something totally new. Into the life of each individual something amazingly alive comes. God's will is for life, for what is good, free, genuine, eternal.

This is how the kingdom announces itself: the rulership of God is not visible through words alone, nor does it emerge from a different religious understanding, but it consists in deed and in truth (John 3:21). People become different because they are now living under a different rulership. This rulership is not a human government but the authority that comes from heaven into our hearts. And since it proclaims life, we are for life. Since this divine dominion rules by righteousness, we become righteous. In Jesus Christ, the Son sent by God, life on earth becomes fundamentally new. Such transformation does not come from your own efforts as you imagine. No, it comes through the strength and grace of God. The deeds of God come to us and a new world is built up through the strength and sheer joy in life: "The kingdom of heaven is at hand! Rise up and get going – away with all other dominion. Let God be your Lord!" This is what it means.

Is this still true for today? Sadly, almost two thousand years have passed and the world is still asleep. Instead of the reign of God, a Christian religion has been established. In the course of time, it has become accepted that there is but one God, the Father; one Lord, Jesus Christ. Right up to this day, the Creator is recognized – and that is good. But the world is still sleeping under a canopy. Under this or that beautiful church roof every kind of dominion, other than God's, has crept in. Today we are subservient to many different authorities. Some of us are directed in one way, others in another. . . . But where is the reign of God?

There are also demonic empires: dominions of death; the rulership of avarice, which is rooted in money; and then all the need and poverty – yes, the need – which drives people to greed and envy and fear. And so we stand again before the question: "Is the kingdom of heaven imminent?" Can we dare to say today, "Be on the watch, all of you! The kingdom is really on the way"? It has not come in nineteen hundred years; truly, it is proclaimed in the gospel, promised by God. But here we are again, subject to so many alien powers, all of them worthless compared with the rulership of God. Will it come one day?

"Yes! The kingdom will indeed come. Watch for it!" How dare I say this? Is it foolhardy of me to say this? No! I am completely certain of it, absolutely sure. Now is the time when

we have to say, "Watch out, everyone. A new reign is about
to begin." God's rule will dissolve all other authorities, even
those we have so far taken to be good. But don't be afraid; the
kingdom of heaven is coming! In today's decisive time, amid
so much disharmony, dejection, commotion, where the urge is
to put oneself first and in the center, to take the lead, to push
agendas through, and for each party or group to be pitted
against the other, each wanting to be in control – just in this
day the kingdom of heaven is again drawing near. Today God
wants to rule, and he is already making a beginning. Doubtless, in the time of Jesus it was a matter for derision when he
said, "It is beginning today!" Today too, many people mock
any proclamation that Jesus will establish his kingdom – but
many also understand. Yes indeed, today is again a decisive
hour! We must be equipped for the rulership of God, and this
will not disgrace us.

We should love nothing more than to fulfill the justice of
God, not in church services (which often attract people as
honey attracts flies) but rather in our daily lives, wherever we
are. That is when we have to work zealously for the commandments of God and his truth, yes, his rights; there we must
show our hunger and thirst for righteousness; there we must
prove whether or not we want God. We cannot prove that
in our churches alone but must do it outside, in the fields, in
business, in daily life, in your family – you husband, you wife,
and you children. Together, we have to look out for the rights
of God. . . . We must gather together again. Who will come
under God's rulership – who?

God is not looking for heroic figures – wonderful
people – who captivate others with their charisma. It must
have been quite baffling to the educated world when Jesus
pronounced, "Blessed are the poor in spirit" – blessed are the

uneducated, those who do not try to understand everything
with their intellect! Blessed are they who do not have to
impress others by showing how smart they are. Blessed are they
who are not always theorizing about spiritual things. What
Jesus is saying is that it is the day laborers who are blessed,
those who live from hand to mouth and yet are skilled with
their hoe or pickax. Blessed are the farm workers with their
plow, who can't think much about anything except how best
to do their work. Blessed are the craftsmen who create their
handicraft and work hard to finish it on time but do not have
time to read many books. Blessed are all such people whom we
label uneducated – for these people are taught by God.

The kingdom of heaven belongs to such as these, those who
are poor in spirit – for it is these who understand God, for they
live according to their hearts. The others live according to
their heads and thus cannot be used. They are too concerned
about what might happen and don't leave the Father freedom
to act. Therefore, those people are blessed who remain as children toward the Father in everything life brings them and
do not set themselves up to be superior, as though the good
fortune of the world lay in that. Praise God that true wisdom
is to be found upon the streets and not in palaces and lecture
halls (1 Cor. 1:18–25). . . .

This is why each person must become poor and remain so,
so that it can never be said to anyone: "First you must acquire
this or that, or else we can't make use of you!" In God's
kingdom only one thing is required: a complete turnabout. If
you are wealthy, let go of those ridiculous possessions! Say to
yourself, "I will not let my money rule me. I won't envy those
who have much. I want only the lordship of God!" If you are
poor, turn completely away from your poverty. "I won't let
cares and sorrows rule me. I want God to rule, also in my

greatest suffering. God will help me again. I will remain under his leadership."

So when you hear about God's kingdom, be true to it; that is the only thing required of us. Be faithful. Where alien influences creep in – away with them – we want God alone! Let nothing else have dominion; everything depends on this. ◆

3

Foolish Wisdom

• • • • •

Blessed are you who are poor, for yours is the kingdom of God.

Blessed are you who hunger now, for you will be satisfied.

Blessed are you who weep now, for you will laugh.

Blessed are you when people hate you, when they exclude you and insult you and reject your name as evil, because of the Son of Man.

Rejoice in that day and leap for joy, because great is your reward in heaven. For that is how their ancestors treated the prophets.

   Luke 6:20–23

Virginia Stem Owens

WHEN I ASSIGNED my freshman English class "The Sermon on the Mount," a selection in their rhetoric textbook taken from the King James Version, I had expected them to have at least a nodding acquaintance with the reading and to express a modicum of piety in their written responses. After all, Texas has always been considered at least marginally part of the Bible Belt.

The first paper I picked up began, "In my opinion religion is one big hoax." I was mildly surprised since this came from a student who had never expressed a single iconoclastic notion the entire semester. I glanced at the opening sentence of the next paper: "There is an old saying that 'you shouldn't believe everything you read' and it applies in this case."

All right, I thought. Maybe this is just a fluke. I reached for the third paper. "It is hard to believe something that was written down thousands of years ago," it began. "In the Bible Adam and Eve were the first two people and if they were then where did black people come from? Also the Bible says nothing about dinosaurs and I think God would of mentioned them."

I put down my red pen. This was no fluke. What I had here was a major trend.

It was not, of course, the loose-jointed logic nor the minimalist approach to spelling and punctuation that surprised me. Although as a teacher I might feel duty-bound to probe their syllogisms and circle their misspellings, the question that I was personally interested in was, Why were these students (a) so angry at what they had read, and (b) so blithe in their dismissal of it? My own introduction to the Sermon on the Mount as a child in Sunday School had been accompanied by pastel poster illustrations of Jesus sitting, like a patient Mister Rogers, on a green hillside surrounded by eager, pink children. It had never occurred to me either to be angry or to turn away from such a scene.

As I read on, the answer to the first part of my question became clear. To wit:

"The stuff the churches preach is extremely strict and allows for almost no fun without thinking it is a sin or not."

"I did not like the essay 'Sermon the Mount.' It was hard to read and made me feel like I had to be perfect and no one is."

"The things asked in this sermon are absurd. To look at a woman is adultery? That is the most extreme, stupid, un-human statement that I have ever heard."

At this point I began to be encouraged. There is something exquisitely innocent about not realizing you shouldn't call Jesus stupid. This was not exactly intellectual agnosticism talking here, usually the perceived foe of the faith. It was just down-home hedonism. It was Herod watching Salome dance. It was the disciples asking "Who then can be saved?" when Jesus deflated their dreams of wealth with the needle's eye. This was the real thing, a pristine response to the gospel, unfiltered through a two-millennia cultural haze.

In fact, the anger was preferable to the blithe dismissal of the text I found in other papers.

"Many believe that this sermon should be taken literally. I believe, on the other hand, that, because the scriptures have been interpreted from so many different languages, we should use them as a guide – not law. Another fallback is that certain Beatitudes are irrelevant to current life-styles. Loving your enemies, for instance, is obviously not observed by the majority today."

Unfortunately, I have yet to come across a student who sees any logical contradiction between this morality-by-consensus stance and their favorite proverb. *Who's to say? It's different things to different people.*

In another paper, however, one which also relied on the irrelevancy premise, I found the most disconcerting assessment of all.

"In this essay the author explains the doctrines of an era in the past which cannot be brought into the future in the same context. This essay now cannot be taken the same way it was written. It can be used as a guideline for good manners."

Good manners! Was this all that remained of the old-fashioned piety I had expected? The Sermon on the Mount reduced to suggestions by Emily Post? . . .

So what do I make of these responses? First of all, I now understand why, in literature classes, one has to explain the simplest biblical allusions, even references to Jonah and the whale or Noah and the ark. Beyond that, however, I find it strangely heartening that, except for the young man who found the Sermon on the Mount a guide to good manners, the Bible remains offensive to honest, ignorant ears, just as it was in the first century. For me, that somehow validates its significance. Whereas the scriptures almost lost their characteristically astringent flavor during the past century, the current widespread biblical illiteracy should catapult us into a situation more nearly approximating that of their original, first-century audience. The Bible will no longer be choked by cloying cultural associations. ◆

Frederick Buechner

IF WE DIDN'T already know but were asked to guess the kind of people Jesus would pick out for special commendation, we might be tempted to guess one sort or another of spiritual hero – men and women of impeccable credentials morally, spiritually, humanly, and every which way. If so, we would be wrong. . . . It's worth noting the ones he did pick out.

Not the spiritual giants, but the "poor in spirit," as he called them, the ones who spiritually speaking have absolutely nothing to give and absolutely everything to receive, like the Prodigal telling his father "I am not worthy to be called thy son," only to discover for the first time all he had in having a father.

Not the champions of faith who can rejoice even in the midst of suffering but the ones who mourn over their own suffering because they know that for the most part they've brought it down on themselves, and over the suffering of others because that's just the way it makes them feel to be in the same room with them.

Not the strong ones but the meek ones in the sense of the gentle ones, that is, the ones not like Caspar Milquetoast but like Charlie Chaplin, the little tramp who lets the world walk over him and yet, dapper and undaunted to the end, somehow makes the world more human in the process.

Not the ones who are righteous but the ones who hope they will be someday and in the meantime are well aware that the distance they still have to go is even greater than the distance they've already come.

Not the winners of great victories over evil in the world but the ones who, seeing it also in themselves every time they comb their hair in front of the bathroom mirror, are merciful when they find it in others and maybe that way win the greater victory.

Not the totally pure, but the "pure in heart," to use Jesus' phrase, the ones who may be as shopworn and clay-footed as the next one but have somehow kept some inner freshness and innocence intact.

Not the ones who have necessarily found peace in its fullness but the ones who, just for that reason, try to bring it about wherever and however they can – peace with their neighbors and God, peace with themselves.

Jesus saved for last the ones who side with heaven even when any fool can see it's the losing side and all you get for your pains is pain. Looking into the faces of his listeners, he speaks to them directly for the first time. "Blessed are you," he says.

You can see them looking back at him. They're not what you'd call a high-class crowd – peasants and fisherfolk for the most part, on the shabby side, not all that bright. It doesn't look as if there's a hero among them. They have their jaws set. Their brows are furrowed with concentration.

They are blessed when they are worked over and cursed out on his account, he tells them. It is not his hard times to come but theirs he is concerned with, speaking out of his own meekness and mercy, the purity of his own heart. ◆

John Dear

I F WE WANT to take Jesus' Beatitudes and Sermon on the Mount seriously, we had best first confess our preference for the false teachings of the culture of violence and war and renounce them once and for all. I call these false spiritual teachings "the anti-Beatitudes," "the anti–Sermon on the Mount." Here they are in a nutshell:

Blessed are the rich.

Blessed are those who never mourn,
who cause others to mourn.

Blessed are the violent, the oppressors,
those who dominate others or run
the domination system.

Blessed are those who hunger and thirst for injustice.

Blessed are those who show no mercy.

Blessed are the impure of heart.

Blessed are the warmakers.

Blessed are those who are never persecuted, who never struggle for justice, who never rock the boat on behalf of the poor and disenfranchised, who are never insulted because of their allegiance to the nonviolent Jesus.

These anti-Beatitudes undergird the spirituality of violence and war that fuels our culture. If we imagine the opposite of what Jesus teaches, it may help us gain a little more clarity and insight into his teachings. As we ponder the culture's "anti-Beatitudes," we realize how profoundly we have bought into the culture of violence, how deeply its false teachings have penetrated our minds and hearts, and how strongly we resist what Jesus has to say. ◆

4

Blessedness

• • • • •

Blessed are you . . .
Matthew 5:3–11

James C. Howell

THE AMERICAN Declaration of Independence submits we have an "unalienable right" to the "pursuit of happiness." How fascinating, then, that Jesus never said, "Blessed are the happy."

They seem blessed! Robert Schuller even wrote a book on the Beatitudes with the catchy, alluring title *The Be Happy Attitudes*. Nothing wrong with happiness! And many Bible versions, with lexicographical backing and sound reasoning, have translated the Greek work *makarios* at the beginning of each of Jesus' Beatitudes not as "blessed" but as "happy." The danger, I suspect, is that the word "happy" has gotten so watered down, so trivialized, so shredded into confetti, that the "happiness" we pursue has virtually nothing to do with what Jesus had in mind when he said "blessed." . . .

The translation itself is not wrong, but we need to beware: ancient people did not harbor a superficial, "fun"-oriented view of happiness, or of being blessed. Robert Wilken summarizes the difference:

> For us the term *happiness* has come to mean "feeling good" or enjoying certain pleasures, a transient state that arrives and departs as circumstances change or fortune intervenes. For the ancients, happiness was a possession of the soul, something that one acquired and that, once acquired, could not easily be taken away. Happiness designated the supreme aim of human life ... living in accord with nature, in harmony with our deepest aspirations as human beings.

Many Americans hear the word "happy" very differently. We fancy the notion of Jesus smiling and providing tips on "how to be happy," and would be disappointed should Jesus not give us a boost in our very Americanized "pursuit of happiness."

But as you have pondered the Beatitudes you may have noticed a couple of problems. Those who are poor, who mourn, who are meek, and who are persecuted and reviled don't sound very "happy," do they? And if it is true that we identify happiness with "fun" (Are my children happy? = Are my children having fun? Is my marriage happy? = Are we having fun?), then doesn't the very question "Am I happy?" derail us from Jesus' path? "Am I happy?" asks about *me*, and turns me in on myself; but isn't Jesus interested in us opening ourselves outward to God and to others? "Happiness" is something I pursue; happiness is up to me. But Jesus' Beatitudes are about what we cannot achieve, what we cannot make happen, what we can only receive as the most startling of gifts. ...

So to be "blessed" isn't catchy advice on how to go and be happy; rather, "blessed" is being swept up in God's decisive

movement in the world. "It's about something that's starting
to happen, not about a general truth of life. It is *gospel*: good
news, not good advice." (N. T. Wright) . . .

But doesn't Jesus really want me to *do* something – to
be poor in spirit? and pure in heart? and to get busy with
peacemaking or purity of heart? Implicitly, yes, Jesus is recom-
mending a way of life, a posture we should assume, habits
we should practice until they are second nature in our lives.
And yet the way we think about this way of life, these habits,
is tricky. Subtly I may calculate to behave a certain way to
get Jesus *for me!* But "whoever would save his life will lose it"
(Mark 8:35). The gift of the Beatitudes is kin to another curious
thought from Jesus: "Do not let your left hand know what your
right hand is doing" (Matt. 6:3). How much more wonderful is
it to be drawn in, almost when we weren't looking? A promise
was uttered, and in response to our good fortune we simply
nodded spontaneously. If I begin to be poor in spirit or meek,
if I hunger and thirst for righteousness or become more pure in
heart, I am startled, and can think of nothing to say but "It is
no longer I who live, but Christ who lives in me" (Gal. 2:20). ◆

Kathy Escobar

ESCENT GOES against my basic nature of
wanting a controlled, predictable, upwardly mobile
kind of life, not only for me but also for my family. I
know from experience that it is far more comforting to be part
of a culture where everyone is focused on building security and
safety. The magnetic pull "up" is strong. However, I continue
to learn how most of Jesus' teachings have a wild, paradoxical

twist: in the kingdom of God, somehow, *down means up*. Much of my previous Christian experience was focused on rising up to be closer to God; now, I'm learning that downward is what draws me nearer to God. When I am with my friends in the darkness and pain, I am acutely aware of God's presence more than in my comfortable places. . . .

Downward mobility is about discovering and revealing what it means to live into the kingdom of God as a Christ-follower. The guiding text for a life of descent is the Beatitudes in Matthew 5:3-12. These passages inspire us toward a better way. Jesus' words of blessing to the poor, marginalized, and downwardly mobile were not a threat or a coercion technique to force us into a miserable life. His call to go downward is a methodology for the abundant life. It is the easier yoke. If we crave God's peace and presence, then I guess we have to trust his methods too. It's easy to think more money, power, or status will give us security and a stronger sense of self, yet Jesus says it will be exactly the opposite: *to find our lives we need to lose them* (Matt. 10:39).

In fact, the more we read the Gospels, allowing the Beatitudes to sink into our bones and be sewn into our skin, the more we realize that there's really nowhere else to go but down.

Down into the mess of real life.

Down into the ugly places of the human experience.

Down into the places where real people in need of God's hope live.

Almost everything I was taught in much of my initial church experience was completely contrary to this. I was taught to:

Pull myself up by my bootstraps, believe more, and figure out a way to be strong.

Not feel too much because pain is somehow bad.

Find ways to rise to the top.

Run with the pack and do not question what they tell me to believe.

Believe that God helps those who help themselves.

Pray harder, memorize more scripture, and keep asking for forgiveness "just in case" there was something still offensive in my heart.

Separate myself from the real world and surround myself with other people like me so that I would be protected from harm. . . .

It is critically important to acknowledge just how prevalent, powerful, and damaging these completely-contrary-to-the-Beatitudes messages really are. . . . It's what Jesus was always working against. It's what we'll always be working against. . . .

As I engage the downward path, I discover that the power systems of the world are inherently inconsistent with the ways of the kingdom, the upside-down kind of living Jesus espouses. Descent is the harder but more meaningful journey. We are battling not only our own fears and inadequacies, but also deeply grooved systems of inequality and power in a culture that thrives on success and strength.

Jesus told us his ways were harder. He said that to follow him meant we were going to have to give up everything familiar, that people would think we were crazy, that we'd be poor, persecuted, and rejected, and that we'd lose our security and so many other things we held dear. At the same time, he told us we'd also find life. ✦

Francis of Assisi

L ET US CONSIDER, my dear brethren, what our
vocation is. It is not only for our own salvation that
God has called us by his mercy, but it is for the salvation of many others. It is in order that we should exhort all
the world, more by example than by words, to do penance and
to keep the divine precepts. We are looked upon as senseless
and contemptible, but let not this depress you; take courage,
and be confident that our Lord, who conquered the world,
will speak efficaciously through you. . . . Go then, and exhort
people to do penance for the remission of their sins, and for
peace. You will find some among the faithful mild and good,
who will receive you with pleasure and willingly listen to you.
Others, on the contrary, people without religion, proud and
violent, will censure you and be very hostile to you. But make
up your minds to bear all this with humble patience, and let
nothing alarm you. In a very short time many learned and
noble persons will join themselves to you, to preach to kings,
to princes, and to nations. Be therefore patient in tribula-
tions, fervent in prayer, and fearless in labor. Be unassuming
in speech, be grave in your manner, and grateful for the favors
and benefits you may receive. The kingdom of God, which is
eternal, will be your reward. I entreat the one and only God,
who lives and reigns in three persons, to grant it to us, as he
doubtless will grant it to us, if we are faithful to fulfil all that
we have voluntarily promised. ◆

5

Poverty of Spirit

◆ ◆ ◆ ◆ ◆

Blessed are the poor in spirit,
for theirs is the kingdom of heaven.
   Matthew 5:3

Philip Yancey

WHY WOULD GOD *single out the poor for special attention over any other group?* I used to wonder. What makes the poor deserving of God's concern? I received help on this issue from a writer named Monika Hellwig, who lists the following "advantages" to being poor:

1. The poor know they are in urgent need of redemption.

2. The poor know not only their dependence on God and on powerful people but also their interdependence with one another.

3. The poor rest their security not on things but on people.

4. The poor have no exaggerated sense of their own importance, and no exaggerated need of privacy.

5. The poor expect little from competition and much from cooperation.

6. The poor can distinguish between necessities and luxuries.

7. The poor can wait, because they have acquired a kind of dogged patience born of acknowledged dependence.

8. The fears of the poor are more realistic and less exaggerated, because they already know that one can survive great suffering and want.

9. When the poor have the gospel preached to them, it sounds like good news and not like a threat or a scolding.

10. The poor can respond to the call of the gospel with a certain abandonment and uncomplicated totality because they have so little to lose and are ready for anything.

In summary, through no choice of their own – they may urgently wish otherwise – poor people find themselves in a posture that befits the grace of God. In their state of neediness, dependence, and dissatisfaction with life, they may welcome God's free gift of love.

As an exercise I went back over Monika Hellwig's list, substituting the word "rich" for "poor," and changing each sentence to its opposite. "The rich do not know they are in urgent need of redemption. . . . The rich rest their security not on people but on things." (Jesus did something similar in Luke's version of the Beatitudes, but that portion gets much less attention: "But woe to you who are rich, for you have already received your comfort.")

Next, I tried something far more threatening: I substituted the word "I." Reviewing each of the statements, I asked myself if my own attitudes more resembled those of the poor or of the rich. Do I easily acknowledge my needs? Do I readily depend on God and on other people? Where does my security rest? Am I more likely to compete or cooperate? Can I distinguish between necessities and luxuries? Am I patient? Do the Beatitudes sound to me like good news or like a scolding?

As I did this exercise I began to realize why so many saints voluntarily submit to the discipline of poverty. Dependence, humility, simplicity, cooperation, and a sense of abandon are qualities greatly prized in the spiritual life, but extremely elusive for people who live in comfort. There may be other ways to God but, oh, they are hard – as hard as a camel squeezing through the eye of a needle. In the great reversal of God's kingdom, prosperous saints are very rare.

I do not believe the poor to be more virtuous than anyone else (though I have found them more compassionate and often more generous), but they are less likely to *pretend* to be virtuous. They have not the arrogance of the middle class, who can skillfully disguise their problems under a façade of self-righteousness. They are more naturally dependent, because they have no choice; they must depend on others simply to survive.

I now view the Beatitudes not as patronizing slogans but as profound insights into the mystery of human existence. God's kingdom turns the tables upside down. The poor, the hungry, the mourners, and the oppressed truly are blessed. Not because of their miserable states, of course – Jesus spent much of his life trying to remedy those miseries. Rather, they are blessed because of an innate advantage they hold over those more comfortable and self-sufficient. People who are rich, successful, and beautiful may well go through life relying on their natural gifts. People who lack such natural advantages, hence under-qualified for success in the kingdom of this world, just might turn to God in their time of need.

Human beings do not readily admit desperation. When they do, the kingdom of heaven draws near. ◆

Eberhard Arnold

A NOTHER THING concerns me very much: the powerlessness of man, even of the man who has been entrusted with some task. Only God is mighty; we are completely powerless. Even for the work that has been given us, we are wholly without power. We cannot fit even one single stone into the church community. We can provide no protection whatsoever for the community when it has been built up. We cannot even devote anything to the cause by our own power. We are completely without power. But I believe that just this is the only reason why God has called us for this service: we know we are powerless. . . .

It is hard to describe how all our own power must be stripped off us, how our own power must be dropped, disman-tled, torn down, and put away. . . . That is not attained so easily and does not happen through a single heroic decision. It must be done in us by God.

This is the root of grace: the dismantling of our own power. Only to the degree that all our own power is dismantled will God go on effecting the results of his Spirit and the construc-tion of his cause through us, in us, and among us – not otherwise. If a little power of our own were to rise up among us, the Spirit and authority of God would retreat in the same moment and to the corresponding degree. In my estimation that is the single most important insight with regard to the kingdom of God. How it actually happens is hard to say. It is as hard to speak of this as it is to speak of the mystic source of all things. The only thing that can be said is that the Holy Spirit produces effects that are deadly for the old life and that at the same time have a wakening and rousing power for the new life which comes from Christ and his Holy Spirit alone.

Let us use this day to give glory to God. Let us pledge to him that all our own power will remain dismantled, and will keep on being dismantled among us. Let us pledge that the only thing that will count among us will be the power and authority of God in Jesus Christ through the Holy Spirit; that it will never again be we that count, but that God alone will rule and govern in Christ and the Holy Spirit. That means we declare our dependence upon grace. This is the testimony we are required to give. ◆

Dorothy Day

"PRECARITY," OR precariousness, is an essential element in true voluntary poverty, a saintly priest from Martinique has written us. "True poverty is rare," he writes. "Nowadays religious communities are good, I am sure, but they are mistaken about poverty. They accept, admit, poverty on principle, but everything must be good and strong, buildings must be fireproof. Precarity is everywhere rejected, and precarity is an essential element of poverty. This has been forgotten. Here in our monastery we want precarity in everything except the church. These last days our refectory was near collapsing. We have put several supplementary beams in place and thus it will last maybe two or three years more. Someday it will fall on our heads and that will be funny. Precarity enables us better to help the poor. When a community is always building, enlarging, and embellishing, there is nothing left over for the poor. We have no right to do so as long as there are slums and breadlines somewhere."

Over and over again in the history of the church the saints have emphasized poverty. Every religious community, begun in poverty and incredible hardship, but with a joyful acceptance of hardship by the rank-and-file priests, brothers, monks, or nuns who gave their youth and energy to good works, soon began to "thrive." Property was extended until holdings and building accumulated; and although there was still individual poverty in the community, there was corporate wealth. It is hard to remain poor. ◆

6

Mourning

· · · · ·

Blessed are those who mourn,
for they will be comforted.
Matthew 5:4

Nicholas Wolterstorff

WHO ARE THE MOURNERS? The mourners are those who have caught a glimpse of God's new day, who ache with all their being for that day's coming, and who break out into tears when confronted with its absence. They are the ones who realize that in God's realm of peace there is no one blind and who ache whenever they see someone unseeing. They are the ones who realize that in God's realm there is no one hungry and who ache whenever they see someone starving. They are the ones who realize that in God's realm there is no one falsely accused and who ache whenever they see someone imprisoned unjustly. They are the ones who realize that in God's realm there is no one who fails to see God and who ache whenever they see someone unbelieving. They are the ones who realize that in God's realm there is no one who suffers oppression and who ache whenever they see someone beat down. They are the ones who realize that in God's realm there is no one without dignity and who ache whenever they see someone treated with indignity. They are the ones who realize that in God's realm of peace there is neither death nor tears and who ache whenever they see someone crying tears over death. The mourners are aching visionaries. ◆

Rabindranath Tagore

THAT THERE COULD be any gap in the unbroken procession of the joys and sorrows of life was a thing I had no idea of. I could therefore see nothing beyond, and this life I had accepted as all in all. When of a sudden death came and in a moment made a gaping rent in its smooth-seeming fabric, I was utterly bewildered. All around, the trees, the soil, the water, the sun, the moon, the stars remained as immovably true as before; and yet the person who was as truly there, who, through a thousand points of contact with life, mind, and heart, was ever so much more true for me, had vanished in a moment like a dream. What perplexing self-contradiction it all seemed to me as I looked around! How was I ever to reconcile that which remained with that which had gone?

The terrible darkness which was disclosed to me through this rent continued to attract me night and day as time went on. I would ever and anon return to take my stand there and gaze upon it, wondering what there was left in place of what had gone. Emptiness is a thing man cannot bring himself to believe in; that which is not, is untrue; that which is untrue, is not. So our efforts to find something, where we see nothing, are unceasing.

Just as a young plant, surrounded by darkness, stretches itself, as it were on tiptoe, to find its way out into the light, so when death suddenly throws the darkness of negation round the soul it tries and tries to rise into the light of affirmation. And what other sorrow is comparable to the state wherein darkness prevents the finding of a way out of the darkness?

And yet in the midst of this unbearable grief, flashes of joy seemed to sparkle in my mind, now and again, in a way which quite surprised me. That life was not a stable permanent fixture was itself the sorrowful tidings which helped to lighten my mind. That we were not prisoners forever within a solid stone wall of life was the thought which unconsciously kept coming uppermost in rushes of gladness. That which I had held I was made to let go – this was the sense of loss which distressed me – but when at the same moment I viewed it from the standpoint of freedom gained, a great peace fell upon me.

The all-pervading pressure of worldly existence compensates itself by balancing life against death, and thus it does not crush us. The terrible weight of an unopposed life force has not to be endured by man – this truth came upon me that day as a sudden, wonderful revelation.

With the loosening of the attraction of the world, the beauty of nature took on for me a deeper meaning. Death had given me the correct perspective from which to perceive the world in the fullness of its beauty, and as I saw the picture of the universe against the background of death I found it entrancing.

At this time I was attacked with a recrudescence of eccentricity in thought and behavior. To be called upon to submit to the customs and fashions of the day, as if they were something soberly and genuinely real, made me want to laugh. I could not take them seriously. The burden of stopping to consider what other people might think of me was completely lifted off my mind. I have been about in fashionable book shops with a coarse sheet draped round me as my only upper garment, and a pair of slippers on my bare feet. Through hot and cold and wet I used to sleep out on the verandah of the third story. There the stars and I could gaze at each other, and no time was lost in greeting the dawn.

This phase had nothing to do with any ascetic feeling. It was more like a holiday spree as the result of discovering the schoolmaster Life with his cane to be a myth, and thereby being able to shake myself free from the petty rules of his school. If, on waking one fine morning we were to find gravitation reduced to only a fraction of itself, would we still demurely walk along the high road? Would we not rather skip over many-storied houses for a change, or on encountering the monument take a flying jump, rather than trouble to walk round it? That was why, with the weight of worldly life no longer clogging my feet, I could not stick to the usual course of convention.

Alone on the terrace in the darkness of night I groped all over like a blind man trying to find upon the black stone gate of death some device or sign. Then when I woke with the morning light falling on that unscreened bed of mine, I felt, as I opened my eyes, that my enveloping haze was becoming transparent; and, as on the clearing of the mist the hills and rivers and forests of the scene shine forth, so the dew-washed picture of the world-life, spread out before me, seemed to become renewed and ever so beautiful. ❖

Frederica Mathewes-Green

ABBA DIOSCORUS was once found weeping by a younger monk. When asked why he did so, Dioscorus replied, "I am weeping for my sins." The young monk knew Dioscorus had led a valiant and holy life for many years, and said, "My father, you do not have any such sins." Dioscorus told him, "Truly, my child, if I were allowed to see my sins, three or four men would not be enough to weep for them."

"If I were allowed to see my sins." The truth is that we cannot bear to see the selfish twists of our heart, our greed and self-pity and manipulativeness. God allows us a measure of merciful ignorance. "I have yet many things to say to you, but you cannot bear them now," Jesus says.

The starting point for the early church was this awareness of the abyss of sin inside each person, the murky depths of which only the top few inches are visible. God, who is all clarity and light, wants to make us perfect as he is perfect, shot through with his radiance. The first step in our healing, then, is not being comforted. It is taking a hard look at the cleansing that needs to be done.

This is not condemnation, but right diagnosis. It is not judgmentalism, because the judgment is evenly applied: all are sinners, all have fallen short. It is not false guilt, because a lot of the guilt we feel is in fact deserved; we *are* guilty. Forgiveness of past sins doesn't cure the sickness in the heart that continues to yearn after more. We will remain sick until that healing begins, and it will be a lifelong process.

What a relief it is to admit this. Like the woman weeping at Jesus' feet, we have nothing more to conceal, no more self-justification, no more self-pity. We are fully known, even in the depths that we ourselves cannot see, cannot bear to see. Instead of hoping that God will love us for our good parts and pass over the rest, we know that he died for the bad parts, and will not rest till they are made right. The depth of our sin proves the height of his love, a height we cannot comprehend until we realize how desperately we need it. We are fully loved, and one day will be fully healed, brought into God's presence without spot or wrinkle or any such thing.

What's more, repentance enlarges the heart until it encompasses all earthly life, and the sorrow tendered to God is no longer for ourselves alone. Knowing our own sin, we pray in solidarity with all other sinners, even those who hurt us. With all creation we groan, crying out to God for his healing and mercy. He who does not desire the death of a sinner, but that he turn from his evil and live, puts his Spirit within us, and we too no longer desire any vengeance. Then our ability to love others, even our enemies, broadens like sunlight on the horizon. ⬥

The Meek

* * * * *

Blessed are the meek,
for they will inherit the earth.
　　Matthew 5:5

John Chrysostom

WHEN THEREFORE your tongue is as Christ's tongue, and your mouth has become the mouth of the Father, and you are a temple of the Holy Ghost, then what kind of honor could be equal to this? For not even if your mouth were made of gold, nor even of precious stones, would it shine like as now, when lit up with the ornament of meekness. For what is more lovely than a mouth that knows not how to insult, but is used to bless and give good words? . . . Reflecting then on these things, become like Him, to the utmost of your power. No longer then will the devil be able so much as to look you in the face, when you have become such a one as this. For indeed he recognizes the image of the King, he knows the weapons of Christ, whereby he was worsted. And what are these? Gentleness and meekness. For when on the mountain Christ overthrew and laid low the devil who was assaulting him, it was not by making it known that he was Christ, but he entrapped him by these sayings, he took him by gentleness, he turned him to flight by meekness. ◆

Elisabeth Elliot

THE WORLD CANNOT fathom strength proceeding from weakness, gain proceeding from loss, or power from meekness. Christians apprehend these truths very slowly, if at all, for we are strongly influenced by secular thinking. Let's stop and concentrate on what Jesus meant when he said that the *meek* would inherit the earth. Do we understand what meekness truly is? Think first about what it isn't.

It is not a naturally phlegmatic temperament. I knew a woman who was so phlegmatic that nothing seemed to make much difference to her at all. While drying dishes for her one day in her kitchen I asked where I should put a serving platter.

"Oh, I don't know. Wherever *you* think would be a good place," was her answer. I wondered how she managed to find things if there wasn't a place for everything (and everything in its place). . . .

Meekness is most emphatically not weakness. Do you remember who was the meekest man in the Old Testament? Moses! (Num. 12:3). My mental image of him is not of a feeble man. It is shaped by Michelangelo's sculpture and painting and by the biblical descriptions. Think of him murdering the Egyptian, smashing the tables of the commandments, grinding the golden calf to a powder, scattering it on the water and making the Israelites drink it. Nary a hint of weakness there, nor in

David, who wrote, "The meek will he guide in judgment" (Psalm 25:9), nor in Isaiah, who wrote, "The meek also shall increase their joy in the Lord" (Isa. 29:19).

The Lord Jesus was the Lamb of God, and when we think of lambs we think of meekness (and perhaps weakness), but he was also the Lion of Judah, and he said, "I am meek and lowly in heart" (Matt. 11:29). He told us that we can find rest for our souls if we will come to him, take his yoke, and learn. What we must learn is meekness. It doesn't come naturally to any of us.

Meekness is teachability. "The meek will he teach his way" (Ps. 25:9). It is the readiness to be shown, which includes the readiness to lay down my fixed notions, my objections and "what ifs" or "but what abouts," my certainties about the rightness of what I have always done or thought or said. It is the child's glad "Show me! Is *this* the way? Please help me." We won't make it into the kingdom without that childlikeness, that simple willingness to be taught and corrected and helped. "Receive with meekness the engrafted word, which is able to save your souls" (James 1:21). Meekness is an explicitly spiritual quality, a fruit of the Spirit, learned, not inherited. It shows in the kind of attention we pay to one another, the tone of voice we use, the facial expression.

One weekend I spoke in Atlanta on this subject, and the following weekend I was to speak on it again in Philadelphia. As very often happens, I was sorely tested on that very point in the few days in between. That sore test was my chance to be taught and changed and helped. At the same time I was strongly tempted to indulge in the very opposite of meekness: sulking. Someone had hurt me. He or she was the one who needed to be change! I felt I was misunderstood, unfairly treated, and unduly berated. Although I managed to keep my mouth shut, both the Lord and I knew that my thoughts did not spring from a depth of lovingkindness and holy charity. I wanted to vindicate myself to the offender. That was a revelation of how little I knew of meekness.

The Spirit of God reminded me that it was he who had provided this very thing to bring that lesson of meekness which I could learn nowhere else. He was literally putting me on the spot: Would I choose, here and now, to *learn of him*, learn his meekness? He was despised, rejected, reviled, pierced, crushed, oppressed, afflicted, yet he did not open his mouth. What was this little incident of mine by comparison with my Lord's suffering? He brought to mind Jesus' willingness not only to eat with Judas, who would soon betray him, but also to kneel before him and wash his dirty feet. He showed me the look the Lord gave Peter when he had three times denied him – a look of unutterable love and forgiveness, a look of meekness which overpowered Peter's cowardice and selfishness, and brought him to repentance. I thought of his meekness as he hung pinioned on the cross, praying even in his agony for his Father's forgiveness for his killers. There was no venom or bitterness there, only the final proof of a sublime and invincible love.

But how shall I, not born with the smallest shred of that quality, I who love victory by argument and put-down, ever learn that holy meekness? The prophet Zephaniah tells us to *seek* it (Zeph. 2:3). We must walk (live) in the Spirit, not gratifying the desires of the sinful nature (for example, my desire to answer back, to offer excuses and accusations, my desire to show up the other's fault instead of to be shown my own). We must "clothe" ourselves (Col. 3:12) with meekness – put it on, like a garment. This entails an explicit choice: I will be meek. I will not sulk, will not retaliate, will not carry a chip.

A steadfast look at Jesus instead of at the injury makes a very great difference. Seeking to see things in his light changes the aspect altogether.

In *Pilgrim's Progress*, Prudence asks Christian in the House Beautiful, "Can you remember by what means you find your annoyances at times, as if they were vanquished?"

"Yes," says Christian, "when I think what I saw at the cross, that will do it." ◆

Richard Rohr

THIS BEATITUDE is a quote from Psalm 37:11: "The humble shall have the land for their own." Some translate it "the nonviolent." The translation perhaps most familiar is "the meek." It is the unique power of the powerless, which people who have always had power never understand. It is claimed by Mary in her famous *Magnificat,* where she mirrors and models the many "barren" women in the Hebrew scriptures: "God has looked upon me in my lowliness. . . . God fills the starving with good things" (Luke 1:48, 53). She represented the pivotal biblical theme of "the poor of Yahweh" (*anawim*), taught especially by the prophets Zephaniah (2:3) and Zechariah (9:9). Surely Mary and Joseph modeled this stance for Jesus as a child. Their offering of two turtle doves at his presentation in the temple (Luke 2:24), which was the offering of the landless peasantry, reveals their social place in Jewish society.

There is, of course, an irony here. If there was one hated group in Palestine of Jesus' day, it was landlords, those who possess the land. Nobody possessed land except by violence, by oppression, by holding on to it and making all the peasants pay a portion of their harvest. Jesus is turning that around and saying no, it's you little ones who are finally going to possess the land. I can hear implicit critique in his voice, but also hope.

Jesus is undoubtedly redefining the meaning of land, building on what every Jew would have known. Hebrew scripture teaches that only God possesses the land (see Ps. 24:1; Lev. 25:23). In the jubilee year, all the land was to be given back to its original occupants (see Lev. 25:8–17). Native Americans understood the freedom of the land, yet European colonizers did not. Private property forces us behind artificial fences, boundaries, and walls. People close to the earth know that only God "owns" the earth, and that we're all stewards, pilgrims, and strangers with a duty and privilege of caring for it. Who will "own" our plot of land fifty years from now? Ownership is clearly not an objective or divine right, but only a legal one. ❖

Teresa of Ávila

I F   W E   T H I N K   the Lord has given us a certain grace, we must understand that it is a blessing which we have received but which he may take away from us again, as indeed, in the great providence of God, often happens.

Have you never observed this yourselves? I certainly have: sometimes I think I am extremely detached, and, in fact, when it comes to the test, I am; yet at other times I find I have such attachment to things which the day before I should perhaps have scoffed at that I hardly know myself. At some other time I seem to have so much courage that I should not quail at anything I was asked to do in order to serve God, and, when I am tested, I find that I really can do these things. And then on the next day I discover that I should not have the courage to kill an ant for God's sake if I were to meet with any opposition about it. Sometimes it seems not to matter in the least if people complain or speak ill of me, and, when the test comes, I still feel like this – indeed, I even get pleasure from it. And then there come days when a single word distresses me and I long to leave the world altogether, for everything in it seems to weary me. And I am not the only person to be like this, for I have noticed the same thing in many people better than myself, so I know it can happen.

That being so, who can say that he possesses any virtue, or that he is rich, if at the time when he most needs this virtue he finds himself devoid of it? No, let us rather think of ourselves as lacking it and not run into debt without having the means of repayment. Our treasure must come from elsewhere and we never know when God will leave us in this prison of our misery without giving us any. If others, thinking we are good, bestow favors and honors upon us, both they and we shall look foolish when, as I say, it becomes clear that our virtues are only lent us. The truth is that, if we serve the Lord with humility, he will sooner or later succor us in our needs. But, if we are not strong in this virtue, the Lord will leave us to ourselves, as they say, at every step. This is a great favor on his part, for it helps us to realize fully that we have nothing which has not been given us. ◆

8

Hungry and Thirsty

♦ ♦ ♦ ♦ ♦

Blessed are those who hunger and thirst for righteousness,
for they will be filled.
Matthew 5:6

William Barclay

A T THE TIME OF JESUS, for a family to eat meat was in Palestine a rare experience. In that ancient world hunger was not something which could be satisfied with a passing snack. It could often be the hunger which threatened life, the starvation in which one had to eat or die. The same is true of thirst. There are few of us who have ever known what it is to be genuinely thirsty. We live in a situation in which we turn a tap and water flows. In that ancient world people were dependent on streams and wells, and there might be a long, long distance between them on a journey, and the waterskin might be empty. Still worse, the sandstorm might come, and all that a man could do was to turn his back to the swirling sand, and hide his head in his hood, while his mouth and his throat and his nostrils and his lungs were filled with the fine sand, which made him choke with thirst. People who lived in conditions like that knew the thirst which had to be satisfied if they were to survive.

What Jesus is saying here is: "Blessed is the one who longs for righteousness as a starving man longs for food, and as the man perishing of thirst longs for water." . . . He is saying: "Do you desire righteousness with that intensity of desire with which a starving person desires food, and the one parched with thirst desires water?" This is a challenge and demand with which Jesus continually confronted people. It was with this challenge that he confronted the rich young ruler (Matt. 19:16–22). The young man came to Jesus pleading to be enabled to find eternal life, real life. . . . In answer to Jesus' questions he claimed that he had kept all the commandments from his youth upwards. Jesus then confronted him with the demand that he should go and sell all that he had and give the proceeds to the poor. In effect Jesus was saying to him: "Do you want eternal life as much as that? Are you prepared to sacrifice the luxuries of this life to gain eternal life?" And, when the matter was put that way, the young man went sorrowfully away. It was with this challenge that Jesus confronted one of the men who wished to follow him. The man said he would follow Jesus anywhere. Jesus answered: "Foxes have holes, and birds of the air have nests; but the Son of Man hath not where to lay his head" (Luke 9:57–58). In effect Jesus said to him: "Do you want to follow me enough to face a life like that?" . . .

[This Beatitude] is for those who desire righteousness as a matter of life and death. In the novel *Quo Vadis* there is a picture of a young Roman called Vinicius. He is in love with a Christian girl, but because he is a pagan she will not return his

love. Without her knowledge he followed her to a little secret
gathering of the Christians, and there he heard Peter preach.
As he listened something happened within him. He knew that
Jesus Christ was the most important reality in life, but "he felt
that, if he wished to follow that teaching, he would have to
place on a burning pile all his thoughts, habits, and character,
his whole nature up to that moment, burn them into ashes, and
then fill himself with a life altogether different, and an entirely
new soul." . . .

By implication, [this Beatitude] lays down the main cause of
failure in the Christian life. That cause of failure is simply that
we do not sufficiently desire to be a Christian. It is the experience of life that, if we desire a thing sufficiently, we will get
it. If we are prepared to bend every energy, to sacrifice everything, to toil with sufficient intensity, to wait with sufficient
patience, we will succeed in getting that on which we have set
our hearts. The great barrier to our becoming fully Christian is
our failure to desire it enough, our deep-rooted unwillingness
to pay the price of it, our fundamental desire not to upset life,
but to keep it as it is.

Luke gives us a different, and a complementary, version
of this Beatitude: "Woe unto you who are full! For you shall
hunger" (Luke 6:25). That means: "Woe to you who are satisfied, who are content with things as they are, who have no
passionate desire for that which you have not got. You may
live comfortably enough just now, but the day comes when
you will discover that you have somehow missed the greatest
things of all."

In classical Greek, verbs of hungering and thirsting
normally take the genitive case after them; the genitive case
is the case which we express by the word *of*. In the phrase, "a
slice of bread," *of bread* is in the genitive case. The reason for

this grammatical usage is that normally we hunger and thirst for part of some supply of food or drink. We do not want the whole loaf; we want a part of the loaf. We do not want the whole pitcher; we want some of the water which is in the pitcher. But, when these verbs do take the direct accusative, it means that the person involved wants *all* the food and *all* the drink there is. If a Greek said, "I hunger for bread," or "I thirst for water" . . . it would mean that he wanted the whole loaf, and the entire contents of the pitcher. In this Beatitude *righteousness* is in the accusative case; and, therefore, if we are to translate this with strict accuracy, we ought to translate it: "Blessed are those who hunger and thirst for *all of righteousness*, for total righteousness."

That is what so seldom happens. There are people against whose moral character no possible fault can be found; they are completely respectable; intemperance, gambling, adultery, swearing, dishonesty, failure to pay their debts could never possibly be attributed to them; but they are cold and hard and without sympathy. No one who had made a mistake could lay his head on their shoulder and sob out his sorry story. They are good, but they are cold. On the other hand there are people who have all kinds of faults; they may drink to excess; their language may at time be lurid; their passions are not always under control; it is easy to point at their moral errors and their failure in the respectable virtues. But, if anyone else is in trouble, they would give him the coat off their back, and hand him their last penny without a thought of grudging it. Their morals may be erratic, but their heart is warm. The truth is that in neither of these cases can you say that these people are *good* in the full sense of the term. Each of them has a *part* of goodness, but not the *whole* of it; each has *fragmentary*, but not *total* goodness. The Christian goodness is a complete goodness in which virtue and love join hands.

We have not yet sought to define what this word *righteousness* means. The word is *dikaiosune*, and it has three meanings which are all possible, and all relevant. It means *justice*; it means righteousness in the sense of *right living*; and it is the word which is used for the *justification* which comes by faith. . . .

It is not necessary that we should choose between these meanings. We may well believe that this Beatitude includes all these things, and that the hunger and thirst of which it speaks are for the vindication of the cause of God and for the justice of all people; for that personal righteousness which loves and obeys God and serves and forgives people; for that right relationship with God in which all the fear and the estrangement have turned into confidence and trust. No person could hunger and thirst for any greater gifts than these.

After the affirmation there comes the promise. "Blessed are they that hunger and thirst after righteousness; *for they shall be filled*." The word which is used for *filled* is an extraordinary word. It is the word *chortazesthai*. Originally this word was used to describe the special fattening of animals for killing. When it did come to be used of humans, it meant to stuff a person full to the point of complete satiety. It always remained something of a colloquial word, and it always retained something of the idea of filling a person full to repletion. If a person hungers and thirst for that righteousness which God alone can give, God will not send him empty away, but God will fill him, until his longings are achieved and his soul is satisfied. ✦

9

The Merciful

• • • • •

Blessed are the merciful,
for they will be shown mercy.
Matthew 5:7

Charles E. Moore

IN JESUS' DAY, the Roman world was merciless to
the slave and the child. Slaves were property, tools to be
exploited, and could be flogged, branded, and tortured.
Unwanted children could be "exposed," simply thrown out
like refuse. The modern world isn't much better; one need only
recall Stalin's purges, or Hitler's Final Solution, or the genocide
in Rwanda.

But even our everyday world can be harsh. Whether it is
the vitriol spewed out on social media and talk radio or our
obsession with litigation, our lives are riddled with judgment,
suspicion, and blame. Screw up, watch out! Someone will take
advantage of you, or at least try to get even. Justice maybe,
mercy hardly ever.

Yet each of us needs mercy from time to time, and all of us are grateful when we receive it. In fact, all of us rely on an intricate fabric of mercy. This is why Jesus says, "Blessed are the merciful, for they shall receive mercy." Mercy begets mercy, and the result is blessedness. In the Bible, God not only delights in mercy, but mercy belongs to his very nature (Mic. 7:18). Nothing is greater than mercy, not even sacrifice (Hos. 6:6). Jesus himself is God's mercy. No wonder Jesus places mercy above sacred institutions and traditions.

But what, exactly, is mercy? The word's root in Hebrew refers to the womb. To have mercy is to have the feeling for another person that a mother has for her children. Mercy assumes a sense of solidarity with and responsibility for those in need. It involves a feeling but is more than a feeling. It is, as William Barclay says, "the ability to get right inside the other person's skin until we can see things with his eyes, think things with his mind, and feel things with his feelings." Mercy suffers with the sufferer. It demands investment and involvement.

Mercy moves us to see the person, not just his problem. The person before me is homeless, or addicted, or untrustworthy and manipulative. I can readily see his poverty, his shame. But mercy moves me to experience his pain and anguish, his loneliness and fear, his sense of worthlessness. Through all this I see his deepest longing – his hope of being and making good. I see him as I try to see myself.

Showing mercy is one thing, being merciful another. Being merciful is not just doing kind deeds. Mercy assumes a certain posture. The merciful know what it means to need mercy; that's why they can't help but respond to the guilt and suffering of others. They, like Jesus, are moved with compassion toward all those who have lost the way. They take upon themselves the distress, humiliation, need, and sin of others. They have a heart for the poor, the hurting, the lonely, and those whose lives are in one way or another a wreck. Instead of judging by appearances, they assume the best in the worst, being patient towards those who lash out because they don't know how to assuage their pain. They understand that there are reasons why people act out as they do. They welcome the prodigal son home despite his sin and despite the wreckage he has caused others. For they too have been welcomed.

In his book *The Name of God Is Mercy*, Pope Francis tells of a time when a younger Capuchin priest came to him in Buenos Aires and told him: "I always have so many people at the confessional, people of all walks of life, some humble and some less humble, but many priests too. . . . I forgive a lot and some-times I have doubts, I wonder if I have forgiven too much." Francis asked him what he did when he had those doubts. The priest replied: "I go to our chapel and stand in front of the tabernacle and say to Jesus: 'Lord, forgive me if I have forgiven too much. But you're the one who gave me the bad example!'"

None of us can get or show mercy enough. Without mercy, our righteousness is in danger of becoming hard, judgmental, impatient, legalistic, quick to anger. Yes, Jesus calls blessed those who hunger and thirst to do God's will, but only if they have big hearts toward those who don't. Why else, other than mercy, did the adulterous woman cleanse Jesus' feet with her tears? "She loved much because she was forgiven much."

John, an old friend of mine saved from drugs, has been befriending homeless people for almost forty years. Some may ask: Is it worth it? What difference does it really make? The more important question is: What difference does it make when we stop bestowing mercy? For when we ignore the needs of others, we lose our capacity for sharing and spreading happiness, and remain under the illusion that happiness has no reference beyond ourselves. We forget what a comfort it can be when we share in the suffering of others. That comfort is something John has received himself countless times. When he sets out on foot, his friends on the street reach out to him, eager to spend their last buck to get him a cup of coffee. John experiences a fullness that many people less touched by human suffering never know. Blessed indeed are the merciful. ◆

Leo Tolstoy

LOVING ACTIVITY GAINS its importance from the fact that it is contagious. External activity expressed in gratuitous gifts of grain and money, according to descriptions and lists, calls forth the worst emotions: greediness, hatred, deception, unkind criticism; private activity calls forth, on the contrary, the best sentiments: love and the desire of sacrifice.

"I have worked, I have struggled, they give me nothing; but they give a reward to that lazy dog, that drunkard! Who told him to get drunk? The thief deserves all he gets!" says the rich and the average muzhik to those whom they refuse assistance.

With no less anger speaks the poor man of the rich who demands an equal share: "We are the poor ones. They suck us dry, and then give them our share. They are so mean," and the like.

Such feelings are elicited by the distribution of gratuitous assistance. But, on the contrary, if one sees how another is sharing with a neighbor, is working for an unfortunate, one has the desire to do likewise. In this lies the strength of loving activity. Its strength is that it is contagious, and, as soon as it becomes contagious, then there is no limit to its spread.

As one candle kindles another, and thousands are lighted from that one, so also one heart inflames another and thousands are set a-glowing. Millions of rubles will do less than will be done by even a small diminution of greediness and increase of love in the mass of the people. If only the love is multiplied then the miracle is accomplished which was performed at the distribution of the five loaves. All are satisfied, and still much remains. ◆

Purity of Heart

•••••

Blessed are the pure in heart,
for they will see God.
Matthew 5:8

Irenaeus

"BLESSED ARE THE PURE of heart, for they shall see God." It is true, because of the greatness and inexpressible glory of God, that "man shall not see me and live," for the Father cannot be grasped. But because of God's love and goodness toward us, and because he can do all things, he goes so far as to grant those who love him the privilege of seeing him. . . . For "what is impossible for men is possible for God." ◆

Søren Kierkegaard

"**D**RAW NIGH TO GOD and he will draw nigh to you. Cleanse your hands, ye sinners, and purify your hearts ye double-minded" (James 4:8). For only the pure in heart can see God, and therefore, draw nigh to him; and only by God's drawing nigh to them can they maintain this purity. And he who in truth wills only one thing can will only the Good, and he who only wills one thing when he wills the Good can only will the Good in truth. . . .

THERE WAS A MAN on earth who seemed to will only one thing. It was unnecessary for him to insist upon it. Even if he had been silent about it, there were witnesses enough against him who testified how inhumanly he steeled his mind, how nothing touched him, neither tenderness, nor innocence, nor misery; how his blinded soul had eyes for nothing, and how the senses in him had only eyes for the one thing that he willed. And yet it was certainly a delusion, a terrible delusion, that he willed one thing. For pleasure and honor and riches and power and all that this world has to offer only appear to be one thing. It is not, nor does it remain one thing, while everything else is in change or while he himself is in change. It is not in all circumstances the same. On the contrary, it is subject to continual alteration. Hence even if this man named but one thing, whether it be pleasure or honor or riches, actually he did not will one thing. Neither can he be said to will one thing when that one thing which he wills is not in itself one: is in itself a multitude of things, a dispersion, the toy of changeableness, and the prey of corruption! In the time of pleasure see how he longed for one gratification after another. Variety was

his watchword. Is variety, then, to will one thing that shall ever
remain the same? On the contrary, it is to will one thing that
must never be the same. It is to will a multitude of things. And
a person who wills in this fashion is not only double-minded
but is at odds with himself. For such a man wills first one thing
and then immediately wills the opposite, because the oneness
of pleasure is a snare and a delusion. It is the diversity of pleasures that he wills. So when the man of whom we are speaking
had gratified himself up to the point of disgust, he became
weary and sated. Even if he still desired one thing – what was it
that he desired? . . .

In the short-lived moment of delusion the worldly goal is
therefore a multitude of things, and thus not one thing. So
far is it from a state of being and remaining one thing, that in
the next moment it changes itself into its opposite. Carried to
its extreme limit, what is pleasure other than disgust? What
is earthly honor at its dizzy pinnacle other than contempt for
existence? What are riches, the highest superabundance of
riches, other than poverty? For no matter how much all the
earth's gold hidden in covetousness may amount to, is it not
infinitely less than the smallest mite hidden in the content-
ment of the poor? What is worldly omnipotence other than
dependence? What slave in chains is as unfree as a tyrant? No,
the worldly goal is not one thing. Diverse as it is, in life it is
changed into its opposite, in death into nothing, in eternity
into damnation – for the one who has willed this goal. Only
the Good is one thing in its essence and the same in each of
its expressions. Take love as an illustration. The one who truly
loves does not love once and for all. Nor does he use a part of
his love, and then again another part. For to change it into
small coins is not to use it rightly. No, he loves with all of his
love. It is wholly present in each expression. He continues to

give it away as a whole, and yet he keeps it intact as a whole, in his heart. Wonderful riches! When the miser has gathered all the world's gold in sordidness – then he has become poor. When the lover gives away his whole love, he keeps it entire – in the purity of the heart. Shall a man in truth will one thing, then this one thing that he wills must be such that it remains unaltered in all changes, so that by willing it he can win immutability. If it changes continually, then he himself becomes changeable, double-minded, and unstable. And this continual change is nothing else than impurity. ◆

Thomas Merton

WHEN WE HAVE a *right* intention, our intention is pure. We seek to do God's will with a supernatural motive. We mean to please him. But in doing so we still consider the work and ourselves apart from God and outside him. Our intention is directed chiefly upon the work to be done. When the work is done, we rest in its accomplishment, and hope for a reward from God.

But when we have a *simple* intention, we are less occupied with the thing to be done. We do all that we do not only for God but so to speak *in* him. We are more aware of him who works in us than of ourselves or of our work. Yet this does not mean that we are not fully conscious of what we do, or that realities lose their distinctness in a kind of sweet metaphysical blur. It may happen that one who works with this "simple" intention is more perfectly alive to the exigencies of his work and does the work far better than the worker of "right" intention who has no such perspective. The man of *right* intentions makes a juridical offering of his work to God and then plunges himself into the work, hoping for the best. For all his right intention he may well become completely dizzy in a maze of practical details. . . .

But the man of *simple intention* works in an atmosphere of prayer: that is to say he is recollected. His spiritual reserves are not all poured out into his work, but stored where they belong, in the depths of his being, with his God. He is detached from his work and from its results. Only a person who works purely for God can at the same time do a very good job and leave the results of the job to God alone. ◆

Brennan Manning

O NE DAY SAINT FRANCIS and Brother Leo were walking down the road. Noticing that Leo was depressed, Francis turned and asked: "Leo, do you know what it means to be pure of heart?"

"Of course. It means to have no sins, faults, or weaknesses to reproach myself for."

"Ah," said Francis, "now I understand why you're sad. We will always have something to reproach ourselves for."

"Right," said Leo. "That's why I despair of ever arriving at purity of heart."

"Leo, listen carefully to me. Don't be so preoccupied with the purity of your heart. Turn and look at Jesus. Admire him. Rejoice that he is what he is – your brother, your friend, your Lord and Savior. That, little brother, is what it means to be pure of heart. And once you've turned to Jesus, don't turn back and look at yourself. Don't wonder where you stand with him.

"The sadness of not being perfect, the discovery that you really are sinful, is a feeling much too human, even bordering on idolatry. Focus your vision outside yourself on the beauty,

graciousness, and compassion of Jesus Christ. The pure of
heart praise him from sunrise to sundown. Even when they feel
broken, feeble, distracted, insecure, and uncertain, they are
able to release it into his peace. A heart like that is stripped and
filled – stripped of self and filled with the fullness of God. It is
enough that Jesus is Lord."

After a long pause, Leo said, "Still, Francis, the Lord
demands our effort and fidelity."

"No doubt about that," replied Francis. "But holiness is not
a personal achievement. It's an emptiness you discover in yourself. Instead of resenting it, you accept it and it becomes the
free space where the Lord can create anew. To cry out, 'You
alone are the Holy One, you alone are the Lord,' that is what it
means to be pure of heart. And it doesn't come by your Hercu-
lean efforts and threadbare resolutions."

"Then how?" asked Leo.

"Simply hoard nothing of yourself; sweep the house clean.
Sweep out even the attic, even the nagging painful consciousness of your past. Accept being shipwrecked. Renounce
everything that is heavy, even the weight of your sins. See only
the compassion, the infinite patience, and the tender love of
Christ. Jesus is Lord. That suffices. Your guilt and reproach
disappear into the nothingness of non-attention. You are no
longer aware of yourself, like the sparrow aloft and free in the
azure sky. Even the desire for holiness is transformed into a
pure and simple desire for Jesus." ◆

II

Peacemaking

· · · · ·

Blessed are the peacemakers,
for they will be called children of God.
　Matthew 5:9

John Dear

WITH THIS BEATITUDE, Jesus calls us all to be peacemakers. That means, of course, we can no longer be warmakers. We cannot support war, participate in war, pay for war, promote war, or wage war. A peacemaker works to end war and create peace. From now on, every Christian is banned from warfare and sets to work making peace and creating a more peaceful world. . . .

This one verse throws out thousands of years of belief in a violent God and . . . does away with any spiritual justification for warfare or that God might bless our troops and our wars. Instead, it opens vast new vistas in our imaginations about what the living God is actually like, and what God's reign might be like. With this Beatitude, we glimpse the nonviolence of heaven and join the global struggle to abolish war and pursue a new world of nonviolence here on earth.

From now on, anyone or anything, including the church, that supports war or violence in any form is not of God, not doing the will of God, and not bearing the good fruit of God. Anyone that makes peace does the will of God and is, therefore, godly.

With this Beatitude, Jesus unpacks the connections made by the prophet Isaiah. In chapter two of the Book of Isaiah, for example, we read an oracle about how all the nations of the world will climb the mountain of God, sit at the feet of God, stop talking, and start listening to God. Isaiah explains how, once we listen to God, we then go down the mountain back into the world, dismantle all our weapons, and refuse to wage war ever again. "They shall beat their swords into plowshares and study war no more," he explains of those who have met God. Isaiah knows, as Jesus proclaims, that God is a God of peace. Once we meet God, we are disarmed and sent forth to make peace. Like Jesus, we do what we have seen done. . . .

Though we're all called to be peacemakers, our peacemaking work may be different given our history, nation, culture, and talents. . . . But the days of claiming to be peacemakers as we wage war need to end. We know the difference now. Peacemakers do not kill or hurt or threaten anyone, individually, nationally, or globally. We do not risk the taking of a single human life, much less millions.

Peacemakers practice nonviolence. We cannot join a military, wage war, work in the nuclear weapons industry, or sell weapons. Nonviolence sets a new boundary line for our lives. As peacemakers, we are nonviolent to ourselves, nonviolent to all others, all creatures, and all creation, and we work publicly for a new world of nonviolence. We are peaceful toward ourselves, and we steadfastly cultivate interior peace. We are peaceful toward all those around us, all creatures, and all creation. We do our part to make a more peaceful world. . . .

This is what Jesus imagines when he proclaims this Beatitude. He wants us to become peacemakers and to discern the particulars of that calling in our own time and place.

When Jesus calls us to become peacemakers, he's calling us to follow him and become with him "the beloved of God." Jesus exemplifies the peacemaking life. At his birth, angels sing to shepherds about the coming of peace on earth. In his baptism, he hears that he is the beloved son of the God of peace. After he rejects the temptations to violence, power, and domination in his desert retreat, he goes forth announcing the coming of God's reign of peace. He forms a community of peace, teaches his followers to practice nonviolence, and sends them out into the empire on a campaign of peace, telling them to announce peace wherever they go. He builds a peace movement to heal the victims of violence and war, dispel from everyone their possession by the empire, and announce the coming of God's reign of nonviolence. When the religious leaders drag a poor woman before him to kill her, he saves her life and forbids killing and condemnations. He heals the deaf, mute, blind, and lame, and even raises the dead. . . .

Christians are people who follow Jesus the peacemaker. That's what it means to be a Christian – not to belong to a cult, sing hymns, make money, lord power over others, or be self-righteous. Christians strive with all their being to make peace in the world as Jesus did. They take his gift of peace to heart and try to carry on his work. ◆

Thomas Merton

INSTEAD OF LOVING what you think is peace, love other people, and love God above all. And instead of hating the people you think are warmakers, hate the appetites and the disorder in your own soul, which are the causes of war. If you love peace, then hate injustice, hate tyranny, hate greed – but hate these things *in yourself* first, not in another. ◆

Peter Kreeft

IN THE GARDEN of Gethsemane, Jesus commanded Peter to put up his sword and reminded him that those who live by the sword perish by the sword. Thus the most just war ever fought, in defense of the most just, most worthy, most innocent man and cause, was also the shortest. Jesus stopped it almost before it started, apparently allowing it to start only to give his disciples and us an object lesson about his methods for ending it. After stopping the war, he healed its lone casualty, Malchus, whose ear had been cut off. Then, having made peace in this local and physical war, he went on to make peace in the universal, spiritual war, the war between man and God, on Calvary.

There too he did not use force but made peace in the most surprising way, by dying. He drained away war down himself, like a sinkhole, or a blotter. He made peace by making himself the universal victim, by suffering all the violence, war, aggression, hate, and harm that the father of lies and of violence could fling at him, by doing nothing in return, by being meek as the slaughtered sheep. *He* was "the meek" who "shall inherit the earth." By his meekness he won the world and the authority to give its rule over to his disciples when the time is ripe.

A strange story indeed – the strangest story ever told. It is symbolized in Revelation by the battle between *therion*, the Great Beast, and *arnion*, the meek little Lamb; and the odds are stacked, for the Beast doesn't stand a chance against the strategy of the Lamb, who wins by losing, triumphs by dying.

Not only does he make peace in a strange way, it is also a strange peace. It is not just peace but *"my* peace I give to you." He gives it "not as the world gives" because that is a different sort of peace. It is not the peace we expect, not a sort of comfortable niceness. Jesus was not nice. Jesus was not an uncle. Jesus was a fire. "I come not to bring peace but a sword" (this refers to the world's peace). Yet "peace I leave with you" (this refers to his peace). . . .

[Jesus] made peace between man and God. From that ultimate peace comes another peace, peace between man and man. In our history it has been so. Not politics but sanctity abolished barbarism and slavery and snobbery. It is the long way round, but it is the surgeon's way: to deal with the root cause of the disease, not just the symptoms. ◆

12

Persecution

• • • • •

Blessed are those who are persecuted because of righteousness, for theirs is the kingdom of heaven.

Blessed are you when people insult you, persecute you, and falsely say all kinds of evil against you because of me. Rejoice and be glad, because great is your reward in heaven, for in the same way they persecuted the prophets who were before you.

Matthew 5:10–12

Jerome

YOU ARE DECEIVED if you think that a Christian can live without persecution. He suffers the greatest who lives under none. Nothing is more to be feared than too long a peace. A storm puts a man on his guard, and obliges him to exert his utmost efforts to avoid shipwreck. ◆

Gene L. Davenport

THE GOSPEL CALLS disciples to insert themselves into the darkness as bearers of the light. In Jesus, the new order has drawn near in the midst of the old. To ignore the call to bear witness in the midst of the darkness is to allow the darkness to go unchallenged, unresisted. To say that we cannot do this or that because the world is the way it is is to ignore or disbelieve the assertion that with the old order there is a new order coming into being. Despite the dominant scheme of the world, now is the time to embrace the new order.

Such intrusion of mercy into the midst of mercilessness, purity of heart into the midst of atheism, and peacemaking into the midst of violence inevitably results in hostility and anger from those who are dominated by the old order. Truly to embrace the new order and to seek to allow God to use one for peacemaking and the establishment of his righteousness is to make oneself vulnerable to prosecution and persecution from the state, the various movements and agencies of the society, and the institutions, including the church, by which the society seeks to order its life. The old age cannot tolerate the infusion of the new. . . .

The darkness can seldom afford simply to ridicule the bearers of the light, but must destroy them, seeking thereby to destroy the light itself. Only when ridicule causes the one who is ridiculed to withdraw, to cease the witness, does the darkness settle for the ridicule – only, that is, when the darkness has won. The faithfulness of the disciple, however, propels the disciple onward, the grace of God upholding him or her in the tenacity of the witness, and the darkness then must take sterner measures. The darkness will seek to destroy. The state will threaten with imprisonment and death, not knowing that the disciple, upheld by the one who liberates the prisoners and restores life to the dead, fears neither of these penalties.

It is not that the disciple will necessarily become a determined lawbreaker, though the breaking of this or that law will be inevitable, but rather that by his or her very bearing in the world, the disciple threatens the structure of the law by threatening the value system, the social structure, and the ideology the law represents and defends. Disciples are never punished by the state simply for violating this or that law, although for purposes of legality an indictment will be based on one or another specific law. They are punished because they threaten the entire system. The true offense is the disciple's very existence. . . .

"Rejoice," in this Beatitude, is an exhortation to act in a way opposite to the way reviling, persecution, and slander normally would lead one to act. Do not be made to doubt or to be ashamed by the reviling; do not respond with violence or revenge to those who persecute you; do not spend a lot of effort and time attempting to correct the lies laid out by the slanderers. The exhortation not to react as children of the darkness would react is not based on any practical consideration such as, "I won't respond to the lie, because to fight a lie is to give credence to it." Nor is it based on any naïve notion that if the disciple ignores the situation, it will go away. Rather, it is rooted simply in the assumption that the way of the light and the way of the darkness are radically different. For the disciple to respond in kind to the onslaughts of the darkness would be to abandon the light, to disbelieve God, and, consequently, to affirm the charges of the revilers. It would be to exchange the God of Israel for the god of the darkness.

To rejoice is to respond in the midst of the darkness as though the whole world already lives in the light. To rejoice is to live in anticipation of deliverance as though deliverance already had taken place, as though the events toward whose culmination we look were already present. ◆

Óscar Romero

A CHURCH THAT does not provoke crisis, a gospel that does not disturb, a word of God that does not rankle, a word of God that does not touch the concrete sin of the society in which it is being proclaimed – what kind of gospel is that? Just nice, pious considerations that bother nobody – that's the way many people would like our preaching to be. Those preachers who avoid every thorny subject so as not to bother anyone or cause conflict and difficulty shed no light on the reality in which they live. ◆

DEAR BROTHERS, do not betray your service to this ministry of God's word. It is very easy to be servants of the word without disturbing the world in any way. We can spiritualize our words so that they lack any commitment to history. We can speak words that sound good in any part of the world because they say nothing about the world. Such words create no problems; they give rise to no conflicts. The word that characterizes the authentic church is the word that causes conflicts and persecutions. It is the searing word of the prophets that announces and denounces: it announces the marvelous works of God so that people will believe and worship God, and it denounces the sins of those who oppose God's kingdom. The true word denounces sins so that they will be uprooted from people's hearts, from their societies, from their laws, and from all those organizations that oppress and imprison and trample upon the right of God and humankind. ✦

THIS IS THE MISSION entrusted to the church, a difficult mission: to uproot sins from history, to uproot sins from politics, to uproot sins from the economy, to uproot sins from wherever they are. What a difficult task!

The church has to confront conflicts caused by great selfishness, great pride, and great vanity because so many people have enthroned the kingdom of sin among us. The church must suffer for speaking the truth, for denouncing sin, and for uprooting sin. No one wants to have a sore spot touched, and therefore a society with so many sores reacts strongly when someone has the courage to touch the sore and say: "You have to treat that. You have to eliminate that. Believe in Christ and be converted." ✦

Jeanne DeCelles

JESUS DID NOT get into trouble with the powers of his day simply by challenging the individual behaviors of his hearers. His downfall came from challenging the very systems of his society. He challenged the cornerstones. Just as the values of Madison Avenue, Wall Street, and the Pentagon conflict with the gospel, so too with Jesus and the institutions of his time: he was in conflict with the power structures of his own day, religious and civil alike.

Confrontation was not popular in first-century Palestine. It is not popular anywhere today. To bring gospel values to bear on labor practices, governmental decisions, and even religious traditions and policies is no more popular for a follower of Jesus than it was for him. He was told that they had their laws. Those who dare to bring his values to today's world are told the same thing. We have our laws and our customs. All the same, the fact that a behavior has reached the status of custom or law does no more to give it validity than it did when Jesus challenged it.

Discipleship does have its costs – anyone who has dared to bring the gospel to bear on his or her own life knows that. Whether we feel it or not may be a good litmus test for discerning if we are truly following on his path, or pursuing a false trail. ◈

Salt and Light

◆ ◆ ◆ ◆ ◆

You are the salt of the earth. But if the salt loses its saltiness, how can it be made salty again? It is no longer good for anything, except to be thrown out and trampled underfoot.

You are the light of the world. A town built on a hill cannot be hidden. Neither do people light a lamp and put it under a bowl. Instead they put it on its stand, and it gives light to everyone in the house. In the same way, let your light shine before others, that they may see your good deeds and glorify your Father in heaven.

Matthew 5:13–16

Charles E. Moore

THE BEATITUDES ARE in the third person, generic and impersonal like proverbs. In verse 11, however, Jesus says, "Blessed are *you*." Now he calls each of us blessed when we are hated or falsely accused or persecuted because we are his followers. In saying this, Jesus well understands the temptation to give up, to backtrack, to play it safe. Great is the temptation to compromise, to find other things besides righteousness to hunger and thirst for, to stop showing mercy, to clutter one's heart with the things of this world, to stand aside amidst conflict and avoid getting involved. It is easy to lose sight of who we are as his followers.

And who are we? Jesus says, "You *are* the salt of the earth" and "You *are* the light of the world." He does not say "you ought to be" or "you should try to be." We are salt and light. Both salt and light are so basic, so ordinary, so essential to life that Jesus sees no need to spell out what he means. Commentators often get carried away with these two metaphors and miss Jesus' main point. He is not just teaching about the importance of social involvement. He assumes his followers are in the world, just as he came into the world. If they were not, they wouldn't be persecuted. His concern is not that his followers get more involved in the world, but that they don't become like the world and lose their true identity. He wants his followers to remain true to who they are – to be what the world, on its own, cannot become.

Watch out, Jesus warns. Don't cease to be one of my little ones. Don't let yourselves get so tangled up in the cares and causes of this world that you get smothered and trodden underfoot. Salt can lose its integrity, its identifying quality. It can become good for nothing. Strictly speaking, salt cannot lose its taste or properties, but it can be compromised, adulterated so as to have no effect. When we add to Jesus' teachings we can dilute their life-giving essence. And though it is the nature of light to shine, it can be obscured by an opaque covering and lose the power to illuminate. This happens when we conform to the thinking and ways of this world and keep our religion in our pocket. Putting a lamp under a bushel might keep it from getting blown out, but the price for such protection is darkness.

Jesus is simply reminding his disciples: Be who you are, wherever you are, no matter what. Practice the greater righteousness I am showing you in this sermon. Be agents of reconciliation, ready to forgive and tear down the walls that divide people. Live lives of sexual integrity. Be honest in all you say and do. Do good to those who threaten you. Treat others as you would have them treat you.

When we align ourselves with Christ and demonstrate our allegiance to him and him alone, when we honestly and consistently seek to live in accordance with his authority, not just in church but in every area of life, we will invariably draw out and enhance the good already in the world. We will season and give life to those around us, and illuminate the darkness. When those around us see our kindness, the depth of love we have for one another, our courage and compassion and joy and readiness to forgive, our acts of mercy for friend and foe, our struggle for peace, and our passion for justice, they will come to know who God is and what he wills. ✦

Jane Tyson Clement

RESOLVE

I'll wash my hands of innocence
and cast the snowy robe aside
and shun the face of purity
to walk where sinners now abide.

The bare and brutal face of hate
I must go forth to look upon

and clasp the hand of treachery
with love as if it were my own.

My sins are inward and refined,
my friends the gentle friends of God;
I must go seek the publicans,
the wild companions of my Lord. ◆

John R. W. Stott

THE BASIC TRUTH which lies behind the metaphors of salt and light and is common to them both is that the church and the world are distinct communities. On the one hand there is "the earth"; on the other there is "you" who are the earth's salt. On the one hand there is "the world"; on the other there is "you" who are the world's light. True, the two communities ("they" and "you") are related to each other, but their relatedness depends on their distinctness. It is important to assert this clearly in our day in which it is theologically fashionable to blur the distinction between the church and the world, and to refer to all humankind indiscriminately as "the people of God."

Further, the metaphors tell us something about both communities. The world is evidently a dark place, with little or no light of its own, since an external source of light is needed to illumine it. True, it is always talking about its enlightenment, but much of its boasted light is in reality darkness. The world also manifests a constant tendency to deteriorate. The notion is not that the world is tasteless and that Christians can make it less insipid . . . but that it is putrefying. It cannot stop itself from going bad. Only salt introduced from outside can do this. The church, on the other hand, is set in the world with a double role, as salt to arrest – or at least to hinder – the process of social decay, and as light to dispel the darkness....

Christian saltiness is Christian character as depicted in the Beatitudes, committed Christian discipleship exemplified in both deed and word. For effectiveness the Christian must retain his Christlikeness, as salt must retain its saltiness.... The influence of Christians in and on society depends on their being distinct, not identical. Martyn Lloyd-Jones emphasizes this: "The glory of the gospel is that when the church is absolutely different from the world, she invariably attracts it. It is then that the world is made to listen to her message, though it may hate it at first." Otherwise, if we Christians are indistinguishable from non-Christians, we are useless. We might as well be discarded like saltless salt, "thrown out and trodden under foot by men." ...

As with salt, so with the light, the affirmation is followed by a condition: *Let your light shine before others.* If salt can lose its saltiness, the light in us can become darkness. But we are to allow the light of Christ within us to shine out from us, so that people may see it. We are not to be like a town or village nestling in a valley whose lights are concealed from view, but like *a city set on a hill* which *cannot be hid* and whose lights are clearly seen for miles around. Again, we are to be like a lighted lamp, "a burning and shining lamp" as John the Baptist was, which is set on a lampstand in a prominent position in the house so that *it gives light to all in the house,* and is not stuck "under the meal-tub" or "under a bucket," where it can do no good.

That is, as the disciples of Jesus, we are not to conceal the truth we know or the truth of what we are. We are not to pretend to be other than we are, but be willing for our Christianity to be visible to all. As Bonhoeffer puts it, "Flight into the invisible is a denial of the call. A community of Jesus which seeks to hide itself has ceased to follow him." Rather are we to be ourselves, our true Christian selves, openly living the life described in the Beatitudes, and not ashamed of Christ. Then people will see us and our good works, and seeing us will glorify God. For they will inevitably recognize that it is by the grace of God we are what we are, that *our* light is *his* light, and that *our* works are *his* works done in us and through us. ✦

Kingdom Commands

The Sermon on the Mount has been a mystery impossible for many of its advocates to understand. There is no new set of laws here, no new commandments or prohibitions replacing the old Ten Commandments. Here the new tree, the new light, the new salt, the new essence reveal God's heart as it was given to humankind in Jesus Christ, and as it will rule in his coming kingdom.

EBERHARD ARNOLD, *Salt and Light*

I F T H E B E A T I T U D E S sound strange, what follows only accentuates how subversive Jesus' teaching is. But Jesus is adamant: he came to fulfill the Law and the Prophets, not contradict them, to bring to completion all that God began to do through Israel. He expects "greater righteousness."

The rest of the Sermon expands on the meaning of this greater righteousness, applying the true intention of the Law of Moses to daily life. First, Jesus counters the legalism of the scribes and Pharisees. The scribes calculated over six hundred commandments and prohibitions in the Old Testament, and the Pharisees aspired to keep them all. Jesus says this entirely misses the mark. In fact, it only hinders obedience. Jesus concentrates on the spirit of the Law rather than on the details of its application.

Second, Jesus places priority on the root of behavior. Hence his emphasis on purity of the heart rather than on external matters like ritual washing of the hands. Likewise, it is not sufficient to refrain from killing, for killing is simply the symptom of a deeper malady.

When Jesus says, "But I say to you . . ." he is not contradicting the Old Testament but reiterating and clarifying the original intent of the Law. He *surpasses* every legality. In other words, Jesus is not issuing new rules or a new moral code but establishing a new relationship between God and his people, and among people.

Jesus brings a different kind of righteousness altogether, a righteousness that makes things right. Doing God's will is not a burden rooted in duty but a creative possibility that liberates us and conquers everything that divides – the sin inside us, the walls between us, and the forces that dehumanize us. ✦

14

The Law

• • • • •

Do not think that I have come to abolish the Law or the Prophets;
I have not come to abolish them but to fulfill them. For truly I
tell you, until heaven and earth disappear, not the smallest letter,
not the least stroke of a pen, will by any means disappear from
the Law until everything is accomplished. Therefore anyone who
sets aside one of the least of these commands and teaches others
accordingly will be called least in the kingdom of heaven, but
whoever practices and teaches these commands will be called
great in the kingdom of heaven.
  Matthew 5:17–19

Barbara Brown Taylor

J ESUS WAS A JEW. While there are lively discussions
  to be had with present-day Jews about just how Jewish he
  was, Matthew's Gospel is unambiguous: Jesus was a son
of Israel, a descendant of the royal house of David, the messiah
come in fulfillment of ancient prophecy, to uphold the divine
law that set his people apart and gave them fullness of life. . . .

I am so sorry to tell you this, but Jesus was just not a very good Protestant. He was a Jew, for whom good works were not optional. He was the loving son of the Light-Giver who gave the law, and he expected those who followed him to follow it too, right down to the last jot and tittle. Later Paul would mount some good arguments about how the law was God's grace for Jews, while God had something different in mind for Gentiles. But however our view of the law has changed through the years, our spiritual ancestors had the good sense to preserve this core teaching of Jesus in the Sermon on the Mount: God expects us to step up. Righteousness is a good thing. Exceeding righteousness is even better. Knowing God's word is no substitute for doing it. Good works count. ◆

Jen Wilkin

"CHRISTIAN, YOU CANNOT obey the Law. Your certain failure is a means to show forth the grace of God when you repent."

"We don't need more lists of how to be a better spouse/parent/Christian. We need more grace."

"My life strategy for today: fail, repent, repeat."

Sounds good, doesn't it? These sorts of statements compose a growing body of commentary that regards the Law of the Bible as a crushing burden, not just for the unbeliever, but for the believer as well. Enough with "checkbox Christianity," these voices tell us. No more "how-tos" on righteousness. In the righteousness department you are an epic fail, so toss out your checklists and your laws, and cast yourself on grace.…

As a response to this skewed view of Law, some have begun to articulate a skewed view of grace – one that discounts the

necessity of obedience to the moral precepts of the Law. I
call this view "celebratory failurism" – the idea that believers
cannot obey the Law and will fail at every attempt. Furthermore, our failure is ultimately cause to celebrate because it
makes grace all the more beautiful.

These days, obedience has gotten a bad name. And failure
has gotten a makeover.

Interestingly, Jesus battled legalism in a different way than
the celebratory failurist does. Rather than tossing out the Law
or devaluing obedience to it, he called his followers to a deeper
obedience (Matt. 5:17–48) than the behavior modification
the Pharisees prized. He called for obedience in motive as
well as in deed, the kind of godly obedience that is impossible for someone whose heart has not been transformed by
the gospel in the power of the Holy Spirit. Rather than abolish
the Law, Jesus deepened his followers' understanding of what
it required, and then went to the cross to ensure they could
actually begin to obey it. . . .

Celebratory failurism asserts that all our attempts to obey
will fail, thereby making us the recipients of greater grace.
But God does not exhort us to obey just to teach us that we
cannot hope to obey. He exhorts us to obey to teach us that, by
grace, we can obey, and therein lies hope. Through the gospel
our God, whose Law and whose character do not change,
changes us into those who obey in both motive and deed.
Believers no longer live under the Law, but the Law lies under
us as a sure path for pursuing what is good, right, and pleasing
to the Lord. Contrary to the tenets of celebratory failurism, the
Law is not the problem. The heart of the Law-follower is.

Obedience is only moralism if we believe it curries favor
with God. The believer knows that it is impossible to curry
favor with God, because God needs nothing from us. He

cannot be put in our debt. Knowing this frees us to obey out of joyful gratitude rather than servile grasping.

Imagine telling your child, "I know you'll fail, but here are our house rules. Let me know when you break them so I can extend grace to you." We recognize that raising a lawless child is not good for the child, for our family, or for society as a whole. We don't train our children to obey us so they can gain our favor. They already have our favor. We, being evil, train and equip them to obey because it is good and right and safe. And how much more does our heavenly Father love us? ◆

Addison Hodges Hart

ACCORDING TO HIS own testimony, Jesus "fulfills" the Torah; he "completes" it. But how? It would seem that he means that the Torah becomes "complete" when it goes into the hearts and lives of his hearers and changes them from the inside out. In other words, when it has a real effect in human hearts and changes human lives, it has been fulfilled: persons become embodiments of the Torah, and the Torah lives in them. This interpretation will be unambiguous in verses 21–48 [of Matthew 5]. . . . There Jesus will crack through the shell of the Law's literal statues, extracting the kernels of their inner meaning, and planting those deep into the motivations and minds of his followers. No longer literal murder, but the anger that prompts it is condemned; no longer simply adultery, but the taproot of lust is dug out; and so forth. In moving the Torah down deep into the inner motivations and passions, Jesus "writes the law upon their hearts." This, then, is the very essence of the new covenant. . . .

So he is willing to suspend any literal judgement in the case of palpable sin, such as in the account of the woman caught in adultery, sparing the sinner with almost carefree mercifulness. But he doesn't spare in the least, for instance, the interior vice of lust. Where contaminating inner drives are concerned, he is ruthless. Where people are concerned, he is generous. The Ten Commandments will get a makeover in the Sermon on the Mount, and in the process Jesus will not be "relaxing" the Law at all. When Jesus goes beneath the surface and forces us to examine our secret thoughts and scrutinize the unpleasant drives, passions, inward suggestions, and numerous "unclean spirits" that move us to malevolent behaviors, he is reinforcing the most pure objective of the Law. . . .

So, in effect, not an iota or a dot of the Law – meaning the moral laws – has been compromised by Jesus' radical approach. If the objective of the eternal Torah is accomplished, and lives are transformed and human beings learn to live in wisdom, then nothing contained in the Law – not even its smallest grammatical marks – have been in vain. The Law is fulfilled when people *do* the commandments as if by nature. "In the kingdom of heaven," says Jesus, "he who does them [the commandments] and teaches them shall be called great." In the words of Jeremiah's prophecy, God will put his laws "within them." They will be transformed from within, and thus will *naturally* grow into righteousness. This describes both Jesus' approach to the Torah – how he interprets it – and how he likewise presents the nature of the kingdom of heaven itself. ❖

Jürgen Moltmann

ANYONE WHO CONSIDERS the Sermon on the Mount to be in principle impossible of fulfillment mocks God; for God is the creator and lover of life, and he gives no commandments that cannot be fulfilled. Anyone who considers that the Sermon on the Mount is fulfillable only in the sentiments of the heart, but not in public action, says that Jesus is wrong; for he preached the sermon precisely in order that it might be put into practice. Anyone who considers that it is fulfillable only for himself personally, but not in the context of his responsibility for other people, does not know God the Creator. Anyone, finally, who believes that only one person – Jesus himself – was able to fulfill the Sermon on the Mount, whereas everyone else is bound to fail in the attempt, thus to become a manifest sinner, is stifling the truth of the community of Christ, about which Paul says: "Bear one another's burdens and so *fulfill* the law of Christ" (Gal. 6:2). ◆

The Greater Righteousness

• • • • •

For I tell you that unless your righteousness surpasses that of the Pharisees and the teachers of the law, you will certainly not enter the kingdom of heaven.
Matthew 5:20

Leo Tolstoy

JUST AS THERE ARE two ways for indicating the road to a traveler, even thus there are two ways for moral guidance in the case of a man who is seeking the truth. One way consists in indicating to the man the objects which he will come across, and then he is guided by these objects.

The other way consists in giving the man the direction by the compass, which he is carrying with him, and on which he observes the one immutable direction, and, consequently, every deflection from it.

The first way of moral guidance is the way of external definitions, of rules: man is given definite tokens of acts which he must perform and which not.

"Observe the Sabbath, be circumcised, do not steal, drink no intoxicating drink, kill no living being, give the tithe to the poor, make your ablutions, and pray five times a day," and so forth – such are the injunctions of external religious teachings – of the Brahmanical, Buddhistic, Muslim, Hebrew, and the ecclesiastic falsely called Christian.

The other way is to indicate to man unattainable perfection, the striving after which man is cognizant of: man has pointed out to him the ideal, in relation to which he is at any time able to see the degree of his divergence from it.

"Love God with all thy heart, and with all thy soul, and with all thy mind, and thy neighbor as thyself." "Be ye perfect, even as your Father which is in Heaven is perfect."

Such is the teaching of Christ.

The verification of the execution of external religious tenets is the coincidence of the acts with the injunctions of these tenets, and this coincidence is possible.

The verification of the execution of Christ's teaching is the consciousness of the degree of its non-correspondence with the ideal perfection. (The degree of approximation is not visible; what is visible is the deflection from perfection.)

A man who professes an external law is a man who is standing in the light of a lamp which is attached to a post. He is standing in the light of this lamp, he sees the light, and he has no other place to go to. A man who professes the teaching of Christ is like a man carrying a lamp before him on a more or less long pole: the light is always before him; it always incites him to follow it, and continually opens up in front of him a new illuminated space which draws him on. . . .

In this consists the difference between the teaching of Christ and all other religious teachings, a difference consisting not in the difference of demands, but in the difference of the way of guiding people. Christ gave no definitions of life. He never established any institutions, he never established marriage. But people who do not understand the peculiarities of Christ's teaching, who are accustomed to external tenets, and who wish to feel themselves in the right, as does the Pharisee, contrary to the whole spirit of Christ's teaching, have out of the letter made an external teaching of rules, and have substituted this teaching for Christ's true teaching of the ideal. . . .

The ideal of perfection which Christ has given us is not a dream or a subject for rhetorical sermons, but a most necessary, most accessible guide of moral life for man, just as the compass is a necessary and accessible implement guiding the navigator; all that is necessary is to believe in the one as in the other. In whatever situation a person may be, the teaching about the ideal, given by Christ, is sufficient in order to obtain the safest indication of those acts which one may and which one may not perform. But it is necessary completely to believe in this teaching, this one teaching, and to stop believing in any other, just as it is necessary for the navigator to believe in the compass, and to stop looking at and being guided by what he sees on both sides. . . .

"Man is weak – he must receive a task which is according to his strength," say people. This amounts to saying: "My hands are weak and I cannot draw a straight line, that is, one which is the shortest distance between two points, and therefore, in order to make it easier for myself, though wishing to draw a straight line, I will take a curved or a broken line as my guide." The weaker my hand is, the more perfect must my guide be.

It is not right, having come to know the Christian teaching of the ideal, to act as though we did not know it, and to substitute external definitions for it. The Christian teaching of the ideal is open to humanity because it can guide it at its present age. Humanity has passed out from external religious injunctions, and nobody believes in them.

The Christian doctrine of the ideal is the only one which can guide humanity. We must not, we should not substitute external rules for the ideal of Christ, but this ideal must be kept firmly before us in all its purity, and, above everything else, we must believe in it. ◆

Oswald Chambers

I S IT TOO STRONG to call this a spiritual torpedo? These statements of Jesus are the most revolutionary statements human ears ever listened to, and it needs the Holy Spirit to interpret them to us; the shallow admiration for Jesus Christ as a teacher that is taught today is of no use.

Who is going to climb that "hill of the Lord"? To stand before God and say, "My hands are clean, my heart is pure" – who can do it? Who can stand in the eternal light of God and have nothing for God to blame in him or in her? – only the Son of God. . . .

Jesus says our disposition must be right to its depths, not only our conscious motives but our unconscious motives. Now we are beyond our depth. Can God make me pure in heart? Blessed be the name of God, he can! Can he alter my disposition so that when circumstances reveal me to myself, I am amazed? He can. Can he impart his nature to me until it is identically the same as his own? He can. That, and nothing less, is the meaning of his cross and resurrection. ◆

16

Anger

$\bullet\ \bullet\ \bullet\ \bullet\ \bullet$

You have heard that it was said to the people long ago, "You shall not murder, and anyone who murders will be subject to judgment." But I tell you that anyone who is angry with a brother or sister will be subject to judgment. Again, anyone who says to a brother or sister, "Raca," is answerable to the court. And anyone who says, "You fool!" will be in danger of the fire of hell.

Matthew 5:21–22

Dallas Willard

ACCORDING TO JESUS, contempt is a greater evil than anger and so is deserving of greater condemnation. Unlike innocent anger, at least, it is a kind of studied degradation of another, and it also is more pervasive in life than anger. It is never justifiable or good. Therefore Jesus tells us, "Whoever says 'Raca' to his brother shall stand condemned before the Sanhedrin, the highest court of the land."

The Aramaic term *raca* was current in Jesus' day to express contempt for someone and to mark out him or her as contemptible. It may have originated from the sound one makes to collect spittle from the throat in order to spit. In anger I want to hurt you. In contempt, I don't care whether you are hurt or not. Or at least so I say. You are not worth consideration one way or the other. We can be angry at someone without denying their worth. But contempt makes it easier for us to hurt them or see them further degraded.

Today, of course, we would not say, "Raca." But we might call someone a twit or a twerp, maybe a dork or a nerd. These are the gentler words in our vocabulary of contempt; when it really gets going, it becomes filthy. Our verbal arsenal is loaded with contemptuous terms, some with sexual, racial, or cultural bearings, others just personally degrading. They should never be uttered.

The intent and the effect of contempt is always to exclude someone, push them away, leave them out and isolated. This explains why filth is so constantly invoked in expressing contempt and why contempt is so cruel, so serious. It breaks the social bond more severely than anger. Yet it may also be done with such refinement.

How often we see it, in the schoolyard, at a party, even in the home or church sanctuary! Someone is being put down or oh so precisely omitted, left out. It is a constant in most of human life. In the course of normal life one is rarely in a situation where contempt is not at least hovering in the wings. And everyone lives in terror of it. It is never quite beyond the margins of our consciousness. . . .

Jesus' comment here is that anyone who says, "Raca," to an associate is rightly to be singled out by the highest authorities in the land – "the council," or Sanhedrin – for appropriate and obviously serious penalties. Contemptuous actions and attitudes are a knife in the heart that permanently harms and mutilates people's souls. That they are so common does not ease their destructiveness. In most professional circles and "high" society, where one might hope for the highest moral sensitivity, contempt is a fine art. Practicing it is even a part of being "in good standing." Not to know whom and how to despise is one of the surest of signs that you are not quite with it and are yourself mildly contemptible.

In his marvelous little talk "The Inner Ring," C. S. Lewis comments that "in all men's lives at certain periods, and in many men's lives at all periods between infancy and extreme old age, one of the most dominant elements is the desire to be inside the local Ring and the terror of being left outside."

To *belong* is a vital need based in the spiritual nature of the human being. Contempt spits on this pathetically deep need. And, like anger, contempt does not have to be acted out in special ways to be evil. It is inherently poisonous. Just by being what it is, it is withering to the human soul. But when expressed in the contemptuous phrase – in its thousands of forms – or in the equally powerful gesture or look, it stabs the soul to its core and deflates its powers of life. It can hurt so badly and destroy so deeply that murder would almost be a mercy. Its power is also seen in the intensity of the resentment and rage it always evokes.

But Jesus notes one stage further in the progression of internal evil that may be there without murder occurring: "And whoever says 'You fool!' shall merit condemnation to the fires of Gehenna."

"You fool!" said with that characteristic combination of freezing contempt and withering anger that Jesus had in mind, is a deeper harm than either anger or contempt alone. . . .

The fool, in biblical language, is a combination of stupid perversity and rebellion against God and all that sensible people stand for. He is willfully perverted, rebellious, knowingly wicked to his own harm. . . . To brand someone "fool" in this biblical sense was a violation of the soul so devastating, of such great harm, that, as Jesus saw, it would justify consigning the offender to the smoldering garbage dump of human existence, Gehenna. It combines all that is evil in anger as well as in contempt. It is not possible for people with such attitudes toward others to live in the movements of God's kingdom, for they are totally out of harmony with it. ◆

Augustine of Hippo

WE ARE NOT delivered from offenses, but it is equally true that we are not deprived of our refuge; our griefs do not cease, but our consolations are equally abiding. And well do you know how, in the midst of such offenses, we must watch lest hatred of anyone gain a hold upon the heart, and so not only hinder us from praying to God with the door of our chamber closed (Matt. 6:6) but also shut the door against God himself; for hatred of another insidiously creeps upon us, while no one who is angry considers his anger to be unjust. For anger habitually cherished against anyone becomes hatred, since the sweetness which is mingled with what appears to be righteous anger makes us detain it longer than we ought in the vessel, until the whole is soured, and the vessel itself is spoiled. . . . It is incomparably more for our soul's welfare to shut the recesses of the heart against anger, even when it knocks with a just claim for admission, than to admit that which it will be most difficult to expel, and which will rapidly grow from a mere sapling to a strong tree. Anger dares to increase with boldness more suddenly than people suppose, for it does not blush in the dark, when the sun has gone down upon it. ✦

Francis de Sales

YOU WILL ASK how to put away anger. My child, when you feel its first movements, collect yourself gently and seriously, not hastily or with impetuosity. Sometimes in a law court the officials who enforce quiet make more noise than those they affect to hush; and so, if you are impetuous in restraining your temper, you will throw your heart into worse confusion than before, and, amid the excitement, it will lose all self-control. . . . If you are like the Psalmist, ready to cry out, "Mine eye is consumed for very anger," go on to say, "Have mercy upon me, O Lord," so that God may stretch forth his right hand and control your wrath. I mean that when we feel stirred with anger we ought to call upon God for help, like the apostles did when they were tossed about with wind and storm. And he is sure to say, "Peace, be still." . . .

Further, directly you are conscious of an angry act, atone for the fault by some speedy act of meekness towards the person who excited your anger. It is a good remedy for anger to make immediate amends by some opposite act of meekness. There is an old saying, that fresh wounds are soonest closed. Moreover, when there is nothing to stir your wrath, lay up a store of meekness and kindliness, speaking and acting in things great and small as gently as possible. ✦

William Blake

A Poison Tree

I was angry with my friend;
I told my wrath, my wrath did end.
I was angry with my foe:
I told it not, my wrath did grow.

And I waterd it in fears,
Night & morning with my tears:
And I sunned it with smiles,
And with soft deceitful wiles.

And it grew both day and night.
Till it bore an apple bright.
And my foe beheld it shine,
And he knew that it was mine.

And into my garden stole,
When the night had veild the pole;
In the morning glad I see;
My foe outstretched beneath the tree. ◆

Right Worship

♦ ♦ ♦ ♦ ♦

Therefore, if you are offering your gift at the altar and there remember that your brother or sister has something against you, leave your gift there in front of the altar. First go and be reconciled to them; then come and offer your gift.

Settle matters quickly with your adversary who is taking you to court. Do it while you are still together on the way, or your adversary may hand you over to the judge, and the judge may hand you over to the officer, and you may be thrown into prison. Truly I tell you, you will not get out until you have paid the last penny.

Matthew 5:23–26

F. B. Meyer

"YOUR GIFT AT THE ALTAR." The altar denotes some act of self-surrender to God's service which we are eager to make. Beside it stands the High Priest, waiting to consummate our gift, adding to it the merit of his intercession. The light of the Shekinah fire (Exod. 13:20–22), which waits to consume the gift, is shining with intense brilliancy. All is prepared for the devout act of the soul which, constrained by the mercies of God, is about to present itself a holy, reasonable, and living sacrifice. Suddenly our great Melchizedek [Jesus (see Heb. 7)] turns a searching light upon the hours which have recently passed. Every incident stands as clearly revealed as the objects in a landscape illumined by the lightning flash at midnight. And we hear his voice say solemnly and searchingly, "Does your brother have something against you?" (Matt. 5:23).

At first we shudder before the inquiry. We are conscious of some hidden wrong. The stiletto with which we struck at him was so sharp and slender that we assured ourselves against ourselves that the thrust must have escaped Christ's notice. But now we are aware that he, whose eyes carry the light with which they see, beheld it. We cannot deceive him, but we evade his inquiry by enumerating the many causes of complaint that we have against the person who has been the subject of our Lord's question.

"He has not treated me as I had every right to expect. He has been ungrateful, ungracious, intolerant. He has not considered my interests. He has taken advantage of my goodwill. I never can get along with him; his temperament and mine are so different. Why did you give him to me as my brother? Had it been anyone else, I could have agreed. Outwardly I have tried to do my best. Can you wonder that I hide a grudge in my heart, and that almost involuntarily it betrays its presence? But, after all, the incident was a very slight one; no doubt he has forgotten it before now. He is accustomed to giving me ugly knocks; probably his skin is too thick to feel so slight an evidence of my unfriendliness."

Again, the searching voice inquires: "Does your brother have something against you?"

"It depends, O Master," we reply, "in what court the case is tried. In any human court so slight a thing as that which stands revealed in this fierce light would be passed over as too trivial for notice. Before a jury of my friends, or even of my acquaintances, it would be admitted that I had not done anything so very wrong. It might be supposed that I was becoming morbid and introspective were I to take action on such a triviality."

Again, that clear, strong voice is heard saying: "We will not quibble. You know that your brother is suffering, and he is losing faith in your profession of religion, that he is being prejudiced against me. Your parrying of my question is your condemnation. You know what you have done. In excusing, you accuse yourself. Leave your gift at the altar. Go first and be reconciled to him. Then return; I will await you. Though hours may pass, you will find me here."

"May I not offer my gift now, and then find my brother? My heart is full of desire. I am eager to be an entire burnt offering to my God. Will not this fervor pass away, and leave me chilled?"

"Not so," the Master answers. "Your present gift will not be acceptable to God. The impetuous desire to make it is of the flesh, not of the Spirit. If it were of the Spirit there would be no doubt about its ultimate permanence. To obey is better than sacrifice, and to hearken than the fat of lambs (1 Sam. 15:22). Be quick. The sky is darkening with night. The road that remains to be traversed by your brother, who has now become your adversary, is short. Agree with him quickly while you are on the way, lest by delay the quarrel between you and him becomes aggravated, and you find yourself in difficulties from which extrication will be impossible. Every moment of delay intensifies the sense of injustice, and makes more difficult your attempt at reconciliation."

"But he has wronged me, gracious Master. Is nothing to be said to him?"

"Not in the first place," is the reply. "It is necessary that you should retract for your part, whatever it may be. Ask his forgiveness for that ruffled feeling, that unkind and harsh bearing, that icy reserve. Pay him any due that he may rightfully claim. Ask his forgiveness as you would ask God's, and your approach will bring a flood of repentant and protesting words, which will show that you have won your brother. But if these do not follow, and he receives your apology as his right, or without remark, still you have done your part, and there is nothing to be said against you further. I will deal with him – then come and offer your gift."

What music then is in that word *Come!* (Matt. 5:24) All heaven speaks in the invitation. Come, says the Master, and render yourself a living sacrifice, which is your reasonable service (Rom. 12:1). Come and let me make of you so much as is possible in your brief life. Come, for all things are ready.

And we discover this – that when we have acted as love should act, not because we *feel* the love, but because the Master bids us, and we simply obey, then the love of God bursts up in our hearts like a hot geyser spring, and we find ourselves able to offer our gifts to God with an emotion of love that we could never have experienced otherwise. ◆

Henri J. M. Nouwen

S O MUCH OF OUR energy, time, and money goes into maintaining distance from one another. Many if not most of the resources of the world are used to defend ourselves against one another, to maintain or increase our power, and to safeguard our own privileged position.

Imagine all that effort being put in the service of peace and reconciliation! Would there be any poverty? Would there be crimes and wars? Just imagine that there was no longer fear among people, no longer rivalry, hostility, bitterness, or revenge. . . . We say, "I can't imagine." But God says, "That's what I imagine, a whole world not only created but also living in my image." ◆

George MacDonald

I READ THEN, in this parable, that a man had better make up his mind to be righteous, to be fair, to do what he can to pay what he owes, in any and all the relations of life – all the matters, in a word, wherein one man may demand of another, or complain that he has not received fair play. Arrange your matters with those who have anything against you, while you are yet together and things have not gone too far to be arranged; you will have to do it, and that under less easy circumstances than now. Putting off is of no use. You must. The thing has to be done; there are means of compelling you.

"In this affair, however, I am in the right."

"If so, very well – for this affair. But I have reason to doubt whether you are capable of judging righteously in your own cause. Do you hate the man?"

"No, I don't hate him."

"Do you dislike him?"

"I can't say I like him."

"Do you love him as yourself?"

"Oh, come, come! No one does that!"

"Then no one is to be trusted when he thinks, however firmly, that he is all right, and his neighbor all wrong, in any matter between them."

"But I don't say I am all right, and he is all wrong; there may be something to urge on his side; what I say is, that I am more in the right than he."

"This is not fundamentally a question of things: it is a question of condition, of spiritual relation and action, towards your neighbor. If in yourself you were all right towards him, you could do him no wrong. Let it be with the individual dispute as it may, you owe him something that you do not pay him, as certainly as you think he owes you something he will not pay you."

"He would take immediate advantage of me if I owned that."

"So much the worse for him. Until you are fair to him, it does not matter to you whether he is unfair to you or not."

"I beg your pardon – it is just what does matter! I want nothing but my rights. What can matter to me more than my rights?"

"Your duties – your debts. You are all wrong about the thing. It is a very small matter to you whether the man give you your rights or not; it is life or death to you whether or not you give him his. Whether he pay you what you count his debt or no, you will be compelled to pay him all you owe him. If you owe him a pound and he you a million, you must pay him the pound whether he pay you the million or not; there is no business parallel here. If, owing you love, he gives you hate, you, owing him love, have yet to pay it. A love unpaid you, a justice undone you, a praise withheld from you, a judgment passed on you without judgment, will not absolve you of the debt of a love unpaid, a justice not done, a praise withheld, a false judgment passed: these uttermost farthings – not to speak of such debts as the world itself counts grievous wrongs – you must pay him, whether he pay you or not. We have a good while given us to pay, but a crisis will come – come soon after all – comes always sooner than those expect it who are not ready for it – a crisis when the demand unyielded will be followed by prison."

The same holds with every demand of God: by refusing to pay, the man makes an adversary who will compel him – and that for the man's own sake. If you or your life say, "I will not," then he will see to it. There is a prison, and the one thing we know about that prison is that its doors do not open until entire satisfaction is rendered, the last farthing paid. ◆

18

Sexual Purity

• • • • •

*You have heard that it was said, "You shall not commit adultery."
But I tell you that anyone who looks at a woman lustfully has
already committed adultery with her in his heart. If your right
eye causes you to stumble, gouge it out and throw it away. It is
better for you to lose one part of your body than for your whole
body to be thrown into hell. And if your right hand causes you to
stumble, cut it off and throw it away. It is better for you to lose
one part of your body than for your whole body to go into hell.*
Matthew 5:27–30

J. Heinrich Arnold

IN A STRUGGLE against temptation, what can we do to
blot out the evil clouding our inner eye, or bring into focus
the love of God we are looking for? In the boxing ring or
on the street, the strong-willed man may be the winner; yet in
the struggle of the human heart, willpower may have nothing
to do with the outcome of a battle.

It is impossible to defeat one's sinful nature by willpower alone, because the will is never wholly free, but bent this way and that by conflicting emotions and other forces at work on it. In an inner struggle it becomes, as the German philosophers say, especially *verkrampft* [cramped], and to enlist it may be of no use at all. In fact, it may end up entrenching in our mind the very evil we are struggling to overcome, or even drive it to the point of becoming reality. In the words of the Swiss-French psychiatrist Charles Baudouin:

> When an idea imposes itself on the mind . . . all conscious efforts the subject makes in order to counteract it are not merely without the desired effect, but will actually go in the opposite direction and intensify it . . . with the result that the dominant idea is reinforced.

Paul writes knowingly of the problem:

> I do not understand what I do. For what I want to do I do not do, but what I hate I do. . . . I have the desire to do what is good, but I cannot carry it out. (Rom. 7:15–18)

Perhaps it is helpful here to distinguish between the will and the deeper, essential longing of our heart: the conscience. Whereas the will reacts to temptation by attempting to inhibit the imagination and desire, the conscience (the early Quakers called it the "inner light") points us to true purity of heart. It is a guide in the innermost recesses of the soul, where Christ himself dwells. And when it takes the upper hand, the worst temptations can be overcome. . . .

Again, as long as we try to conquer evil by sheer willpower, evil will get the better of us. To quote Baudouin's colleague Émile Coué, "When the will and the imagination are at war, the imagination gains the upper hand without exception." Yet as soon as we give ear to that innermost longing of heart that cries out for Jesus, the evil in us will retreat. And if we trust in this deeper will and pray, "Not my will, but your will, Jesus. Your purity is greater than my impurity; your generosity will overcome my envy; your love will triumph over my hatred," it will gradually subside altogether.

We must believe: Jesus really is faithful to us, even though we are unfaithful, and he is not a distant savior who reaches down from above, but a man who, as Paul writes, died on the cross "in human weakness" and now lives "by the power of God." . . .

Is purity a practical goal, or just a wonderful ideal? In struggling to answer this vital question over many years, I always find myself returning to the one who calls us to a pure heart in the first place. If Jesus – the only sinless man to have ever walked the earth – struggled with temptation, how much understanding he must have for our lapses and failings! Yet he still demands of us, "Be perfect," and tells us that only the pure in heart will "see God."

The Swedish writer Selma Lagerlöf tells the story of a knight who, having lit a candle at the tomb of Jesus on one of the Crusades, vows to bring back this flame, unextinguished, to his home town in Italy. Though robbed by highwaymen and met by every possible calamity and danger on his journey, the knight is set on one thing only: to guard and protect his small flame. At the end of the story, we see how single-minded devotion transfigures this knight completely: having left home a ruthless warrior, capable of the worst deeds, he has returned a new man.

If, like this knight, we set our hearts on one thing alone, we too can be wholly transfigured: "When he appears we will be like him, and we shall see him as he is. Everyone who has this hope in him purifies himself, just as he is pure" (1 John 3:2–3). But as long as we remain divided, we will (to quote my father's book *Inner Land*) also remain "weak, flabby, and indolent; incapable of accepting God's will, making important decisions, and taking strong action. . . . Purity of heart is nothing else than the absolute integrity needed to overcome enervating desires."

Before we dismiss this "absolute integrity" as another impossible ideal, let us look at what the apostle Paul says about purification. He takes it for granted that we will always have arguments and obstacles in our minds, and that we will always be subject to temptation. Yet he goes on to describe our fight against evil as a victorious one in which every thought is "taken captive to obey Christ" (2 Cor. 10:5). Again, the victory may not be easily gained. We must face the fact that the struggle is a full-fledged war that has been waged continually since the fall of man, and that since the resurrection and the coming down of the Holy Spirit at Pentecost, it has only intensified. The wonderful thing about Paul's words is his certainty that our thoughts can be taken captive to obey Christ. ✦

Francis Chan

"LORD, PLEASE kill me before I cheat on my wife." This is a prayer that I prayed many times when I was first married. I'm not saying that it was mature or biblical, but it gives you a glimpse into my mind. I did not ever want to bring shame to the church, and I knew that this potential for evil was in me. . . .

I remember reading, many years ago, an article about a man who had a fatal heart attack while having sex with a prostitute. I imagined how terrifying it must have been for that man to enter into the presence of a holy God at that moment. If nothing else keeps you from adultery, maybe the fact that Almighty God could take your life amidst the very act would terrify you enough to repent.

It was years later that a friend of mine, a fellow pastor, committed adultery with his assistant. I didn't see him for months after it happened. When he came into my office, he looked awful. He proceeded to tell me the whole story. He explained how one thing led to another, and before he knew it he had committed the act he preached against for years.

What impacted me most was when he explained his thoughts and feelings after sinning. He told me of how he kept looking at his revolver, tempted to pull the trigger. He reasoned that everyone would be happier if he was dead. The other woman's husband would be happier. His own wife and kids would be happier. His church would be happier. It was only by the grace of God that he was still alive.

Of course, taking his own life in the aftermath of adultery would only be multiplying the sin. But I was struck by the misery he felt. He seriously thought it would be better to be dead than to have done this and to live with the consequences! His misery was both a wake-up call and a warning to me. Fear can be a great grace.

My pursuit of sexual purity has been a discipline. I have said with the apostle Paul, "I discipline my body and keep it under control, lest after preaching to others I myself should be disqualified" (1 Cor. 9:27).

I live each day with severe caution. I rarely counsel women, and never alone. I won't go anywhere with a woman alone. In twenty-three years, I have never even been in a car alone with another woman (aside from relatives). It has felt silly at times to inconveniently tell women they had to drive separately even though we are going to the same location, but I believe it's been worth it. My wife has access to all of my email accounts and phone records, and I don't have a Facebook profile. There are no secrets between us.

I have alcoholic friends who were supernaturally delivered from any desire for alcohol. I have other friends who pray for deliverance, but are tempted daily. They refuse to have any alcohol in their homes, and stay away from tempting situations. After reading John Piper's letter to a would-be adulterer, it sounds like his story has been one of supernatural deliverance, while mine has been one of discipline and daily strength. I believe God is glorified by both.

Early on in my Christian journey, I focused only on running away from sin. I believe it was good and right, but not complete. It was later that I discovered the truth of Galatians 5:16, "Walk by the Spirit, and you will not gratify the desires of the flesh."

God calls us not only to run away from temptation, but to run toward him. He promises that when we are walking by the Spirit, we *will not* gratify the flesh. As I have followed God's Spirit into meaningful ministry, it has been amazing to see the craving for sin diminish. The thrill of the Holy Spirit manifesting himself through me to bless others fills me thoroughly, crowding out sinful desires that might otherwise have had room to grow (1 Cor. 12:7).

It's like playing in an intense basketball game. I get tunnel vision. Winning is all I think about. My mind does not wander one bit. In the same way, when my wife and I are intensely pursuing God's cause and kingdom, our minds don't wander toward sin. Soldiers stay focused when they are in battle.

"No soldier gets entangled in civilian pursuits, since his aim is to please the one who enlisted him" (2 Tim. 2:4). It's when we relax, when we forget we are actually on a mission, that trouble comes. ◆

19

Marriage

• • • • •

It has been said, "Anyone who divorces his wife must give her a certificate of divorce." But I tell you that anyone who divorces his wife, except for sexual immorality, makes her the victim of adultery, and anyone who marries a divorced woman commits adultery.

Matthew 5:31–32

Johann Christoph Arnold

THE QUESTION OF DIVORCE and remarriage is one of the toughest issues that face the Christian church in our time. It is harder and harder to find couples who affirm the words, "What God has joined together, let no one put asunder" – couples who believe that marriage means faithfulness between one man and one woman until death parts them (Matt. 19:6).

The majority of Christians today believe that divorce and remarriage are morally and biblically permissible. They argue that though God hates divorce, he allows it as a concession to our sinful condition. Because of our hardness of heart, they explain, marriages can "die" or dissolve. In other words, God recognizes our frailty and accepts the fact that in a fallen world the ideal cannot always be realized. Through God's forgiveness, one can always start again, even if in a new marriage.

But what about the bond that is promised between two and made – whether knowingly or unknowingly – before God? Does God's forgiveness ever mean we can deny it? Does he ever allow unfaithfulness? Just as the unity of the church is eternal and unchangeable, so true marriage reflects this unity and is indissoluble. Like the early Christians, I believe that as long as both spouses are living, there can be no remarriage after divorce. What God has joined together in the unity of the Spirit is joined together until death parts a couple. Unfaithfulness, whether by one or by both partners, cannot change this. No Christian has the freedom to marry someone else as long as his or her spouse is still living. The bond of unity is at stake.

Jesus is clear that it was because of hard-heartedness that Moses, under the law, allowed divorce (Matt. 19:8). However, among his disciples – those born of the Spirit – hard-heartedness is no longer a valid excuse. Moses said, "Anyone who divorces his wife must give her a certificate of divorce." But Jesus said, "Anyone who divorces his wife, except for sexual immorality, makes her the victim of adultery, and anyone who marries a divorced woman commits adultery." The disciples understood this decisive word of Jesus clearly: "If this is the situation between a husband and wife, it is better not to marry" (Matt. 19:10). Moses gave allowance to divorce out of sheer necessity, but this hardly changes the fact that from the beginning marriage was meant to be indissoluble. A marriage cannot be dissolved (even if it is broken), neither by the husband who abandons his adulterous wife, nor by the wife who abandons her adulterous husband. God's order cannot be abolished that easily or lightly. . . .

Even if Jesus allows divorce for reasons of sexual immorality or adultery, it should never be the inevitable result or an excuse to remarry. Jesus' love reconciles and forgives. Those who seek a divorce will always be left with the stain of bitterness on their conscience. No matter how much emotional pain an unfaithful spouse causes, the wounded partner must be willing to forgive. Only when we forgive can we ever hope to receive the forgiveness of God for ourselves (Matt. 6:14–15). Faithful love, to our spouse but especially to Christ, is the only answer to a broken bond. . . .

Though God hates divorce, he will also judge every unloving or dead marriage, and this should be a warning to each of us. How many of us have been cold-hearted or loveless to our spouses at one time or another? How many thousands of couples, rather than loving each other, merely coexist? True faithfulness is not simply the absence of adultery. It must be a commitment of heart and soul. Whenever husband and wife lack commitment to each other, live parallel lives, or become estranged, separation and divorce lurk around the corner.

It is the task of every church to fight the spirit of adultery wherever it raises its head. Here I am not only speaking of adultery as a physical act; in a sense, anything inside a marriage that weakens love, unity, and purity, or hinders the spirit of mutual reverence, is adultery, because it feeds the spirit of adultery. That is why God speaks of the unfaithfulness of the people of Israel as adultery (Mal. 2:10–16).

In the Old Testament, the prophets use faithfulness in marriage as a picture of God's commitment to Israel, his chosen people – his bride (Hos. 3:1). In a similar way, the apostle Paul compares marriage to the relationship of unity between Christ, the bridegroom, and his church, the bride. Only in the spirit of these biblical images can we clearly consider the question of divorce and remarriage.

When a church fails to nurture the marriages of its own members, how can it claim innocence when these marriages fall apart? When it shies away from testifying that "what God has joined together, no one should put asunder," how can it expect its married members to remain committed for life?

In considering these questions, there are two pitfalls we must avoid. First, we can never agree to divorce; second, we must never treat those who suffer its need and pain with legalism or rigidity. In rejecting divorce, we cannot reject the divorced person, even if remarried. We must always remember that though Jesus speaks very sharply against sin, he never lacks compassion. But because he longs to redeem and heal every sinner, he requires repentance for every sin. This is also true for every broken marriage.

Clearly, we must never judge. At the same time, however, we must be faithful to Christ above everything else. We must embrace his whole truth – not just those parts of it that seem to fit our needs (Matt. 23:23–24). . . .

Naturally, if divorce is to be avoided, the church must offer its members guidance and practical support long before their marriages collapse. As soon as there are indications that a marriage is at risk, it is best to be honest and open about it. Once a couple drifts too far apart, it may take space as well as time for them to find each other's hearts again. In a situation like this, as in one where a spouse has become abusive, temporary separation may be necessary. Especially when this is the case, the church must find concrete ways to help both spouses – first in seeking repentance and then in finding the mutual trust and forgiveness necessary to restore the marriage.

It is sad that in today's society, faithfulness is so rare that it has come to be seen as a "heroic" virtue. Shouldn't it be taken for granted as the bedrock of our faith? As followers of Christ, shouldn't each of us be willing to hold firm through thick and thin until death, to Christ, to his church, and to our husband or wife? Only with this resolve can we hope to remain faithful to our marriage vows.

The way of discipleship is a narrow way, but through the cross anyone who hears the words of Jesus can put them into practice. If Jesus' teaching on divorce and remarriage is hard, it is only because so many in our day no longer believe in the power of repentance and forgiveness. It is because we no longer believe that what God joins together can, by his grace, be held together; and that, as Jesus says, "With God, all things are possible."

Nothing should be too hard for us when it is a requirement of the gospel (Matt. 11:28–30). If we look at Jesus' teaching on divorce and remarriage in this faith, we will see that it is one of great promise, hope, and strength. It is a teaching whose righteousness is much greater than that of the moralists and philosophers. It is the righteousness of the kingdom, and it is based on the reality of resurrection and new life. ◆

David Fleer

PREACHERS TODAY DON'T much quote anymore, "God hates divorce." Now they quote, "Judge not, lest you be judged."

Times have changed. . . . Now, when former partners find themselves "on radically different life paths" and discover "no more potential for life in their relationship," they can go their blessed way. The off ramp reads, "Times have changed."

Early in my first ministry the exit I was tempted to take was marked, "Let bygones be bygones" when one Sunday William came forward and stood before the congregation. He said, with only a little prodding, that if he'd offended anyone, he was sorry and that he'd like to be considered a member in good standing. He wanted to start out fresh and his fiancée, Rebecca, was studying to become a Christian. But the congregation's elders, who knew William, hesitated. They wondered if there might need to be fruit demonstrating repentance. After all, his affairs and divorce had left his first wife devastated and the congregation reeling. But I stood firm and said, "Do we believe in grace or not? If God can forgive him, then why can't we?" He married Rebecca, and they had a child and then divorced for what seemed good cause. And he married again, and this one lasted a while longer—another child, last I heard. That's life; look around.

The off ramp I helped construct read, "You've heard that it was said, 'Whoever marries a divorced woman commits adultery,' but I say to you, let bygones be bygones, it doesn't matter, time to move on. . . ."

This passage on marriage and divorce is full of exits that want to lure us away.

From the simple, "That can't mean what it says . . . ,"

To the theoretical, "It's symbolic of what should be but isn't. An ideal we cannot reach . . . ,"

To the historic personal, "What about battered wives who didn't leave an abusive relationship because they were told it was 'the Lord's will'?" . . .

But, what if we stay on the road? Avoid these off ramps? Walk with Jesus, at least for a while, see where he is headed?

What we find, down the road, is that other religious folk seem as troubled over this matter as we are and try to push Jesus into an exit lane. Down the road, we overhear this revealing conversation:

> RELIGIOUS LEADERS TO JESUS: "Is it lawful to divorce for any reason at all? Would you please clarify for us your opinion on the text you earlier quoted, Deuteronomy? May a man divorce his wife 'for a matter of indecency.' Yes or no?"

> JESUS: "Let's not talk about exceptions. Let's talk about intentions. Let's talk about beginnings, about Genesis. What God has joined together let no man. . . ."

> RELIGIOUS LEADERS: "You're not answering the question. Yes or no: May a man divorce his wife 'for any matter of indecency'?"

When smoke finally clears, Jesus is standing next to a wife, saying, "You're not getting rid of her so quickly. You'll not uproot her, cast her away without resources, abandoned, tainted, all because your 'dish was spoiled' or 'she didn't age as expected.'"

In this conversation Jesus isn't dodging bullets, digressing, or taking an off ramp. Jesus is reprogramming our way of thinking to change our way of living.

Jesus isn't parading down the road with a book of codes under one arm and drawing lines in the sand with the other. He's walking with people in need, the hopeless and helpless, women and men on the margins.

Jesus is standing with a wife about to be exchanged. He says, "Not so fast, mister."

Stay with Jesus on the road – in this tough section of town – and listen to the context of his words. Jesus says, "No lust," "no anger," "pray for your enemies." . . . These are not ideals beyond reach, an interim ethic, all about the hereafter. This is reprogramming for the community who call themselves the church of Christ. ✦

Dietrich Bonhoeffer

ARRIAGE IS MORE than your love for each other. It has a higher dignity and power. For it is God's holy ordinance, by means of which he wills to perpetuate the human race until the end of time. In your love you see your two selves as solitary figures in the world; in marriage you see yourselves as links in the chain of the generations, which God causes to come and go to his glory and calls into his kingdom. In your love you see only the heaven of your bliss, through marriage you are placed at a post of responsibility toward the world and to humankind.

Your love is your own private possession; marriage is more than a private affair, it is an estate, an office. As the crown makes the king, and not just his determination to rule, so marriage, and not just your love for each other, makes you husband and wife in the sight of God and man. As you first gave the ring to one another and received it a second time from the hand of the parson, so love comes from you, but marriage from above, from God. As God is infinitely higher than man, so the sanctity, the privilege, and the promise of marriage are higher than the sanctity, the privilege, and the promise of love. It is not your love which sustains the marriage, but from now on the marriage that sustains your love.

God makes your marriage indissoluble. "Those whom God has joined together, let no man put asunder." God is joining you together; it is his act, not yours. Do not confound your love with God. God makes your marriage indissoluble, he protects it from every danger from within and without. What a blessed thing it is to know that no power on earth, no human frailty can dissolve what God holds together. Knowing that, we may say with all confidence, what God has joined together man *cannot* put asunder. No need now to be troubled with those anxious fears so inseparable from love. You can say to each other now without a shadow of doubt: "We can never lose each other now. By the will of God we belong to each other till death us do part." ◆

20

Truthfulness

• • • • •

Again, you have heard that it was said to the people long ago, "Do not break your oath, but fulfill to the Lord the vows you have made." But I tell you, do not swear an oath at all: either by heaven, for it is God's throne; or by the earth, for it is his footstool; or by Jerusalem, for it is the city of the Great King. And do not swear by your head, for you cannot make even one hair white or black. All you need to say is simply "Yes" or "No"; anything beyond this comes from the evil one.

Matthew 5:33–37

Peter Riedemann

NOWADAYS there is much controversy about taking oaths, with everyone asserting their own opinion. They all lack the truth and with their fabricated delusions seek to lead many astray. They cause hearts to be burdened and led into sin. Therefore I feel urged to reveal what is false, deceitful, and senseless, and to point to the truth. I do not want to quarrel with them, for that is not my way, nor the way of the church of God, but I wish to protect devout people from being tainted by those who represent these many false teachings.

They say first that in the Old Testament, God himself commanded his people to swear by his name. Now the Son is not against the Father; what the Father once commanded, the Son has not changed.

To this we say that, truly, we know the Son is not against the Father. Otherwise, his kingdom would fall. Father and Son are one, and for this reason the Son wants us to be one in him. Christ is one with the Father, and Christ is in the Father, and the Father is in Christ. Therefore, it is not Christ but the Father in him who has now established and not annulled his law. He has brought it, as Paul says, from the shadow into the light of truth. . . .

Someone may ask, "Should we understand the scriptures only literally?" We say no! Here, as in all scripture, we must let the Holy Spirit, through whom scripture was inspired, be the judge. But who can judge in this way without having the Holy Spirit? A carnal person understands nothing of the things of the Spirit of God, but the spiritual person judges all things spiritually. Those who have Christ will easily recognize what is meant here about him. They will discover that Christ brings the truth out of the shadow and says, "People were commanded not to swear falsely, but I say to you, do not swear at all." It is primarily Christ's purpose, as Matthew 5 shows, to lead us to a more perfect righteousness than that to which God's people of old were led. . . .

That is one reason Christ forbids swearing. He wants to invite his people, those who have been called by him, to be more faithful to what they have been taught and to live more righteously than the people of the old covenant. Truth is revealed to them; it has come more fully to light in Christ. A second reason is our weakness. In our own strength, we are unable to do either small or great things unless God works in us. This we see from Christ's words: "You shall not swear by your head, because you cannot cause even one hair to become white or black." In another place he says, "Which of you by being anxious can add one cubit to his height?" (Matt. 6:27).

Because we of ourselves have no strength or ability, God wishes us to give the honor to him who can do everything. He is a jealous God and does not give his glory to another. Now whoever swears to do this or that robs God of his rightful honor. Such a person swears to do a certain thing in spite of a lack of ability and without knowing whether God wants to do that thing in him. That is why James says, "You ought to say, 'If it is God's will, I shall do this or that'" (James 4:15). Therefore, all God-fearing persons will beware of such swearing, however much they may be slandered. . . .

So it is clear that God does not want us to swear by temple, altar, heaven, earth, our own head, or any created thing. Even less should we swear by his name! The words of James confirm this: "Above all, dear brothers, do not swear, neither by heaven, nor by earth, nor by anything else. Let your yes be yes, and your no be no" (James 5:12). James wishes that there be no oaths, whether small or large, in order to avoid hypocrisy. Let people twist it, disguise it, and dress it up as much as they will; yet there is nothing good in swearing an oath. Christ says that our way of speaking should be simply yes and no. Whatever is more than that is evil. The evil one is the devil, who tears out the good from the hearts of people, and plants evil.

Those who are devoted to God will live according to his truth. They will allow the truth to rule and guide them, and will obey what it inspires, speaks, and acts through them. They will believe the truth and follow it for its own sake, for God himself is truth and is dwelling in them. Therefore, God's followers do not need or desire an oath. ◆

Scot McKnight

L ET'S BE CLEAR HERE: *Jesus is talking about legal oaths* and *Jesus is against legal oaths*. This passage isn't simply a clever way of asking, "We should all be honest, shouldn't we?" As if he is saying, "The world would be a better place if we all told the truth." But to make this point, he chose a narrow slice of life, namely, a legal oath. No, our zeal to "apply" fails us here. Jesus is talking about oaths, legally binding oaths. That's what he quoted from Moses, that's what he ridicules in his four kinds of oaths, and that's what he prohibits at the end of the passage.

But he is not talking just about legal oaths. Jesus wants utter honesty from his followers, and he illustrates a world where utter honesty has been compromised by speaking about oaths. So the way to read this passage is this: *because he values honesty so much, he uses a concrete example of a world that establishes dishonesty.* Jesus wants a world of utter honesty, and that would mean, among other things, nonparticipation in the use of oaths. We live this text into our world when we live with utter honesty and work against systems where dishonesty has become systemic. . . .

We live this text out when we begin to see how complicit we are in legal systems that encode ethics out of sync with the kingdom ethic of Jesus. We live this text out when we learn the simplicity of honesty, when we learn that our yes really does mean yes and our no really does mean no, and when we learn that our yes obligates us and that our no obligates us. I would argue, then, that followers of Jesus are to tell a judge who requests an oath that they are bound by Jesus not to use oaths because their words are honest.

Notice the order: it is because the kingdom is a world of utter honesty . . . that followers of Jesus choose not to participate in a system, like oaths, where dishonesty becomes systemic. Again, he is sketching a world in which utter honesty rules. ◆

Francis de Sales

L ET YOUR WORDS be kindly, frank, sincere, straightforward, simple, and true; avoid all artifice, duplicity, and pretense, remembering that, although it is not always well to publish abroad everything that may be true, yet it is never allowable to oppose the truth. Make it your rule never knowingly to say what is not strictly true, either accusing or excusing, always remembering that God is the God of truth. If you have unintentionally said what is not true, and it is possible to correct yourself at once by means of explanation or reparation, do so. A straightforward apology has far greater weight than any falsehood. . . . We are told in holy scripture that God's Holy Spirit will not abide with the false or doubleminded. Depend upon it: there is no craft half so profitable and successful as simplicity. Worldly prudence and artifice belong to the children of this world; but the children of God go straight on with a single heart and in all confidence; falsehood, deceit, and duplicity are sure signs of a mean, weak mind. ◆

Eberhard Arnold

JESUS IS SAYING TO US: "When you are truly living, you are truthful and genuine in all your words. They are concise and clear, firm and plain, and you are courageous in all you say." Then you will not hide as soon as you hear something unfavorable about yourself, but you will come forward courageously and face what you have done. You will own up to what you are. You will confess your own weakness and acknowledge God's strength and spirit. So you will be glad when you are revealed in your weakness, for you no longer seek your own honor. It is a phantom: your honor is a shadow, a delusion, a breath that must pass away like morning mist over a meadow when the sun appears. ◆

Thomas Merton

IN THE END, the problem of sincerity is a problem of love. A sincere person is not so much one who sees the truth and manifests it as he sees it, but one who loves the truth with a pure love. But the truth is more than an abstraction. It lives and is embodied in people and things that are real. And the secret of sincerity is, therefore, not to be sought in a philosophical love for abstract truth but in a love for real people and real things – a love for God apprehended in the reality around us.

It is difficult to express in words how important this notion is. The whole problem of our time is not lack of knowledge but lack of love. If we only loved one another we would have no difficulty in trusting one another and in sharing the truth with one another. ◆

21

Nonresistance

· · · · ·

You have heard that it was said, "Eye for eye, and tooth for tooth." But I tell you, do not resist an evil person.
Matthew 5:38

Giovanni Papini

I N S P I T E O F its apparent absurdity, the only way is that commanded by Jesus. If a man gives you a blow and you return another blow, he will answer with his fists, you in turn with kicks, weapons will be drawn and one of you may lose your life, often for a trivial reason. If you flee, your adversary will follow you and emboldened by his first experience will knock you down. Turning the other cheek means not receiving the second blow. It means cutting the chain of the inevitable wrongs at the first link. Your adversary who expected resistance or flight is humiliated before you and before himself. He was ready for anything but this. He is thrown into confusion, a confusion which is almost shame. He has the time to come to himself; your immobility cools his anger, gives him time to reflect. He cannot accuse you of fear because you are ready to receive the second blow, and you yourself show him the place to strike.

Every person has an obscure respect for courage in others, especially if it is moral courage, the rarest and most difficult sort of bravery. An injured man who feels no resentment and who does not run away shows more strength of soul, more mastery of himself, more true heroism than he who in the blindness of rage rushes upon the offender to render back to him twice the evil received. Quietness, when it is not stupidity, gentleness, when it is not cowardice, astound common souls as do all marvelous things. They make the very brute understand that this man is more than a man. The brute himself, when not incited to follow by a hot answer or by cowardly flight, remains paralyzed, feels almost afraid of this new, unknown, puzzling force, the more so because among the greatest exciting factors for the one who strikes is his anticipated pleasure in the angry blow, in the resistance, in the ensuing struggle.

Man is a fighting animal; but with no resistance offered, the pleasure disappears; there is no zest left. There is no longer an adversary, but a superior who says quietly, "Is that not enough? Here is the other cheek; strike as long as you wish. It is better that my face should suffer than my soul. You can hurt me as much as you wish, but you cannot force me to follow you into a mad, brutal rage. The fact that someone has wronged me cannot force me to act wrongly."

Literally to follow this command of Jesus demands a mastery possessed by few, of the blood, of the nerves, and of all the instincts of the baser part of our being. It is a bitter and repellent command; but Jesus never said it would be easy to follow him. He never said it would be possible to obey him without harsh renunciations, without stern and continuous inner battles; without the denial of the old Adam and the birth of the new man. And yet the results of nonresistance, even if they are not always perfect, are certainly superior to those of resistance or flight. The example of so extraordinary a spiritual mastery, so impossible and unthinkable for common people, the almost superhuman fascination of conduct so contrary to usual customs, traditions, and passions; this example, this spectacle of power, this puzzling miracle, unexpected like all miracles, difficult to understand like all prodigies, this example of a strong, sane human being who looks like anyone else, and yet who acts almost like a god, like a being above other beings, above the motives which move everyone else – this example if repeated more than once, if it cannot be laid to supine stupidity, if it is accompanied by proofs of physical courage when physical courage is necessary to enjoy and not to harm – this example has an effectiveness which we can imagine, soaked though we are in the ideas of revenge and reprisals. We imagine it with difficulty; we cannot prove it because we have had too few of such examples to be able to cite even partial experiments as proofs of our intuition.

But if this command of Jesus has never been obeyed or too rarely obeyed, there is no proof that it cannot be followed, still less that it ought to be rejected. It is repugnant to human nature, but all real moral conquests are repugnant to our nature. They are salutary amputations of a part of our soul – for some of us the most living part of the soul – and it is natural that the threat of mutilation should make it shudder But whether it pleases us or not, only by accepting this command of Christ can we solve the problem of violence. It is the only course which does not add evil to evil, which does not multiply evil a hundredfold, which prevents the infection of the wound, which cuts out the malignant growth when it is only a tiny pustule. To answer blows with blows, evil deeds with evil deeds, is to meet the attacker on his own ground, to proclaim oneself as low as he. To answer with flight is to humiliate oneself before him, and incite him to continue. To answer a furiously angry man with reasonable words is useless effort. But to answer with a simple gesture of acceptance, to endure for three days the bore who inflicts himself on you for an hour, to offer your chest to the person who has struck you on the shoulder, to give a thousand to the man who has stolen a hundred from you, these are acts of heroic excellence, supine though they may appear, so extraordinary that they overcome the brutal bully with the irresistible majesty of the divine. Only he who has conquered himself can conquer his enemies. Only the saints can charm wolves to mildness. Only he who has transformed his own soul can transform the souls of his brothers, and transform the world into a less grievous place for all. ◆

Fyodor Dostoyevsky

AT SOME THOUGHTS one stands perplexed, especially at the sight of men's sin, and wonders whether one should use force or humble love. Always decide to use humble love. If you resolve on that, once and for all, you may subdue the whole world. Loving humility is marvelously strong, the strongest of all things, and there is nothing else like it. ◆

Harry Emerson Fosdick

THE IDEA THAT Jesus taught nonresistance as an absolute ethic is part of the sentimentalizing of him which has characterized much modern Christianity. "Tenderness of heart," wrote Renan, "was in him transformed into an infinite sweetness, a vague poetry, and a universal charm." If Jesus was anything like that, one wonders why they crucified him. He stirred some people to loyalty so intense that they willingly died for him and others to hatred so fierce that they would not rest until they killed him. Some called him a blasphemer, some a sorcerer in league with the devil, but apparently they never thought of him in terms of "infinite sweetness, vague poetry, universal charm." Moneychangers driven from the temple courts and self-complacent moralists castigated by his stinging condemnation faced another kind of man than that – a formidable personality who certainly did attack evil. What he meant by "Do not resist one who is evil" cannot be adequately understood apart from its setting in his life. ◆

Howard Thurman

"NO ONE EVER wins a fight" – thoughtfully, and with eyes searching the depths of me, my grandmother repeated the words. I was something to behold. One eye was swollen, my jacket was ripped with all the buttons torn from their places, and there was a large tear in the right knee of my trousers. It was a hard and bitter fight. I had stood all I could, until at last I threw discretion to the winds and the fight was on. The fact that he was larger and older and had brothers did not matter. For four blocks we had fought and there was none to separate us. At last I began to gain in power; with one tremendous effort I got him to the ground and, as the saying went, "made him eat dirt." Then I had come home to face my grandmother. "No one ever wins a fight," were her only words as she looked at me. "But I beat him," I said. "Yes, but look at you. You beat him, but you will learn someday that nobody ever wins a fight."

Many years have come and gone since that afternoon in early summer. I have seen many fights, big and little. I have lived through two world wars. The wisdom of these telling words becomes clearer as the days unfold. There is something seductive about the quickening sense of power that comes when the fight is on. There is a bewitching something people call honor, in behalf of which they often do and become the dishonorable thing. It is all very strange. How often honor is sacrificed in defense of honor. Honor is often a strange mixture of many things – pride, fear, hate, shame, courage, truth, cowardice – many things. The mind takes many curious twistings and turnings as it runs the interference for one's survival. And yet the term survival alone is not quite what is meant. People want to survive, yes, but on their own terms. And this is most often what is meant by honor.

"No one ever wins a fight." This suggests that there is always some other way; or does it mean that man can always choose the weapons he shall use? Not to fight at all is to choose a weapon by which one fights. Perhaps the authentic moral stature of a man is determined by his choice of weapons which he uses in his fight against the adversary. Of all weapons, love is the most deadly and devastating, and few there be who dare trust their fate in its hands. •

22

Overcoming Evil

◆ ◆ ◆ ◆ ◆

If anyone slaps you on the right cheek, turn to him the other cheek also. And if anyone wants to sue you and take your shirt, hand over your coat as well. If anyone forces you to go one mile, go with him two miles. Give to the one who asks you, and do not turn away from the one who wants to borrow from you.
Matthew 5:39–42

E. Stanley Jones

JESUS IS NOT teaching passive resistance, but an active resistance on a higher level. The account does not say, "If a man smite you on one check, let him smite the other also," but it does say, "Turn to him the other also." It is this audacious offensive of love that forces the man to go further and thus to break down. He tries to break your head, and you, as a Christian, try to break his heart. In turning the other cheek you wrest the offensive from him and assume moral charge of the situation. You choose your own battleground, and your own weapons, you refuse his and compel him to stand on ground with which he is not familiar and to face weapons he does not know how to face. If a man compels you to go with him one mile you are his slave; but if you voluntarily go with him two, then you rise from your slavery, confer a bounty on him and thus become his master. If he sues you at law and takes away your coat, you are his servant, but if you confer on him your cloak also, you assume the mastery by your own moral daring.

Allowing a man to smite you on one cheek, and letting him have the coat, and submitting to him when he compels you to go one mile does little or no good. The fact is that it does harm to the man who does it and to the man who submits to it. It is the other cheek, the cloak also, and the second mile that do the trick. It is this plus that turns the scale. The one cheek, the coat, and the one mile – this is passive resistance; but turning the other cheek, giving the cloak also, and going the second mile – this is an active resistance on the plane of unquenchable good will. . . .

When the battle closed in between Jesus and the Jewish and Roman authorities, he was not passive. He was entirely active and assumed moral command in every situation. When they came to arrest him in the garden, and Peter with his sword struck off the ear of the servant of the high priest, using the same weapons as his enemies, Jesus rebuked Peter and pronounced the doom of those who came to arrest him with swords by saying, "They that take the sword shall perish with the sword." They came to arrest him and obtain a sentence against him, and the first thing they confronted was the fact that they heard the sentence of doom passed upon themselves. He then assumes further moral command by stooping down, picking up the severed ear of his enemy and restoring it. In the moment of passing under their power he arises in sublimity, assumes moral command and stands, not as a helpless prisoner, but as a giver of bounty....

Jesus, after talking about turning the other cheek and going the second mile, immediately adds that we are to love our enemies and do good to them that despitefully use us. He links the passive resistance of evil and the active love of the enemy who does the evil and makes them one. Without this active love the method of conquering by turning the other cheek is savorless salt. It may do harm. Without this active love, going one mile, and even going two, may do harm to the oppressor and the oppressed in that it may produce contempt in the mind of the oppressor and may further weaken the oppressed. One may allow himself to be smitten on the other cheek, but in his heart of hearts he may be saying, "Yes, but I hate you and will get even with you if I can." That kills the active element that would work on the heart of the oppressor and renders the method sterile. Love gives the method life. That which made the death of Jesus different, in addition to the character of the sufferer, was the fact that out from him went an active love toward the men who put him to death and which expressed itself in the prayer for his enemies, "Father, forgive them." That spirit wrested the offensive from their hands and turned the tragedy into a triumph....

"Try this method of love on the tiger and see what will happen," said a questioner one day in order to floor me. He was quite right. It would not work on a tiger. But it will work on a man.... In every man there are two men – one that is evil, whom you are not to resist, on his level, with his weapons – "resist not him that is evil" – and another man, who is not evil, but who is susceptible to the appeal of loving suffering. Get to that man and you win, says Jesus. No, this method of love will not work with a tiger, but Jesus' assumption is that men are not tigers, and there is that in every man which is capable of response. Even if he does not respond and the method fails, still you have grown tall in the process of stooping. You win in either case. ◆

Dietrich Bonhoeffer

MARTIN LUTHER distinguished between personal sufferings and those incurred by Christians in the performance of duty as bearers of an office ordained by God, maintaining that the precept of nonviolence applies to the first but not the second. In the second case we are not only freed from obligation to eschew violence, but if we want to act in a genuine spirit of love we must do the very opposite, and meet force with force in order to check the assault of evil. It was along these lines that the Reformers justified war and other legal sanctions against evil. But this distinction between person and office is wholly alien to the teaching of Jesus. He says nothing about that. He addresses his disciples as people who have left all to follow him, and the precept of nonviolence applies equally to private life and official duty. He is the Lord of all life, and demands undivided allegiance.

Furthermore, when it comes to practice, this distinction raises insoluble difficulties. Am I ever acting only as a private person or only in an official capacity? If I am attacked am I not at once the father of my children, the pastor of my flock, and a government official? Am I not bound for that very reason to defend myself against every attack, for reason of

responsibility to my office? And am I not also always an individual, face to face with Jesus, even in the performance of my
official duties? ...

How then can the precept of Jesus be justified in the light
of experience? It is obvious that weakness and defenselessness
only invite aggression. Is then the demand of Jesus nothing
but an impracticable ideal? Does he refuse to face up to realities – or shall we say, to the sin of the world? There may of
course be a legitimate place for such an ideal in the inner life
of the Christian community, but in the outside world such an
ideal appears to wear the blinkers of perfectionism and to take
no account of sin. Living as we do in a world of sin and evil, we
can have no truck with anything as impracticable as that.

Jesus, however, tells us that it is just *because* we live in the
world, and just *because* the world is evil, that the precept of
nonresistance must be put into practice. Surely we do not wish
to accuse Jesus of ignoring the reality and power of evil! Why,
the whole of his life was one long conflict with the devil. He
calls evil evil, and that is the very reason why he speaks to his
followers in this way. How is that possible?

If we took the precept of nonresistance as an ethical blueprint for general application, we should indeed be indulging
in idealistic dreams: we should be dreaming of a utopia with
laws which the world would never obey. To make nonresistance
a principle for secular life is to deny God by undermining
his gracious ordinance for the preservation of the world. But
Jesus is no draftsman of political blueprints; he is the one who
vanquished evil through suffering. It looked as though evil
had triumphed on the cross, but the real victory belonged to
Jesus. And the cross is the only justification for the precept
of nonviolence, for it alone can kindle a faith in the victory

over evil which will enable us to obey that precept. And only such obedience is blessed with the promise that we shall be partakers of Christ's victory as well as of his sufferings.

The passion of Christ is the victory of divine love over the powers of evil, and therefore it is the only supportable basis for Christian obedience. Once again, Jesus calls those who follow him to share his passion. How can we convince the world by our preaching of the passion when we shrink from that passion in our own lives? On the cross Jesus fulfilled the law he himself established and thus graciously keeps his disciples in the fellowship of his suffering. The cross is the only power in the world which proves that suffering love can avenge and vanquish evil. ◆

Martin Luther King Jr.

THROUGH VIOLENCE you may murder the liar, but you cannot murder the lie, nor establish the truth. Through violence you may murder the hater, but you do not murder hate. In fact, violence merely increases hate. So it goes. Returning violence for violence multiplies violence, adding deeper darkness to a night already devoid of stars. Darkness cannot drive out darkness; only light can do that. Hate cannot drive out hate; only love can do that. ◆

Love of Enemy

• • • • •

You have heard that it was said, "Love your neighbor and hate your enemy." But I tell you, love your enemies and pray for those who persecute you, that you may be children of your Father in heaven. He causes his sun to rise on the evil and the good, and sends rain on the righteous and the unrighteous. If you love those who love you, what reward will you get? Are not even the tax collectors doing that? And if you greet only your own people, what are you doing more than others? Do not even pagans do that?
Matthew 5:43–47

Martin Luther King Jr.

CERTAINLY THESE are great words, words lifted to cosmic proportions. And over the centuries, many persons have argued that this is an extremely difficult command. Many would go so far as to say that it just isn't possible to move out into the actual practice of this glorious command. They would go on to say that this is just additional proof that Jesus was an impractical idealist who never quite came down to earth. So the arguments abound. But far from being an impractical idealist, Jesus has become the practical realist. The words of this text glitter in our eyes with a new urgency. Far from being the pious injunction of a utopian dreamer, this command is an absolute necessity for the survival of our civilization. Yes, it is love that will save our world and our civilization, love even for enemies.

Now let me hasten to say that Jesus was very serious when he gave this command; he wasn't playing. He realized that it's hard to love your enemies. He realized that it's difficult to love those persons who seek to defeat you, those persons who say evil things about you. He realized that it was painfully hard, pressingly hard. But he wasn't playing. And we cannot dismiss this passage as just another example of Oriental hyperbole, just a sort of exaggeration to get over the point. This is a basic philosophy of all that we hear coming from the lips of our Master. Because Jesus wasn't playing; because he was serious. We have the Christian and moral responsibility to seek to discover the meaning of these words, and to discover how we can live out this command, and why we should live by this command. . . .

Within the best of us, there is some evil, and within the worst of us, there is some good. When we come to see this, we take a different attitude toward individuals. The person who hates you most has some good in him; even the nation that hates you most has some good in it; even the race that hates you most has some good in it. And when you come to the point that you look in the face of every man and see deep down within him what religion calls "the image of God," you begin to love him in spite of – no matter what he does, you see God's image there. There is an element of goodness that he can never slough off. Discover the element of good in your enemy. And as you seek to hate him, find the center of goodness and place your attention there and you will take a new attitude.

Another way that you love your enemy is this: When the opportunity presents itself for you to defeat your enemy, that is the time which you must not do it. There will come a time, in many instances, when the person who hates you most, the person who has misused you most, the person who has gossiped about you most, the person who has spread false rumors about you most, there will come a time when you will have an opportunity to defeat that person. It might be in terms of a recommendation for a job; it might be in terms of helping that person to make some move in life. That's the time you must do it. That is the meaning of love. In the final analysis, love is not this sentimental something that we talk about. It's not merely an emotional something. Love is creative, understanding goodwill for all men. It is the refusal to defeat any individual. When you rise to the level of love, of its great beauty and power, you seek only to defeat evil systems. Individuals who happen to be caught up in that system, you love, but you seek to defeat the system. . . .

The first reason that we should love our enemies, and I think this was at the very center of Jesus' thinking, is this: that hate for hate only intensifies the existence of hate and evil in the universe. If I hit you and you hit me and I hit you back and you hit me back and go on, you see, that goes on ad infinitum. It just never ends. Somewhere somebody must have a little sense, and that's the strong person. The strong person is the person who can cut off the chain of hate, the chain of evil. And that is the tragedy of hate, that it doesn't cut it off. It only intensifies the existence of hate and evil in the universe. Somebody must have religion enough and morality enough to cut it off and inject within the very structure of the universe that strong and powerful element of love. . . .

There's another reason why you should love your enemies, and that is because hate distorts the personality of the hater. We usually think of what hate does for the individual hated or the individuals hated or the groups hated. But it is even more tragic, it is even more ruinous and injurious to the individual who hates. You just begin hating somebody, and you will begin to do irrational things. You can't see straight when you hate. You can't walk straight when you hate. You can't stand upright. Your vision is distorted. There is nothing more tragic than to see an individual whose heart is filled with hate. He comes to the point that he becomes a pathological case. . . . So Jesus says love, because hate destroys the hater as well as the hated.

Now there is a final reason I think that Jesus says, "Love your enemies." It is this: that love has within it a redemptive power. And there is a power there that eventually transforms individuals. That's why Jesus says, "Love your enemies." Because if you hate your enemies, you have no way to redeem and to transform your enemies. But if you love your enemies, you will discover that at the very root of love is the power of redemption. You just keep loving people and keep loving them, even though they're mistreating you. Here's the person who is a neighbor, and this person is doing something wrong to you and all of that. Just keep being friendly to that person. Keep loving them. Don't do anything to embarrass them. Just keep loving them, and they can't stand it too long. Oh, they react in many ways in the beginning. They react with bitterness because they're mad because you love them like that. They react with guilt feelings, and sometimes they'll hate you a little more at that transition period, but just keep loving them. And by the power of your love they will break down under the load. That's love, you see. It is redemptive, and this is why Jesus says love. There's something about love that builds up and is creative. There is something about hate that tears down and is destructive. So love your enemies. ❖

Helmut Thielicke

HOW DID JESUS come to love his enemies? What actually happened when Jesus practiced that deepest of all love that made it possible for him to pray for his enemies even on the cross? What he said was: "... for they know not what they do." And surely he could say this only if he saw in them something completely different from a sadistic, excited mob of people, a wild crowd of human beasts. He could say this only if he saw in all who stood slavering and shouting around his cross – lost and strayed children of God.

His gaze penetrated the outer dirty surface and saw beneath it something entirely different, something these people were *really* meant to be, that God *really* intended them to be, the plan he had for them. Every person is ultimately a thought of God; true, a dreadfully distorted and almost unrecognizable one, but nevertheless a thought of God. And when the church of Jesus Christ sends its pastors into the cells of even the worst criminals and malefactors and in the night before their execution, in the moment before the law demands its retribution, invites them to the royal table of the Lord, then there occurs the same event that took place in Jesus' prayer for his tormentors and persecutors. Then the church of Jesus bears witness that it still sees in the criminal this thought of God, declares that he is a child of God, recognizes a sonship which he has lost, but therefore once possessed, and now offers it to him again in the name of the sufferings and death of his Savior.

Ralf Luther once expressed it this way: "To love one's enemy does not mean to love the mire in which the pearl lies, but to love the pearl that lies in the mire." So love for one's enemy is not based on an act of will, a kind of "self-control" by which I try to suppress all feelings of hatred (this would only lead to complexes and false and forced actions), but rather upon a *gift*, a gift of *grace* that gives me new eyes, so that with these new eyes I can see something divine in others. . . .

When the people who were looked upon with the eyes of Jesus realized that those eyes recognized in them their lost and buried sonship, they were suddenly changed and then were able to recover. The eyes of Jesus and the eyes of a disciple not only see the pearl but also "release" it, help to *bring out* the sonship of God in the other person.

And every one of us can have the same experience, if we would. What an indescribable liberation it is for a fallen, hate-filled, embittered, evil person to meet a person whose eyes do not stop at his sordid exterior, and thus merely force him to make his armor of mire and spite thicker and more impenetrable and cover himself with another isolating layer of defiance and stubbornness! What a liberation for him to meet someone who sees through that armor. . . .

This Jesus, who stands over there amongst our enviers and haters, is asking that we take our stand with him and discover the terribly ravaged sonship within our brothers and sisters and with love woo it from its grave.

Don't you see? *This* is the gospel – with all its difficult and strange talk of loving one's enemies. That's what it is. This world which is choking and dying of hate and revenge is waiting for the new and renewing eyes of his disciples. It is waiting for the eyes that see man's sonship and therefore also see the bridge that leads to the neighbor's heart and even to the enemy's heart.

That neighbor of yours who gets on your nerves – he is waiting for that look. That fellow worker with whom you are at odds, that son of yours who is breaking your heart and whom you hardly know what to do with, that husband who has changed so sadly and disappointed you so bitterly, and all the others who bring tension and discord into your life. All of them are waiting for you to discover in them what Jesus saw in them and what gave him the strength to die for them. All of them, friends and enemies, the good and the bad, are beloved, straying, erring children of the Father in heaven who is seeking them in pain and agony. ✦

Nikolaj Velimirović

B LESS MY ENEMIES, *O Lord. Even I bless them and do not curse them.*

Enemies have driven me into your embrace more than friends have.

Friends have bound me to earth, enemies have loosed me from earth and have demolished all my aspirations in the world.

Enemies have made me a stranger in worldly realms and an extraneous inhabitant of the world.

Just as a hunted animal finds safer shelter than an unhunted animal does, so have I, persecuted by enemies, found the safest sanctuary, having ensconced myself beneath your tabernacle, where neither friends nor enemies can slay my soul.

Bless my enemies, O Lord. Even I bless them and do not curse them.

They, rather than I, have confessed my sins before the world.

They have punished me, whenever I have hesitated to punish myself.

They have tormented me, whenever I have tried to flee torments.

They have scolded me, whenever I have flattered myself.

They have spat upon me, whenever I have filled myself with arrogance.

Bless my enemies, O Lord. Even I bless them and do not curse them.

Whenever I have made myself wise, they have called me foolish.

Whenever I have made myself mighty, they have mocked me as though I were a dwarf.

Whenever I have wanted to lead people, they have shoved me into the background.

Whenever I have rushed to enrich myself, they have prevented me with an iron hand.

Whenever I thought that I would sleep peacefully, they have wakened me from sleep.

Whenever I have tried to build a home for a long and tranquil life, they have demolished it and driven me out.

Truly, enemies have cut me loose from the world and have stretched out my hands to the hem of your garment.

Bless my enemies, O Lord. Even I bless them and do not curse them. ❖

Perfect Love

• • • • •

Be perfect, therefore, as your heavenly Father is perfect.
    Matthew 5:48

Addison Hodges Hart

WHEN JESUS SPEAKS of "perfection," he is saying something about our "love." The word for "perfect" in Greek is *teleios,* and it refers to making something "complete," or bringing something to the "end" and "goal" for which it exists and toward which it tends. It likewise means "maturity." When Jesus says, "You, therefore, must be perfect, as your heavenly Father is perfect," he is referring to the subject of the passage, which is "love." The disciple must be as "perfect" in love – that is, as "complete" or as fully loving of all – as God himself is. . . .

The objection that most people have to Jesus' exhortation to love all – as also the objection many have to "forgiveness" – is often based on the false idea that Jesus is saying that one must *feel love* for all. And, of course, that is impossible for us to do. But we can be prepared *to do good* to all who cross our path or come within the sphere of our influence, *regardless of how we might feel about them.* Indeed, the point of the passage, and its parallel in Luke (6:32–36), is precisely that we should work against our prejudices, anger, dislikes, hatreds, and maybe even our desires for revenge, and do good anyway. "Love" is "doing good," pure and simple, and doing it to all – "the evil and the good," "the just and the unjust," or, in Luke's terms, "sinners." Frankly, we can do it. We just *choose* not to do so time and time again. ◆

Jürgen Moltmann

I F WE WANT TO KNOW what it means to be "a child of God," then we have to look at Jesus, the Son. He called God his Father and became the friend of the enemies of his class and his nation, a friend of sinners and tax collectors. He called God his Father and went to his death without defending himself, praying for his murderers as he died. The disciples who followed him were therefore right to call him "Son of God," for he was no one else's son and belonged to no other party.

In community with that Son of God from Nazareth we discover who God the Father is, and find out what it means to be his child on earth. We have been enemies of our enemies long enough. In the discipleship of Jesus we experience the liberating power of love, love that is quite literally disarming.

The love which Jesus put in the place of retaliation is love of our enemy. Mutual love is nothing special. It only means repaying good with good. But love of our enemy is not love

as repayment; it is prevenient and creative love. Anyone who
repays evil with good is truly free. He no longer merely reacts.
He creates something new. He follows nothing but his own
resolve, and no longer lets the rules of action be dictated by
his opponent. Jesus did not die cursing his enemies, but with a
prayer for them on his lips. He gave his life for the people who
condemned him and put him to death. In his life, his sufferings, and his death, he revealed to us the perfection of God.
"Be perfect as your heavenly Father is perfect."

But in what does God's perfection consist? Certainly not
in perfectionism in any sense. It lies in the love which is long-
suffering, patient, and kind, which bears no grudge, which
endures all things, believes all things, hopes all things (1 Cor.
13). God loves his enemies, blesses them, does good to them,
and does not set evil against evil: that is his perfection. And
it is from this that we all live. From this the whole world lives,
even if it does not know it. God sustains and preserves everything, because he has hope for everyone. His perfection is his
limitless capacity for suffering. He is all-powerful because he
is all-enduring. His uniqueness is the unfathomably creative
power of his love.

If this were not so, none of us would be able to talk about
the love of God he or she has experienced, for he loved us
when we were still his enemies. While we were godless, Christ
died for us. And his Spirit disarms us when we want to be
the enemies of other people. God's children – that means the
enemies whom God has overcome. They are disarmed. They
become creative. They can no longer repay evil with evil. They
must always discover some way of doing good in return for the
evil done to them. We escape from the vicious circle of mutual
deterrents and follow another law, the law of the creative God.
We see the sun of a new day. It dawns on the evil and the good,

making no distinction between them. God gives life and the warmth of life to all of us – to the evil first of all, because they need it most. We feel the rain which falls on the parched earth and makes it fruitful. In the same way God lets the rain fall on the just and the unjust, so that they too may live – here first of all on the just, because they need it. These are the great images for the new orientation towards God which liberates us. . . .

Nor does God come to us by way of anything less than love for our enemy. God does not ask about good and evil, because even my good is not good before him. God's love seeks the enemy and is perfected in the enemy. If it were not for this, none of us could talk about God's love at all. Apart from this, none of us becomes the child of this God. This is the way Jesus, in his life and death, brought God to us. God's children are *enemies who have been overcome.* God's children live from a hard and costly love. It cost God the death of the Son. Through him, children of God are liberated from ever narrower spirals of hate in the heart and enmity in the world. They emerge from these prisons and see the sun of a new day, which rises in the morning over the evil and the good. ◆

Chiara Lubich

THE FIRST AND MOST significant characteristic of God the Father's love is that it is absolutely free. It is totally opposite to the world's love. The world's love is based on getting something back and feelings of attraction (we love people who love us and people we like). The Father's love is completely selfless. He gives himself to the people he has made however they react. It is a love whose nature is to take the initiative, giving all that it has. Consequently, it is a love that builds and transforms. Our heavenly Father does not love us because we are good or spiritually beautiful and so deserve his attention and kindness. On the contrary, by loving us, he himself creates in us the goodness and spiritual beauty of grace, making us his friends and his children. . . .

How shall we live the Word of Life? We should behave as true children of our heavenly Father, imitating his love, above all in those characteristics we have emphasized here: its being freely given and universal. Like this we'll try to be the first to love, with a love that is generous, in solidarity with the other, open to all, aware particularly of the voids we find around us.

We'll try to love without looking for results. We'll make an effort to be the instruments of the open-handedness of God, sharing with others the gifts of nature and grace we have received from him.

If we let ourselves be guided by this word of Jesus, we will have new eyes and a new heart for every neighbor coming across our path, every time this chance is offered by our daily life. And wherever we are (home, school, work, hospital, and so on) we will feel urged to be distributors of this love which belongs to God and which Jesus brought to earth, the only love that can transform the world. ◆

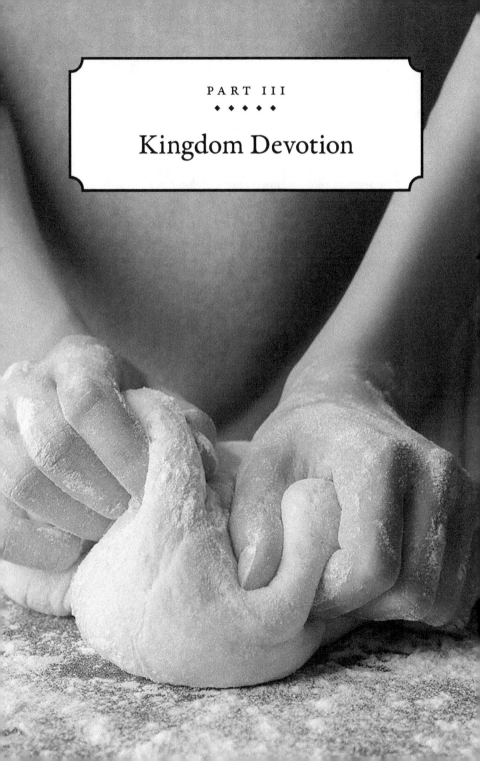

PART III

· · · · ·

Kingdom Devotion

The Sermon on the Mount is not a high-tension moralism; it is the revelation of God's real power in human life. If we take our surrender to God seriously and allow him to enter our lives as light, as the only energy which makes new life possible, then we will be able to live the new life.

EBERHARD ARNOLD, *Salt and Light*

WHILE THE PREVIOUS SECTION covered what Jesus' disciples are to do in matters pertaining to the Law, this section focuses on the meaning of righteousness with regard to religious practice, which Jesus said must exceed that of the scribes and Pharisees. In this context, Jesus addresses three specific acts of worship – almsgiving, prayer, and fasting – that were marks of piety in Judaism. Jesus' three examples cover the whole range of religious activity: our duty towards others, our relationship with God, and our own inner state of being.

Jesus neither discounts nor disparages acts of piety, but he confronts religious hypocrisy. Religiosity which concentrates on public display is a far cry from heartfelt devotion to God. Though it is not wrong to be seen praying, it is wrong to pray in order to be seen. Attention to God, not people's admiration, is what matters.

The Lord's Prayer is set within this context. Its two halves correspond roughly to the first and second tables of the Ten Commandments. The first half highlights God and his kingdom. The second addresses God's provision for humankind: daily bread, forgiveness, guidance, protection, and deliverance. All our needs are covered here.

The Lord's Prayer assumes that we are to do our part as well. God's name is holy, but we are expected to make his name known by the holiness of our lives. God brings his kingdom, but we are to manifest its presence here on earth. God fulfills his will, but we are to commit ourselves to obeying it. He provides for our daily bread, but we are to work for it with the strength he gives. He forgives us our trespasses, but we are to forgive those who trespass against us. ✦

From the Heart

$\blacklozenge$ $\blacklozenge$ $\blacklozenge$ $\blacklozenge$ $\blacklozenge$

Be careful not to practice your righteousness in front of others to be seen by them. If you do, you will have no reward from your Father in heaven. . . .

When you fast, do not look somber as the hypocrites do, for they disfigure their faces to show others they are fasting. Truly I tell you, they have received their reward in full. But when you fast, put oil on your head and wash your face, so that it will not be obvious to others that you are fasting, but only to your Father, who is unseen; and your Father, who sees what is done in secret, will reward you.

Matthew 6:1, 16–18

Sinclair Ferguson

JESUS DOES NOT draw a dichotomy between "outward" and "inward." The truly righteous person shows his righteousness in righteous deeds. Furthermore, true righteousness is expressed, says Jesus, in the disciplines of the

believer. Jesus calls these "acts of righteousness." He does not
say, "Be careful not to do 'acts of righteousness.'" He does not
even say, "Be careful not to do your 'acts of righteousness'
before men." He actually says, "Be careful not to do your 'acts
of righteousness' before men, *to be seen by them.*"

In saying this, Jesus is directing attention to motives. *Why*
we do something is significant as well as *what* we do.

Jesus also clears away another general misconception by what
he says here. The principle he expounds in Matthew 6:1 is illustrated in three different ways: *giving* (6:2–4), *praying* (6:5–15),
and *fasting* (6:16–18). He indicates in what he says about each of
these activities that sacrifice, self-discipline, and self-denial are
called for in the Christian life. He assumes that our lives will be
well regulated and properly structured, and that we will show
an increasing mastery of our own desires. Jesus does not assume
that these things will come "naturally." Rather, he sees them as
quite deliberate activities in the life of his disciples.

To an unusual degree today, Christians mistakenly think
that the freedom of Christian experience means that we no
longer need to make any effort to be spiritual. We simply "do
what we feel," and "be ourselves." To live any other way – for
example, to set aside definite and sacrificial amounts of money
for the Lord's work, or to set aside specific time during the
day for prayer, or to engage in deliberate acts of self-denial as
we seek the Lord's face – is seen as "legalism" and "bondage."
Jesus, on the other hand, assumes that these disciplines are
basic to any spiritual vitality. And he was no legalist! . . .

Each illustration indicates that our fundamental relationship is to God. Jesus describes a man who is the essence of
charity – or so he would like others to think. He plans to give
a gift. So he hires a musician – a trumpeter. After all, if he is
going to give to the poor, he will need to call their attention to

his provision. Why else would a man hire a trumpeter and give his gift publicly? Why else, indeed!

But, says Jesus, this is not a gift in the sight of God. It is *a purchase!* The man is not *helping* the poor half as much as he is *using* the poor to help him. He has received his reward in full. The language Matthew uses here is the same language that appeared on settled accounts in the ancient world. When such men are seen by their fellows, then God writes over their lives, "Paid in full."

We do not need trumpets any longer. We call press conferences instead. Why is it that donors (large and small) seem to feel a need for people to know of their donations? Of course, *the amount* remains undisclosed. After all, one shouldn't give to the needy in public! People might think we did it for the sake of our reputation.

Even those of us who are in no position to call press conferences or hand out press releases can still find ways of "letting it slip" that we give to "the cause." Sometimes the most subtle way to do so is by letting others know how much blessing we have received since we started to give a certain percent of our income (our *gross* income, of course!). How subtle our desire for reputation is.

Give! Jesus says. But when you do so, *forget about yourself.* And *forget about others.* Keep it between yourself and the Lord, and do it "as unto the Lord."

Jesus talks about another man. He is not ashamed that he is a man of prayer. . . . Unfortunately, he prays more in public than he does in private. Also, he prays more eloquently, more fervently, more intimately in public than he does in private. Can it possibly be that all of his zeal for prayer is motivated by his desire "to be seen by men"? He certainly receives what he wants. . . .

Jesus' view of the Pharisees should act as a warning beacon to evangelical Christians. There may be a special temptation to which those who are zealous for holy living can fall prey: retaining the outward shell of spiritual life; emphasizing the importance of certain supposed "marks of grace," but lacking the power and grace of God. Many Christians begin well in their quest for holy lives, as the Pharisees did, but become ensnared by their desire to have a reputation before men rather than before God. ◆

Abraham Joshua Heschel

ABOVE ALL, the Torah asks for *love: thou shalt love thy God; thou shalt love thy neighbor.* All observance is training in the art of love....

A moral deed unwittingly done may be relevant to the world because of the aid it renders unto others. Yet a deed without devotion, for all its effects on the lives of others, will leave the life of the doer unaffected. The true goal is to *be* what we *do.* The worth of a religion is the worth of the individual living it. A mitzvah, therefore, is not mere doing but an act that embraces both the doer and the deed. The means may be external, but the end is personal. Your deeds be pure, so that ye shall be holy.

A hero is he who is greater than his feats, and a pious person is he who is greater than his rituals. The deed is definite, yet the task is infinite....

Even before Israel was told in the Ten Commandments what *to do* it was told what *to be: a holy people.* To perform deeds of holiness is to absorb the holiness of deeds. We must learn how to be one with what we do. This is why in addition to halacha, *the science of deeds,* there is agada, *the art of being....*

The more we do for God's sake, the more we receive for our sake. What ultimately counts most is not the scope of one's deeds but their impact upon the life of the soul. "He who does a mitzvah lights a lamp before God and endows his soul with more life."

We are more than what we do. What we do is spiritually a minimum of what we are. Deeds are outpourings, not the essence of the self. They may reflect or refine the self, but they remain the functions, not the substance of inner life. It is the inner life, however, which is our most urgent problem. ◆

John Flavel

HE WHO PERFORMS duty without the heart, that is, heedlessly, is no more accepted with God than he who performs it with a double heart, that is, hypocritically.... A neglected heart is so confused and dark that the little grace which is in it is not ordinarily discernible: the most accurate and laborious Christians, who take most pains and spend most time about their hearts, do yet find it very difficult to discover the pure and genuine workings of the Spirit there. How then shall the Christian who is comparatively negligent about heart-work ever be able to discover it? Sincerity, which is the thing sought, lies in the heart like a small piece of gold on the bottom of a river; he who would find it must stay till the water is clear, and then he will see it sparkling at the bottom. That the heart may be clear and settled, how much pains and watching, care and diligence, are requisite! ◆

26

When You Give

• • • • •

Be careful not to practice your righteousness in front of others to be seen by them. If you do, you will have no reward from your Father in heaven. So when you give to the needy, do not announce it with trumpets, as the hypocrites do in the synagogues and on the streets, to be honored by others. Truly I tell you, they have received their reward in full. But when you give to the needy, do not let your left hand know what your right hand is doing, so that your giving may be in secret. Then your Father, who sees what is done in secret, will reward you.

Matthew 6:1–4

Leo Tolstoy

A MAN OF THE MODERN WORLD who profits by the order of things based on violence, and at the same time protests that he loves his neighbor and does not observe what he is doing in his daily life to his neighbor, is like a brigand who has spent his life in robbing people, and who, caught at last, knife in hand, in the very act of striking his shrieking victim, should declare that he had no idea that what he was doing was disagreeable to the man he had robbed and was prepared to murder. Just as this robber and murderer could not deny what was evident to everyone, so it would seem that a man living upon the privations of the oppressed classes cannot persuade himself and others that he desires the welfare of those he plunders, and that he does not know how the advantages he enjoys are obtained. . . .

We know very well that we are only allowed to go on eating our dinner, to finish seeing the new play, or to enjoy to the end the ball, the Christmas fête, the promenade, the races, or the hunt, thanks to the policeman's revolver or the soldier's rifle, which will shoot down the famished outcast who has been robbed of his share and who looks round the corner with covetous eyes at our pleasures, ready to interrupt them instantly, were not the policeman and the soldier there, prepared to run up at our first call for help.

And therefore just as a brigand caught in broad daylight in the act cannot persuade us that he did not lift his knife in order to rob his victim of his purse, and had no thought of killing him, we too, it would seem, cannot persuade ourselves or others that the soldiers and policemen around us are not to guard us, but only for defense against foreign foes, and to regulate traffic and fêtes and reviews; we cannot persuade ourselves and others that we do not know that people do not like dying of hunger, bereft of the right to gain their subsistence from the earth on which they live; that they do not like working underground, in the water, or in stifling heat, for ten to fourteen hours a day, at night in factories to manufacture objects for our pleasure. One would imagine it impossible to deny what is so obvious. Yet it is denied. ◆

John Chrysostom

INDEED, THIS ALSO IS THEFT: not to share one's possessions. Perhaps this statement seems surprising to you, but do not be surprised. I shall bring you testimony from the divine scriptures, saying that not only the theft of others' goods but also the failure to share one's own goods with others is theft and swindle and defraudation. What is this testimony?

Accusing the Jews by the prophet, God says, "The earth has brought forth her increase, and you have not brought forth your tithes; but the theft of the poor is in your houses" (see Mal. 3:8–10). Since you have not given the accustomed offerings, God says, you have stolen the goods of the poor. He says this to show the rich that they hold the goods of the poor even if they have inherited them from their fathers or no matter how they have gathered their wealth. And elsewhere the scripture says, "Deprive not the poor of his living" (Sirach 4:1). To deprive is to take what belongs to another; for it is called deprivation when we take and keep what belongs to others. By this we are taught that when we do not show mercy, we will be punished just like those who steal. For our money is the Lord's, however we may have gathered it. If we provide for those in need, we shall obtain great plenty.

This is why God has allowed you to have more: not for you to waste on prostitutes, drink, fancy food, expensive clothes, and all the other kinds of indolence, but for you to distribute to those in need. Just as an official in the imperial treasury, if he neglects to distribute where he is ordered, but spends instead for his own indolence, pays the penalty and is put to death, so also the rich man is a kind of steward of the money which is owed for distribution to the poor. He is directed to distribute it to his fellow servants who are in want. So if he spends more on himself than his need requires, he will pay the harshest penalty hereafter. For his own goods are not his own, but belong to his fellow servants.

Therefore let us use our goods sparingly, as belonging to others, so that they may become our own. How shall we use them sparingly, as belonging to others? When we do not spend them beyond our needs, and do not spend for our needs only, but give equal shares into the hands of the poor. If you are affluent, but spend more than you need, you will give an account of the funds which were entrusted to you. ◆

Mother Teresa

SOME TIME AGO I made a trip to Ethiopia. Our sisters were working there during that terrible drought. Just as I was about to leave for Ethiopia, I found myself surrounded by many children. Each one of them gave something. "Take this to the children! Take this to the children!" they would say. They had many gifts that they wanted to give to our poor. Then a small child, who for the first time had a piece of chocolate, came up to me and said, "I do not want to eat it. You take it and give it to the children." This little one gave a great deal, because he gave it all, and he gave something that was very precious to him.

Have you ever experienced the joy of giving? I do not want you to give to me from your abundance. I never allow people to have fundraisers for me. I don't want that. I want you to give of yourself. The love you put into the giving is the most important thing.

I don't want people donating just to get rid of something.
There are people in Calcutta who have so much money that
they want to get rid of it. They sometimes have money to spare,
money that they try to hide.

A few days ago I received a package wrapped in plain paper.
I thought that it might contain stamps, cards, or something
like that, so I put it aside. I planned to open it later when I had
the time. A few hours later I opened it without even suspecting
its contents. It was hard for me to believe my eyes. That
package contained twenty thousand rupees. It didn't have a
return address or any note, which made me think that it might
be money owed to the government.

I don't like people to send me something because they want
to get rid of it. Giving is something different. It is sharing.

I also don't want you to give me what you have left over. I
want you to give from *your want* until you really feel it!

The other day I received fifteen dollars from a man who
has been paralyzed for twenty years. The paralysis only allows
him the use of his right hand. The only company he tolerates is
tobacco. He told me, "I have stopped smoking for a week. I'm
sending you the money I've saved from not buying cigarettes."
It must have been a horrible sacrifice for him. I bought bread
with his money, and I gave it to those who were hungry. So
both the giver and those who received experienced joy.

This is something all of us need to learn. The chance to
share our love with others is a gift from God. May it be for us
just as it was for Jesus. ◆

When You Pray

• • • • •

And when you pray, do not be like the hypocrites, for they love to pray standing in the synagogues and on the street corners to be seen by others. Truly I tell you, they have received their reward in full. But when you pray, go into your room, close the door and pray to your Father, who is unseen. Then your Father, who sees what is done in secret, will reward you. And when you pray, do not keep on babbling like pagans, for they think they will be heard because of their many words.
    Matthew 6:5–7

Karl Barth

I T I S N O T permissible to consider prayer as a good work to be done, as a pious, nice, and pretty duty to be performed. Prayer cannot be for us a means of creating something, of making a gift to God and to ourselves; we are in the position of persons who can only receive, who are obliged to speak now to God, since they have no one else whom they can address. Luther has said that we must all be destitute, for we are faced by a great void and have everything to receive and learn from God.

Prayer as a human act cannot be a gossiping, a series of phrases or mumblings. . . . Prayer must be an act of affection; it is more than a question of using the lips, for God asks the allegiance of our hearts. If the heart is not in it, if it is only a form which is carried out more or less correctly, what is it then? Nothing! All prayers offered solely by the lips are not only superfluous, but they are also displeasing to God; they are not only useless, but they are offensive to God. At this point it is also important to remark with Calvin that prayer uttered in a language that we do not understand or which the congregation at prayer does not understand is a mockery to God, a perverse hypocrisy, for the heart cannot be in it. We must think and speak in a comprehensible tongue, in a language which has meaning for us.

Let our prayer not be offered according to our good pleasure; otherwise there would be then on our part inordinate desires. Let it be patterned after the rule given by the One who knows our needs better than we ourselves. God has directed us first to submit ourselves to him in order that we may present our requests. So that we may conform to this order, we must eliminate in our prayers all questions like this: Does God listen to us? On this point Calvin is categorical: "Such a prayer is not a prayer." Doubt is not permitted, for it goes without saying that we shall be heard. Even before we pray we must assume the attitude of someone who has been heard. ✦

Daniel M. Doriani

S OME PEOPLE THINK that God is too busy or indifferent to hear every prayer. They hope to shake him from his lethargy, to shout above his deafness, or to locate the formula that captures his attention. The problem in prayer is not that God is too busy for us, but that we feel too busy for him. God does not remove himself from us; we remove ourselves from him.

We do not need to master techniques that guarantee effective prayer. We should reject the idea that our prayers must be "good enough" to merit God's attention. Our words will never be good enough to merit God's attention! But God is kind and compassionate enough to listen.

The pagans had their ideas about how to garner God's attention, and we have ours. Some Christians think that their fervor, their sincerity, or their technique may gain them God's ear. Some think, "If I rise early in the morning and pray on my knees, in the cold, without coffee, then God will hear me."

But such prayer performances may not be seeking God at all. They may be seeking God's benefits or may even be trying to manipulate him. Instead of pleading for mercy, they attempt to force God to be merciful. Persistent prayer is certainly good, but God does not answer prayer because our persistence impresses him. He answers prayer because he loves us. True prayer seeks to commune with God, not to extract benefits from him.

True prayer rests in God's generosity, not in our efforts to earn rewards. True prayer waits on God's wisdom, rather than assuming that we can accurately assess our needs. True prayer trusts God and finds its confidence in him. ◆

Abraham Joshua Heschel

A PERSON HAS GRACE when the throbbing of his heart is audible in his voice, when the longings of his soul animate his face. Now, how do our people pray? They recite the prayer book as if it were last week's newspaper. They ensconce in anonymity – as if prayer were an impersonal exercise – as if worship were an act that came automatically. The words are there but the souls who are to feel their meaning, to absorb their significance, are absent. They utter shells of syllables, but put nothing of themselves into the shells. In our daily speech, in uttering a sentence, our words have a tonal quality. There is no communication without intonation. It is the intonation that indicates what we mean by what we say, so that we can discern whether we hear a question, an exclamation, or an assertion.

It is the *intonation* that lends grace to what we say. But when we pray, the words faint on our lips. Our words have no tone, no strength, no personal dimension, as if we did not mean what we said; as if reading paragraphs in Roget's *Thesaurus*. It is prayer without grace. Of course, they are offered plenty of responsive reading, but there is little responsiveness to what they read. No one knows how to shed a tear. No one is ready to invest a sigh. Is there no tear in their souls?

Is there no balm in Gilead?
Is there no physician there?
Why then is not the health
Of the daughter of my people recovered?

Assembled in the synagogue everything is there – the body, the benches, the books. But one thing is absent: soul. It is as if we all suffered from *spiritual absenteeism*. In good prayer, words become one with the soul. Yet in our synagogues, people who are otherwise sensitive, vibrant, arresting sit there aloof, listless, lazy. *The dead praise not the Lord* (Ps. 115:17). Those who are spiritually dull cannot praise God. ◆

Madeleine L'Engle

WORD

I, who live by words, am wordless when
I try my words in prayer. All language turns
To silence. Prayer will take my words and then
Reveal their emptiness. The stilled voice learns
To hold its peace, to listen with the heart
To silence that is joy, is adoration.
The self is shattered, all words torn apart
In this strange patterned time of contemplation
That, in time, breaks time, breaks words, breaks me,
And then, in silence, leaves me healed and mended.
I leave, returned to language, for I see
Through words, even when all words are ended.
I, who live by words, am wordless when
I turn me to the Word to pray. Amen. ◆

Amy Carmichael

THERE IS A WAY into the greenwood which is not much used in these days of feverish rush. Its name in the scriptures is meditation. ("Let my meditation be sweet unto him.") We should plow a deeper furrow if we knew more of that way. We should be quieter then, and there is nothing creative in noise. "Friend, when dost thou *think?*" asked the old Quaker after listening to a modern time-table; we cannot think by machinery. We cannot consider the lilies without giving time to the lilies. Often our flash of haste means little. To read a book in an hour (if the book has taken half a lifetime to write) means nothing at all. To pray in a hurry of spirit means nothing. To live in a hurry means to do much but effect little. We build more quickly in wood, hay, and stubble than in gold, silver, precious stones; but the one abides, the other does not.

If he who feels the world is too much with him will make for himself a little space, and let his mind settle like a bee in a flower on some great word of his God, and brood over it, pondering it till it has time to work in him, he will find himself in the greenwood.

He will meet his Lord there, and then quite certainly he will soon be looking with his Lord's eyes upon the world. ✦

Mother Teresa

LISTEN IN SILENCE, because if your heart is full of other things you cannot hear the voice of God. But when you have listened to the voice of God in the stillness of your heart, then your heart is filled with God. This will need much sacrifice, but if we really mean to pray and want to pray we must be ready to do it now. These are only the first steps toward prayer, but if we never make the first step with a determination, we will not reach the last one: the presence of God.

This is what we have to learn right from the beginning: to listen to the voice of God in our heart, and then in the silence of the heart God speaks. Then from the fullness of our hearts, our mouth will have to speak. That is the connection. In the silence of the heart, God speaks and you have to listen. Then in the fullness of your heart, because it is full of God, full of love, full of compassion, full of faith, your mouth will speak.

Remember, before you speak, it is necessary to listen, and only then, from the fullness of your heart you speak and God listens. ✦

The Father Knows

• • • • •

Do not be like them, for your Father knows what you need before you ask him.

Matthew 6:8

Martin Luther

YOU DO NOT need to convince God with words, or instruct him at length; for he knows beforehand better what you need than you do yourselves. Just as if you were to come before a prince or a judge who knew your case better than you could describe it to him, and you would undertake to make a long story to inform him about it, he would rightly laugh at you, or rather be offended at you. Yes, we do not know, says Saint Paul, how we are to pray; so that, if he hears us and gives us something, he gives it above what we can understand or hope for.

Therefore sometimes he lets us ask for something that he does not soon give, or indeed does not give at all, as knowing very well what we need or what would be useful to us or not; what we ourselves do not see, and at last must ourselves confess that it would not have been good for us if he had given to us in accordance with our prayer. Therefore we need not teach him or prescribe with our long babbling what and how he is to give to us: for he will give in such a way that his name may be hallowed and his kingdom and his will may be advanced and promoted, etc.

But do you say: Why then does he let us pray and present our need, and does not give it to us unasked, since he knows and sees all our need better than we do? He gives surely to the whole world daily so much good freely, as sun, rain, corn, money, body, life, etc., which no one asks or is grateful for; as he knows that they cannot get along for a single day without light, eating and drinking; why does he then tell us to pray for these things?

Answer: He does not require it, indeed, for the reason that we are to teach him this with our praying, viz., what he is to give us, but in order that we may acknowledge and confess what kind of blessings he is bestowing upon us, and yet much more he can and will give; so that we by our praying are rather instructing ourselves than him. For thereby I am turned about, that I do not go along like the ungodly that never acknowledge this or offer thanks for it; and my heart is thus turned to him and aroused, so that I praise and thank him, and have recourse to him in time of need and look for help from him; and the effect of all this is that I learn more and more to acknowledge what kind of a God he is; and because I address my supplications to him, he is the more disposed to answer me abundantly.

See, this is now a genuine supplicant, not like those other useless talkers, who babble indeed a great deal, but never acknowledge this. But he knows that what he has is the gift of

God, and he says from his heart: Lord, I know that I cannot of myself produce or get a piece of my daily bread, or shield myself against any kind of need or misfortune; therefore I will await it and beseech it from thee, as thou dost teach me, and dost promise to give me, as he who is ready with favors regardless of my thoughts, and who anticipates my need.

See, such acknowledgment in prayer is pleasing to God, and is the true, highest and most precious worship which we can render to him; for thereby the honor and gratitude that are due are given to him. This the others do not do, but they seize and devour all the gifts of God, just as hogs; they appropriate one country, city, house, after another; never think of paying any regard to God; want meanwhile to be holy with their great intonations and babbling in the churches. But a Christian heart, that learns out of the word of God, that we have everything from God and nothing from ourselves, such a heart accepts this in faith and familiarizes itself with it, so that it can look to him for everything and expect it from him. Thus praying teaches us, so that we recognize both ourselves and God, and learn what we need and whence we are to seek for it and get it. ◆

Helmut Thielicke

JESUS' SAYING is so thoroughly comforting and true to life: "Your Father knows what you need *before* you ask him." And we may add: The Father knows what you need even *contrary* to what you ask. "You can talk as you please in your prayers, you can chatter like the heathen and argue like a lawyer, but not for one second will God be diverted from the *one* theme of your life which you keep evading; not for one moment does he lose sight of the sore spot, the real need in your life, which, of course, you don't like to talk about, because you would rather put your fellow men on the carpet. It is true that it is not easy to talk about; but this, too, your Father knows."

Jesus shows us that the Father knows our deepest needs and secrets. And that means that he looks upon us human beings as a mother looks upon her child who is sick or in pain. The little child cannot tell what is wrong with him, and simply looks upon his mother with great, appealing eyes. But the mother knows what is wrong with him even though he cannot speak about it, and therefore she takes hold at the right spot. As a father, as a mother pities her children, so the Lord pities those who fear him and cry out to him in trouble, even though it may often be the wrong trouble they are crying about.

Here we can only cry out: Thank God that our prayer does not depend on our expressing the *correct* desires, that it does not depend on our making a *correct* "diagnosis" of our needs and troubles and then presenting God with a properly phrased and a clearly outlined prayer-proposition. Thank God that this is not so and that it doesn't need to be so, but that he knows us *before* we pray, that the Father is always there with his goodness *before* we come with our many words or with our great silences. . . .

So these words of Jesus, "Your Father knows what you need before you ask him," contain a twofold comfort.

First, God is always there before we pray. The purpose of our praying and asking is not that we must scrupulously look after our own interests and be careful lawyers in presenting our own cause, in order that God may not forget this or that concern which means so much to us. No, the Father has a far deeper interest in us than we ourselves: we are his children, after all;

we are Jesus' brothers. Therefore he knows all about it, and he can still make something out of our stupid, idiotic prayers.

Second, when God seems not to hear our prayers, this is not because he is indifferent to us or hard of hearing or even a hostile power. No, then the reason is that he knows our trouble and everything we need far more deeply than we ourselves, that he knows this as a father knows it, and that often enough he therefore prescribes quite different and more bitter healing remedies for our illness than are pleasing to our lickerish tooth and our terrible shortsightedness.

This is the comfort with which the Lord's Prayer begins, and this is the first thing we must understand when we begin to pray. ◆

Christoph Friedrich Blumhardt

WE CAN SHARE our needs with the Father in a few words, without making a fuss, and rest assured that God already knows what we need and what he will do to help us. We don't have to explain our requests in great detail to God, or try and make quite sure that he knows our needs. God knows about even the smallest matters and takes them straight into his heart. We can turn to him by glancing heavenward, with no words at all. We can do this even when we pray about something concrete and tangible, or about something that specifically troubles us. We may realize that what we thought we needed is actually not necessary and that we can find a way right in the midst of how things are now.

This doesn't mean that we just let things happen – as if everything will come of its own accord without our longing for it. Nor should we just cast a brief and hurried request at God's feet. When this happens, we too easily lose sight of God, assume that everything comes to us without his help, and we forget to thank him. Then we cease to have a believing heart and are consequently not true children of God.

Jesus said, "Before you ask him." Therefore we *do* need to make our requests known to him, otherwise many things will not be given that could have been given. It never displeases God when we come to him with our heartfelt requests. A real child asks for *everything*, knowing God has an ear for him. We should bring all our burdens and needs to him, for at the very least this helps to make us ever more aware that in all things God is the giver.

God always has our interests in mind. He carries our various needs with fatherly concern, eagerly waiting for us to come to him. He has not forgotten us. And when we feel tempted to think so, then all the more we should remember that he knows it all and cares for us. In fact, he knows much more about us and our needs than we do. Simple, childlike prayer is enough to move his heart, give you something out of the fullness of his compassion, and save you from all sorts of fear and trouble. ◆

Teach Us to Pray

• • • • •

One day Jesus was praying in a certain place. When he finished, one of his disciples said to him, "Lord, teach us to pray, just as John taught his disciples."
Luke 11:1

Andrew Murray

"LORD, TEACH US *to pray*." Yes, to pray. This is what we need to be taught. Though in its beginnings prayer is so simple that the feeble child can pray, yet it is at the same time the highest and holiest work to which we can rise. It is fellowship with the Unseen and Most Holy One. The powers of the eternal world have been placed at its disposal. It is the very essence of true religion, the channel of all blessings, the secret of power and life. Not only for ourselves, but for others, for the church, for the world, it is to prayer that God has given the right to take hold of him and his strength. It is on prayer that the promises wait for their fulfilment, the kingdom for its coming, the glory of God for its full revelation. And for this blessed work, how slothful and unfit we are. It is only the Spirit of God can enable us to do it aright. How speedily we are deceived into a resting in the form, while the power is wanting. Our early training, the teaching of the church, the influence of habit, the stirring of the emotions – how easily these lead to prayer which has no spiritual power, and avails but little. True prayer, that takes hold of God's strength, that availeth much, to which the gates of heaven are really opened wide – who would not cry, Oh for someone to teach me thus to pray?

Jesus has opened a school, in which he trains his redeemed ones, who specially desire it, to have power in prayer. Shall we not enter it with the petition: Lord, it is just this we need to be taught! O teach us to *pray*.

"Lord, teach *us* to pray." Yes, us, Lord. We have read in your Word with what power your people of old used to pray, and what mighty wonders were done in answer to their prayers. And if this took place under the old covenant, in the time of preparation, how much more will you not now, in these days of fulfilment, give your people this sure sign of your presence in their midst. We have heard the promises given to the apostles of the power of prayer in your name, and have seen how gloriously they experienced their truth: we know for certain, they can become true to us too. We hear continually even in these days what glorious tokens of your power you still give to those who trust you fully. Lord, these all are people of like passions with ourselves; teach us to pray so too. The promises are for us, the powers and gifts of the heavenly world are for us. O teach us to pray so that we may receive abundantly. To us too you have entrusted your work, on our prayer too the coming of your kingdom depends, in our prayer too you can glorify your

name; "Lord teach us to pray." Yes, us, Lord; we offer ourselves
as learners; we would indeed be taught by you. "Lord, teach us
to pray."

"Lord, *teach* us to pray." Yes, we feel the need now of being
taught to pray. At first there is no work appears so simple; later
on, none that is more difficult; and the confession is forced
from us: We know not how to pray as we ought. It is true we
have God's Word, with its clear and sure promises; but sin
has so darkened our mind, that we know not always how to
apply the Word. In spiritual things we do not always seek the
most needful things, or fail in praying according to the law of
the sanctuary. In temporal things we are still less able to avail
ourselves of the wonderful liberty our Father has given us to
ask what we need. And even when we know what to ask, how
much there is still needed to make prayer acceptable. It must be
to the glory of God, in full surrender to his will, in full assurance of faith, in the name of Jesus, and with a perseverance
that, if need be, refuses to be denied. All this must be learned.
It can only be learned in the school of much prayer, for practice
makes perfect.... Let but the deep undertone of all our prayer
be the teachableness that comes from a sense of ignorance, and
from faith in him as a perfect teacher, and we may be sure we
shall be taught, we shall learn to pray in power. Yes, we may
depend upon it, he *teaches* to pray.

"*Lord*, teach us to pray." None can teach like Jesus, none
but Jesus; therefore we call on him, "Lord, teach us to pray." A
pupil needs a teacher, who knows his work, who has the gift of
teaching, who in patience and love will descend to the pupil's
needs. Blessed be God! Jesus is all this and much more. He
knows what prayer is. It is Jesus, praying himself, who teaches
to pray. He knows what prayer is. He learned it amid the trials
and tears of his earthly life. In heaven it is still his beloved

work: his life there is prayer. Nothing delights him more than to find those whom he can take with him into the Father's presence, whom he can clothe with power to pray down God's blessing on those around them, whom he can train to be his fellow-workers in the intercession by which the kingdom is to be revealed on earth. . . . He teaches, by giving not only thoughts of what to ask or how to ask, but by breathing within us the very spirit of prayer, by living within us as the Great Intercessor. We may indeed and most joyfully say, "Who teaches like him?" Jesus never taught his disciples how to preach, only how to pray. ◆

Elton Trueblood

C HRIST TELLS HIS FOLLOWERS something in general about prayer, including certain dangers, and then he provides a concrete illustration of what he is saying. The pattern is introduced by the words, "Pray then like this." The strongest reason for supposing that he was not providing a stereotype, to be memorized and used on all occasions, is that he had just warned his followers, when they prayed, not to "heap up empty phrases as the Gentiles do." It is easy to see what he had in mind. The formation of official prayers to be rattled off, frequently with no concern for their meaning, is one of the most common features in the history of religious practices, some of which are included in "Gentile" religions. Unless we are very careful, this is what will happen to the finest and best. Some boast that they can race through their prescribed devotion in record time. The prayer wheel can be turned faster and faster! . . . One of the chief ways to deny Christ is to turn any of his words into what he called "empty phrases." ◆

Pope Benedict XVI

OUR PRAYING can and should arise above all from our heart, from our needs, our hopes, our joys, our sufferings, from our shame over sin, and from our gratitude for the good. It can and should be a wholly personal prayer. But we also constantly need to make use of those prayers that express in words the encounter with God experienced both by the church as a whole and by individual members of the church. For without these aids to prayer, our own praying and our image of God become subjective and end up reflecting ourselves more than the living God. In the formulaic prayers that arose first from the faith of Israel and then from the faith of praying members of the church, we get to know God and ourselves as well. They are a "school of prayer" that transforms and opens up our life.

In his Rule, Saint Benedict coined the formula *Mens nostra concordat voci nostrae* – our mind must be in accord with our voice. Normally, thought precedes word; it seeks and formulates the word. But praying the Psalms and liturgical prayer in general is exactly the other way round: the word, the voice, goes ahead of us, and our mind must adapt to it. For on our own we human beings do not "know how to pray as we ought" (Rom. 8:26) – we are too far removed from God, he is too mysterious and too great for us. And so God has come to our aid: he himself provides the words of our prayer and teaches us to pray. Through the prayers that come from him, he enables us to set out toward him; by praying together with the brothers and sisters he has given us, we gradually come to know him and draw closer to him. . . .

Jesus thereby involves us in his own prayer; he leads us into the interior dialogue of triune love; he draws our human hardships deep into God's heart, as it were. This also means, however, that the words of the Our Father are signposts to interior prayer, they provide a basic direction for our being, and they aim to configure us to the image of the Son. The meaning of the Our Father goes much further than the mere provision of a prayer text. It aims to form our being, to train us in the inner attitude of Jesus. ✦

Our Father

. . . . .

Our Father in heaven . . .
Matthew 6:9

Cyprian of Carthage

AND SO, DEAR FRIENDS, since we call God our Father, let us remember to act like children of God, so that he may find pleasure in having us as his children, just as we do in having him as our Father. ◆

N. T. Wright

THE WORD "FATHER" concentrates our attention on the doubly revolutionary message and mission of Jesus. It is the Exodus-message, the message that tyrants and oppressors rightly fear. But it isn't a message of simple human revolution. Most revolutions breed new tyrannies; not this one. This is the Father's revolution. It comes through the suffering and death of the Son. That's why, at the end of the Lord's Prayer, we pray to be delivered from the great tribulation; which is, not surprisingly, what Jesus told his disciples to pray for in the garden. This revolution comes about through the Messiah, and his people, sharing and bearing the pain of the world, that the world may be healed. This is the kingdom-message, the Advent-message.

But if we in turn are to be the messengers, we need to learn to pray this prayer. We, too, need to learn what it means to call God "Father," and we mustn't be surprised when we find ourselves startled by what it means. The one thing you can be sure of with God is that you can't predict what he's going to do next. That's why calling God "Father" is the great act of faith, of holy boldness, of risk. Saying "Our Father" isn't just the boldness, the sheer cheek, of walking into the presence of the living and almighty God and saying "Hi, Dad." It is the boldness, the sheer total risk, of saying quietly "Please may I, too, be considered an apprentice son." It means signing on for the kingdom of God. . . .

When we call God "Father," we are called to step out, as apprentice children, into a world of pain and darkness. We will find that darkness all around us; it will terrify us, precisely because it will remind us of the darkness inside our own selves. The temptation then is to switch off the news, to shut out the pain of the world, to create a painless world for ourselves. A good deal of our contemporary culture is designed to do exactly that. No wonder people find it hard to pray. But if, as the people of the living creator God, we respond to the call to be his sons and daughters; if we take the risk of calling him Father; then we are called to be the people through whom the pain of the world is held in the healing light of the love of God. And we then discover that we want to pray, and need to pray, this prayer. Father; Our Father; Our Father in heaven; Our Father in heaven, may your name be honored. That is, may you be worshipped by your whole creation; may the whole cosmos resound with your praise; may the whole world be freed from injustice, disfigurement, sin, and death. . . .

Jesus took the risk of referring to God obliquely. In John's gospel, one of his regular ways of talking about God was "the Father who sent me." He wanted people to discover who the Father really was by seeing what he, Jesus, was doing. When we call God "Father," we are making the same astonishing, crazy, utterly risky claim. The mission of the church is contained in that word; the failure of the church is highlighted by that word. But the failure, too, is taken care of in the prayer, and in the cross. Our task is to grow up into the Our Father, to dare to impersonate our older brother, seeking daily bread and daily forgiveness as we do so: to wear his clothes, to walk in his shoes, to feast at his table, to weep with him in the garden, to share his suffering, and to know his victory. ◆

Hannah Whitall Smith

"BEHOLD," says the apostle John, "what manner of love the Father hath bestowed upon us, that we should be called the sons of God." The "manner of love" bestowed upon us is the love of a father for his son, a tender protecting love, that knows our weakness and our need, and cares for us accordingly. He treats us as sons, and all he asks in return is that we shall treat him as a father, whom we can trust without anxiety. We must take the son's place of dependence and trust, and must let him keep the father's place of care and responsibility. Because we are the children and he is the Father, we must let him do the father's part. Too often we take upon our own shoulders the father's part, and try to take care of and provide for ourselves. But no good earthly father would want his children to take upon their young shoulders the burden of his duties, and surely much less would our heavenly Father want to lay upon us the burden of his. . . .

If ever an earthly father was worthy of the confidence of his children, surely much more is our heavenly Father worthy of our confidence. And why it is that so few of his children trust him can only be because they have not yet found out that he is really their Father. ◆

Teresa of Ávila

AVOID BEING BASHFUL with God, as some people are, in the belief that they are being humble. It would not be humility on your part if the king were to do you a favor and you refused to accept it; but you would be showing humility by taking it, and being pleased with it, yet realizing how far you are from deserving it. A fine humility it would be if I had the emperor of heaven and earth in my house, coming to it to do me a favor and to delight in my company, and I were so humble that I would not answer his questions, nor remain with him, nor accept what he gave me, but left him alone. Or if he were to speak to me and beg me to ask for what I wanted, and I were so humble that I preferred to remain poor and even let him go away, so that he would see I had not sufficient resolution. Have nothing to do with that kind of humility, daughters, but speak with him as with a father, a brother, a lord, and a spouse – and, sometimes in one way and sometimes in another, he will teach you what you must do to please him. ◆

Dom Hélder Câmara

ARE WE REALLY convinced that God is the Father of us all? Not merely "my" Father, but "our" Father. If he is "ours," then we are all brothers and sisters. . . .

When I was in Rio de Janeiro, one day a man came to see me. He was from Fortaleza, the town where I was born and grew up. He hadn't been able to find a job. I tried to help him. I wrote to a friend of mine who owned a big shop: "Dear friend, see if you can take Antonio on. He's my brother, my blood-brother. He hasn't any work and he's hungry. Can you give my brother, my blood-brother Antonio, a job?"

My friend was on the telephone to me immediately: "Look, your brother Antonio's just arrived. I've given him a job. But, Dom Hélder, how can your brother have possibly fallen into such poverty – your own brother?"

"Is he really with you already?"

"Yes, he is. And I've also given him some clothes and shoes since he was looking like a tramp. But I suspect you told me he's your brother so that I wouldn't be able to refuse."

"Not at all. He is my brother, I tell you."

"Brother, brother: I know, all the world's your brother!"

"Honestly, he is my brother. We've got the same Father."

"Didn't you tell me: blood-brother?"

"We call those blood-brothers who have the same blood of the same father in their veins. So there you are: Christ shed the same blood for you, for me, for Antonio. So we're brothers in the blood of Christ."

Yes, the Lord requires that, having prayed and, precisely because we have prayed, being filled with the Spirit of God, we turn our gaze on our human brothers and sisters. ◆

31

God's Name

• • • • •

Hallowed be your name . . .
Matthew 6:9

William H. Willimon and Stanley Hauerwas

CHRISTIANS, LIKE JEWS, know no strong distinction between our worship and our ethics. We are a people whose moral lives are shaped liturgically. Our ethics is a byproduct of our worship. Time and again you can see this dynamic in the scripture. First Peter sings joyfully, "But you are a chosen race, a royal priesthood, a holy nation, God's own people." Then, "in order that you may proclaim the mighty acts of him who called you out of darkness into his marvelous light" (1 Pet. 2:9).

See the connection? We have been chosen, ordained, adopted as "God's own people" *in order that* we might proclaim God's mighty acts in word and deed.

Again, after telling us that "once you had not received mercy, but now you have received mercy," Peter immediately demands, "Beloved, I urge you as aliens and exiles to abstain from the desires of the flesh that wage war against the soul. Conduct yourselves honorably" (1 Pet. 2:11–12).

You will note the use of strange political designations of Christians as "aliens" and "exiles," even going so far as to call the Christian life "war." The Lord's Prayer is like a bomb ticking in church, waiting to explode and demolish our temples to false gods. It may have slipped past you, but any time you make a statement like "Holy be your name," you have made a revolutionary claim that promises to land you in the middle of conflict, maybe even war.

In the face of this culture's pervasive hedonism, our idolatry of the flag, our worship of ourselves and our assorted deities, give your life to the holy God of Israel whose name is to be hallowed in all that we do and the world will begin calling you "alien" and "exile." Our culture has a way of driving out of the discussion those who do not bow at the culture's altars.

When we pray, "Holy be your name," we are both asking God to make his name holy and pledging ourselves not to misuse God's name. This is what the Ten Commandments are getting at when they prohibit our taking God's name "in vain." It is commonplace to hear God's name taken in vain today. Though it may well be blasphemy, saying "God damn" may not be the greatest blasphemy against the name of God. The German soldiers who went into battle in World War II bearing *Gott mit Uns* ("God with Us") on their helmets are a greater blasphemy to the holy name of God. To invoke the name of the free, mighty God as patron of our causes is to take the name of God in vain.

Those who are being formed by praying, "Our Father who art in heaven, holy be your name" are not permitted to abuse the holiness of God by attempting to put a leash on God, then dragging God into our crusades and cruelties. The holy God will not be jerked around in this way. So when a president prays a public prayer, calling upon God to bless our troops going into war, that is blasphemy. God's name is not to be used as a rubber stamp for our causes.

It is, after all, a matter of honor. God alone is to be honored. The good news is that the honor we owe God is praise and prayer. Such praise protects us from the false honor – both tempting and destructive – that the world offers us. We so desperately desire status. We so want to be noticed by others without having to notice them in return. Yet in honoring God's name we are giving the only honor worth having. We are thus "saved" from the worldly desire for honor that tempts us to kill in God's name in order to secure honor for ourselves.

A college student was the first person in his family to go to college. When someone offered this student some illegal drugs saying, "Go ahead, try it. It'll make you feel good," the student replied, "No."

"Don't be so uptight," said the drug dealer. "Nobody is going to know that you tried a little dope, got a little high."

"That's not the point," said the student. "The point is that my mother cleaned houses and washed floors to send me to this college. I am here because of her. I am here for her. I wouldn't do anything that might demean her sacrifice for me."

That comes close to how we are to react to the holy God. Christians don't steal, don't cheat in their marriages, don't bless war, but not in order to get on the good side of God, since, in Christ, we have been made right with God. We are to live in the light of our knowledge of God's name, God's holy name. . . .

We live as we pray. ◆

Alfred Delp

T HIS PHRASE, *hallowed be thy name,* teaches us to pray for the worthy ideal, for the unassailable, holy, venerated standard. Unless they have something of supreme value, something at the center of their being which they can venerate, human beings gradually deteriorate. Human nature is so constituted that it must have something holy that it can worship, otherwise it becomes cramped and distorted, and instead of a holy object of veneration something else will take its place. I ought to know for I have just emerged from a murderous dialogue with such a self-appointed object of veneration. [Ed. note: Delp, a resister arrested by the Nazis and sentenced to death, is writing from prison.] These substitute values are far more autocratic and demanding than the living God himself. . . .

The word of God should evoke and receive the great veneration this phrase suggests: praise, reverence, awe. . . . The name of God is the holy of holies, the central silence, the thing that above all others calls for humble approach. We not only ought to believe in the truth at the center of our being, in the purpose of our existence, but we should also bear testimony to this belief by the proper fulfillment of our life's purpose. We should subjugate everything to this law of holiness and reject everything that does not harmonize with it. God, the great object of human veneration, will then also be our whole life. "There is no healing in any other name" (Acts 4:12). How little there is to say once we have said this. And how much that is said is mere cant. We have so many pious phrases that are utterly without genuine reverence for God. Religious chastity and silence go well together.

Let us resume the practice of giving names to life and to things. I have been a mere number long enough to know what it means to be nameless and what effect it has on life. As long as life itself has no name, or at least none that it honors, people and things will continue to lose their identity in the dreadful regimentation and anonymity into which we have sunk. Life has a sensitive nervous system through which everything is connected. Since the name of God is no longer the first and foremost of all names in the land and the voice of the people, then everything else that was once precious and prized has lost its name and been subjected to false and falsifying labels. The cliché, the label, the uniform, the slogan, the "dominant trend of the masses" – these are our rulers. And pity the one who dares to differ, to proclaim his own thoughts or use his own name. ✦

Leonardo Boff

W E D O N O T sanctify the name of God when we regard him as a "stopgap" for human weaknesses; in other words, if we call upon him and remember him only when we need help, when our infantile desires collapse around us. We then venerate God only as our own ego and put him at the service of our own interests. . . . We offend God not by denying him but by an egocentric supplication that implies that we do not recognize him as God, as someone different from ourselves and beyond the reach of our manipulations.

We do not sanctify God when our religious language (the language we use in our piety, liturgy, and theology) speaks of him as though he were an entity of this sublunary world: completely known, exhaustively defined, his will completely understood, as though we had had a personal interview with him. . . .

We are not sanctifying the name of God when we erect church buildings, when we elaborate mystical treatises, or when we guarantee his official presence in society by means of religious symbols. His holy name is sanctified only to the extent that these expressions are related to a pure heart, a thirst for justice, and a reaching out for perfection. It is in these realities that God dwells; these are his true temple, where there are no idols. Origen said well, in commenting on this supplication of the Lord's Prayer: "They who do not strive to harmonize their conception of God with that which is just take the name of the Lord God in vain." ◆

God's Kingdom

◆ ◆ ◆ ◆ ◆

Your kingdom come...
Matthew 6:10

Eberhard Arnold

WHENEVER WE COME before God we should ask for the bread we need, the forgiveness of our sins, protection from temptation, and reconciliation with others. All this belongs to true prayer. But most importantly, we need to ask that God's will is done and that his kingdom comes. Our personal prayers remain selfish unless they are placed in the larger context of God's rulership being established on earth. This is the only way in which we may bring our personal needs before God; they must be placed in the setting of his great and all-inclusive power.

We should see these personal requests to God as part of the one object of our prayer: that the Spirit come down and fill us and change everything from the bottom up. We should be brief and to the point when we ask God for this one, all-important thing. . . .

Prayer must never supplant work. If we sincerely ask God for his will to be done, for his nature to be revealed in our work, for his rule to bring humankind to unity, justice, and love, then our life will be one of work. Faith without works is dead. Prayer without work is hypocrisy. Unless we actively work to build for God's kingdom, the Lord's Prayer – "Your kingdom come" – is a lie on our lips. The purpose of Jesus' prayer is to bring us to the point where its meaning is lived out, where it actually happens and becomes part of history. Each of us needs to find a way to devote our whole working strength so that God is honored, his will is done, and his kingdom comes. Unless our love for Jesus results in deeds, our connection to the Tree of Life will wither. . . .

If our prayer is genuine, if we really want nothing but the kingdom of God, then we will think of all the regions of the world. We will call on God to intervene in the history of the nations, the history of classes and ranks, the history that has brought injustice to a climax. We will call on him to come with his judgment and to let his righteousness and peace break in like the dawn. This should be our prayer and the prayer of the church.

When we call on God, we are asking him to do something that we cannot, to bring into being something that we ourselves do not know how to create. We are seeking for the impossible to happen, for something to be changed irrevocably that we could never change. We are asking for a history to unfold for which we ourselves could never be responsible.

The question is: Do we have the faith that through our prayer the status quo can be shattered? Can we believe that at our call Christ will come among us to judge and save? When we ask for the Holy Spirit, are we ready for God to strike us like a burst of flaming lightning, so that at last we experience Pentecost? Do we really believe that God's kingdom is imminent? Are we capable of believing that through our pleading this kingdom will break in? Are we able to believe that as a result of our prayer the entire history of the world will be turned topsy-turvy?

Let us come to God in the absolute certainty that Jesus' words are true: "The kingdom of God has drawn near!" and, "If you have faith, nothing will be impossible for you." Wonders will occur, mountains will be torn from their place, and the whole situation as it is on earth will be changed. Mighty things will happen when we have faith.

It is dangerous to call on God in this way, for it means we are ready, not only to be lifted up from our place, but to be hurled down from our place. So let us concentrate all our powers on Jesus' nearness, on the silent coming of the Holy Spirit, ready for everything to be changed by his intervention.

God is above everything. Christ is stronger than all other spirits. When our faith, life, and deeds are in Jesus, all our prayers are answered. If everything we do has only one goal – that his kingdom comes and his will is done on earth – then the things we pray for will happen. God will show us that he is greater than our hearts can grasp. Much more will happen than we could dare put into words. God's answer will surpass our boldest prayer. And so that we know it is God who does it all, it will happen while we are still praying, or even before we have spoken our prayer. Anyone who knocks at God's door and seeks nothing but God alone will receive what he asks for in the twinkling of an eye. ◆

Christoph Friedrich Blumhardt

I DON'T QUITE TRUST IT when people console me with hopes of eternity. If I cannot see any help in this world, who can guarantee it to me in eternity? Or has the Savior come only into eternity? I say he has come to us! Therefore the comfort of eternity is not sufficient. Can we only reach the goal as soon as we leave this life behind? I don't believe so. God does not work in such a mechanical way. We cannot just merrily skip around in the world and lightly assume that when we die everything will be all right in eternity. Oh no!

Still, Christians everywhere are almost exclusively concerned with the life beyond: they believe that God is powerless on earth, and they declare it to be fanaticism if one sees the light of the living God here on earth and believes that finally even death will be abolished. People everywhere remain under the illusion that God stays eternally in heaven. . . .

Tear yourselves away from this unbelief! If all we aspire to is to get out of this world in order to be free in the next, then we pay tribute to sin and death. It shows the greatest disdain for all the words of God in scripture when we reject the joyous hope of God's coming reign by resigning ourselves to our fate on this earth and letting things continue as they are. Because our religious lives are bankrupt, people think that God is also bankrupt and unable to accomplish anything on earth.

Our happiness depends upon God exercising his power, not us exercising ours. He must accomplish his will, and we must believe that he will do this. This is why God created us. And those who serve the power of God in their hearts pull a little of it down into our world. They represent God by drawing down his power to help. . . .

Need and misery will not be overcome until the barriers between eternity and this world are broken through again. An opening must be made from above downward, not from below upward.

Today's Christianity sees it just the other way round. We Christians would rather find an opening out of this world. We only want to fly up and out of this world, as doves fly into the sky, and be saved. According to the Bible, however, the openings must be broken through from above in order that help can fly down to our earth. But nowadays it takes a terrible struggle to bring this about. Do you know why? Because nobody believes it! We all want to get to heaven and be saved, even though we haven't the slightest idea of what lies beyond. So many people today want things to end. Even so, when they get to "the other side," they will surely rub their eyes sore. One should think very carefully about these matters, and it is a great pain to me that Christians generally do not understand them. That is why we are in such a bad way.

I know that people will say, "There goes Blumhardt again with his cute stories." But please prove to me which of the two is biblical: our death and flight into heaven, or God's future here on earth. From the first to the last chapter, the Bible deals with the coming of God into this world, and there is nothing about this business of dying. Every word in the Bible guarantees the deeds of God right here where I stand. Down here is where Jesus appeared, not above in the invisible world, not around the throne of God. Here on earth is where he wants to dwell again. Here on earth is where we may find him. Here on earth is where he came and will come again. . . . We should lay claim to our right on this earth – the right to victory over sin and death here on earth – not because of our faith, but because of God's power to make things right. ♦

DO YOU WANT to have "religion," to wheedle your way out of everything and say, "God does all things for us! Oh, how I am looking forward to heaven; how nice it will be there"? . . . Where shall God be revealed? On earth. Not in heaven. He does not need you there where there are already plenty of angels to honor him. Your place is on earth! This is the salvation the angels long to observe (1 Pet. 1:10–12).

Take it seriously. Our deeds and life, our redemption, belong to the earth. "Your kingdom come, your will be done on earth as it is in heaven." This is not the hopeless place that people think it is. Much can be done on this earth. What counts is a new creation. Christ's future belongs to it! More can happen here for God than if a hundred thousand people die "saved." But who can understand this? ♦

33

God's Will

◆ ◆ ◆ ◆ ◆

Your will be done,
on earth as it is in heaven.
  Matthew 6:10

Meister Eckhart

NOTHING MAKES a true man but the giving up of
his will. The only perfect and true will comes from
entering into God's will and being without self-will.
For the whole perfection of man's will means being in harmony
with the divine will by willing what God wills, and the way he
wills it.

At the time when the angel appeared to our dear Mary,
nothing that she had done would ever have made her the
mother of God; but as soon as she gave up her will, at that
same hour she became mother of the Eternal Word and
conceived God in that hour.

Never has God given himself nor will he ever give himself
to an alien will. Only where he finds his will does he impart
himself and leave himself, with all that he is.

This is the true inner detachment: In it, the spirit stands
immovable in the face of everything that befalls it, whether it
is good or bad, honor or disgrace or calumny, just as a broad
mountain stands immovable in the face of a little breeze.

Just people hunger and thirst so very much for the will of
God, and it pleases them so much, that they wish for nothing
else and desire nothing different from what God decrees
for them.

If God's will should please you in this way, you would feel
just as if you were in heaven, regardless of what happens or
does not happen to you. But those who desire something
different from God's will get what they deserve: they are
always in misery and trouble; people do them a great deal of
violence and injury, and they suffer in every way.

We deafen God day and night with our words, "Lord, thy
will be done." But then when God's will does happen, we are
furious and don't like it a bit. When our will becomes God's
will, that is certainly good; but how much better it would be
if God's will were to become our will. But as it is now, when
you are sick, of course you don't want to be well against God's
will, but you wish that it were God's will for you to get well.
And when things are going badly for you, you wish that it were
God's will for you to get along easily! But when God's will
becomes your will, then if you are ill – it will be in God's name!
If your friend dies – it will be in God's name!

Anyone who by God's grace unites his will purely and
completely with God's will has no need other than to say in his
ardent longing: "Lord, show me what is thy dearest will and

give me strength to do it!" And God will do this, as truly as he lives, and to such a one he will give in great abundance and all perfection.

There is nothing a man is able to offer God that is more pleasing to him than this kind of detachment. God cares less for our watching, fasting, or praying than for this detachment. God needs nothing more from us than a quiet heart. . . .

I dare to say that such people are happy in these times; for everything that happens to them is what they want. They love God in everything, and because of that their joy is in everything and about everything, at all times in the same way.

This is man's perfection: to be detached from and stripped of everything created; to conduct oneself uniformly in everything and toward everything, to be neither broken by misfortune nor puffed up by good fortune; not to feel greater joy about this than about that – neither greater joy nor greater fear.

For the one who truly loves, everything apart from God, who is the true being, becomes a nothing – nothingness itself.

No one must imagine that it is impossible to attain this, for it is God who does it. Some may say they do not have it. To this I say that I am sorry. But if you do not desire it, I am still more sorry. If you cannot have it, then do have a longing for it! And if you cannot have the longing, then at least long to have the longing!

Because of this the prophet says, "I long, O Lord, to have a longing for thy righteousness."

That we may desire God in the sense that he may be born in us – may God help us to this! ◆

Robert McAfee Brown

THIS IS A PRAYER some people pray without admitting it, a prayer that a few other people are honest enough to acknowledge is what they really desire. It goes, "Our Father who art in heaven . . . stay there!" We can cope with a God who is sequestered in some corner of heaven (or even center stage), but *far off* – which is where we like our gods to be – safely removed from our dwelling place and therefore no threat to us. ✦

François Fénelon

CHRISTIAN PERFECTION is not that rigorous, tedious, cramping thing that many imagine. It demands only an entire surrender of everything to God from the depths of the soul, and the moment this takes place, whatever is done for him becomes easy. They who are God's without reserve, are in every state content; for they will only what he wills, and desire to do for him whatever he desires them to do; they strip themselves of everything, and in this nakedness find all things restored a hundredfold. Peace of conscience, liberty of spirit, the sweet abandonment of themselves and theirs into the hand of God, the joy of perceiving the light always increasing in their hearts, and finally the freedom of their souls from the bondage of the fears and desires of this world, these things constitute that return of happiness which the true children of God receive a hundredfold in the midst of their crosses, while they remain faithful.

They are sacrificed, it is true, but it is to that which they love best; they suffer, but they will to endure all that they do receive, and prefer that anguish to all the false joys of the world; their bodies are subject to excruciating pain; their imaginations are troubled; their minds become languid and weak, but the will is firm and peacefully quiet in the interior of the soul, and responds a joyful *Amen*! to every stroke from the hand that would perfect the sacrifice.

What God requires of us is a will which is no longer divided between him and any creature; a simple, pliable state of will which desires what he desires, rejects nothing but what he rejects, and wills without reserve what he wills, and under no pretext wills what he does not. In this state of mind, all things are proper for us; our amusements, even, are acceptable in his sight.

Blessed is he who thus gives himself to God! ◆

Chiara Lubich

VERY OFTEN we Christians are blind people who have abdicated our supernatural dignity, for we repeat, maybe every day, in the "Our Father": "Your will be done on earth as it is in heaven." But we neither understand what we say, nor do we do (for our part at least) what we implore.

God sees and knows the course we must follow every instant of our lives. For each of us he has established a celestial orbit in which the star of our freedom ought to turn, if it abandons itself to the One who created it. Our orbit, our life, does not conflict with other orbits or with the paths of myriad other beings, children of the Father like us, but harmonizes with them in a firmament more splendid than that of the stars, because it is spiritual. God must move our life and draw it into a divine adventure, which is unknown to us; one in which, at the same time spectators and actors of the marvelous plans of love, we give moment by moment the contribution of our free will.

We can give! Not: we must give! Or worse: let us resign ourselves to giving!

He is Father and therefore is Love. He is Creator, Redeemer, Sanctifier. Who better than he knows what is good for us?

"Lord, may your will really be done, may it be done now and always! May it be done in me, in my children, in others, in their children, in the whole of humanity.

"Be patient and forgive our blindness, for we do not understand and we force heaven to remain closed and prevent it pouring its gifts upon the earth. For, by shutting our eyes, we say with the way we live that it is night and there is no heaven.

"Draw us into the ray of your light, of our light, decreed by your love when, out of love, you created us.

"And force us to kneel every minute in adoration of your will – the one good, pleasing, holy, rich, fascinating, fruitful will. Thus, when the hour of suffering arrives, we may also see your infinite love beyond it. And we may (being full of you) see with your eyes already on this earth and observe from above the divine pattern that you have woven for us and for our brothers and sisters, in which everything turns out to be a splendid design of love. And may our eyes be spared, at least a little, from seeing the knots lovingly tied by your mercy, tempered by justice, that have been placed where our blindness has broken the thread of your will.

"May your will be done in the world and then peace will certainly descend upon the earth, for the angels said to us: 'On earth peace among those whom he favors!'

"And if you said there is only one who is good, the Father, then there is only one will that is good: your Father's will." ◆

Daily Bread

• • • • •

Give us today our daily bread.
Matthew 6:11

Gregory of Nyssa

WHEN WE SAY TO GOD, "Give bread," we do not ask for delights, riches, and flowery robes. We do not seek the beauty of gold, the glow of precious stones, and vessels of silver. We do not request an abundance of land, the command of armies, superiority in war, and governance over nations. We do not desire horses, cattle, and herds of other grazing animals. We do not aspire to possess a host of slaves, pomp in the marketplace, and acclamation by setting up monuments or public portraits. We do not yearn for silk garments and musical ensembles. We ask for none of these by which the soul is distracted from the divine and noble cares. We pray only for bread.

Do you perceive the breadth of divine wisdom and the wealth of teachings contained in these brief words? It is as if the Divine Word cries aloud to his listeners all but the following: Stop, O people, from pouring your desires into vain things. Stop adding to the causes of suffering on your own selves. Your obligation to human nature is only a small thing. To your flesh you owe food, a modest and easily accessible thing, if your purpose is to meet only a need.

Why do you multiply burdens on yourself? For what reason do you subject yourself to the yoke of so many debts? Why do you mine for silver and dig for gold and search after transparent stones? Certainly, because through these things to be able to procure enjoyment of the belly – this insatiable tax collector – to whom the only obligation is really bread which fulfills what is needed for the body.

You trade as far as India. You risk life in unknown seas and commit yourself to annual voyages to fetch products to season your food. You are not mindful of the fact that the pleasure of spices reaches no further than the palate. The same is true of whatever is lovely or aromatic or savory: it provides only some quick and fleeting sensation of delight. What passes beyond the palate is marked by no difference, since nature equally changes all things into a foul odor. Do you see the outcome of artful cookery? Do you see the final result of gourmet allurements?

Instead ask for bread to meet life's needs. You are obligated by nature to the body only in this regard. Whatever else is contrived by the minds of pleasure seekers, it belongs to the extraneous act of sowing weeds. The seed of the housemaster is wheat (Matt. 13:3) and from wheat bread is made. But luxury is derived from the weeds that the enemy has sown among the wheat. Human beings have left aside what is necessary by nature and, as the Divine Word somewhere says, they are choked by the pursuit of vain cares (Matt. 13:22). Thus they remain unfruitful because the soul is continuously engaged with useless cares. . . .

You are the true director of your prayer if your abundance does not come from what belongs to others; if your income is not derived from tears; if no one goes hungry because of your satiety; if no one groans on account of your fullness. Indeed, this is the bread from God, the fruit of justice, the stalk of peace, the bread that is pure and unmixed with the seeds of weeds.

However, if you till the land of others with unjust intent, and back up your unjust claim with documents, and then go on to pray to God, "Give me bread," the one who hears your voice is another, not God. For the fruit of injustice is derived from the opposite, evil nature. He who is attentive to justice derives his bread from God. But he who cultivates injustice is fed by the evil contriver of injustice.

Therefore, look to your own conscience. Bring your request for bread to God, knowing that there is no communion between Christ and Belial. And if you offer gifts acquired by injustice, your gift amounts to the yelp of a dog or the pay of a harlot. Even if you increase your gifts motivated by love of honor, you will hear the words of the prophet who abhors the offerings of such people: "What to me," says the Lord, "is the multitude of your sacrifices? I am filled with holocausts of burnt offerings of rams. The fat of lambs and blood of bulls and he-goats, I do not desire. Incense," he says, "is an abomination to me" (Isa. 1:11, 13). He who sacrifices a bull, God accounts as one who instead kills a dog (Isa. 66:3). But if you have your bread from God, that is, from just toils, then you are permitted to offer to him of the fruits of justice. ◆

Leonardo Boff

THE NEED FOR BREAD is an individual matter, but the satisfaction of that need cannot be an individual effort; it must be that of a community. Thus we do not pray "my Father," but "our Father." . . . We have a Father who belongs to all of us, because he is *our* Father; we are all his offspring, and thus we are all brothers and sisters. Mere personal satisfaction of hunger without considering the others would be a breach of that fellowship.

A person is not just interested in deadening hunger and surviving "somehow." Eating means more than a mere satisfaction of nutritional requirements; it is a communitarian act and a communion rite. Eating is not as enjoyable or fully human if done in sight of the misery of others, the Lazaruses at the foot of the table, waiting for the leftover crumbs. Daily bread provides a basic and necessary happiness for life. If there is to be any happiness, it must be communicated and shared. That is how it is with bread: it is *human* bread to the extent that it is shared and supports a bond of communion. Then happiness is found, and human hunger is satisfied.

Beneath the bread that we consume daily is hidden a whole network of anonymous relationships of which we need to remind ourselves. Before it reaches our table it receives the labor of many hands. The seed is planted in the ground; it has to be tended as it grows. Many hands harvest the grain or maneuver the powerful machinery. Many other hands store the grain and make the bread. Then there are the thousands of distribution points. In all this we find the greatness and the wretchedness of human nature. There can be relationships involving exploitation. Tears are shed over every loaf that we so calmly eat, but we also sense the fellowship and the sharing. Daily bread encompasses the entire human universe in its lights and shadows.

This bread that is jointly produced must be distributed and consumed in concert with others. Only then can we truthfully ask for *our* daily bread. God does not hear the prayer that asks only for *my* bread. A genuine relationship with God calls for maintaining a relationship with others. When we present God with our own needs, he wants us to include those of our brothers and sisters. Otherwise the bonds of fellowship are severed and we live only for ourselves. We all share the same basic necessity; collective satisfaction of that need makes us brothers and sisters.

When the bread that we eat is the result of exploitation, it is not a bread blessed by God. It may supply the chemical needs of nutrition but fail to nourish human life, which is human only when lived within the framework of justice and fraternity. Unjust bread is not really our bread; it is stolen; it belongs to someone else. . . .

This petition for bread has an eminently concrete meaning in our own day. There are millions who sort through garbage piles in search of bare necessities. Hundreds of thousands die every year for lack of sufficient bread. The specter of malnutrition and hunger becomes more and more a threat to the entire human race. To these millions of starving persons the plea for bread has a direct, immediate meaning. The words recall, to those whose hunger is satisfied, the admonition of God himself: "Share your food with the hungry" (Isa. 58:7). How bluntly it was put by Saint Basil the Great in the fourth century:

The bread that is spoiling in your house belongs to the hungry. The shoes that are mildewing under your bed belong to those who have none. The clothes stored away in your trunk belong to those who are naked. The money that depreciates in your treasury belongs to the poor! ◆

F. B. Meyer

ANSWER THIS PRAYER so far as you may; and just because the world is so hungry, and weary, and famishing, go forth and be its breadwinners and its breadgivers. As far as you can, help to alleviate the despair and hopelessness, the misery and the sin of people, by passing on the Bread of God, the Bread of Life, the Bread of Love, the Bread of Hope, upon which you feed. Share your last crust with another. If you get a glint of light, flash it on. If you get a new truth, communicate it. If you get a baptism of the Holy Spirit, never rest until others rejoice in it too. ◆

Forgive Us

• • • • •

And forgive us our debts . . .
  Matthew 6:12

M. Scott Peck

UNPLEASANT THOUGH IT may be, the sense
of personal sin is precisely that which keeps our sin
from getting out of hand. It is quite painful at times,
but it is a very great blessing because it is our one and only
effective safeguard against our own proclivity for evil. Saint
Thérèse of Lisieux put it so nicely in her gentle way: "If you are
willing to serenely bear the trial of being displeasing to yourself, you will be for Jesus a pleasant place of shelter."

Little, if anything, constructive is usually accomplished
by attempting to distinguish between "good" Christians and
"bad" Christians or between true and false Christians. Yet
it is hard to imagine how someone could be a genuine Christian who lacks, as many do, a sense of his or her own personal

sin – who is not "for Jesus a pleasant place of shelter." It is a basic Christian doctrine that we are all sinners. By "all" we do not mean everyone other than ourselves; we mean everyone, but primarily ourselves. The major prerequisite for membership in the true Christian Club is the self-acknowledgment of sin. Housecleaning, like charity, should begin at home, and we usually have quite enough to do being our own watchdog without having to be anyone else's. . . .

The Christian doctrine of sin is hardly as gloomy as many are apt to believe. To the contrary, it is an extraordinarily gentle teaching with the happiest of endings. For whenever we experience contrition – the experience of being displeased with oneself of which Saint Thérèse spoke – we are forgiven. And nowhere is the sweet beauty of forgiveness better described than in the following story, given me by a friend, of a little Filipino girl who talked to Jesus.

The word began to get around that this little girl talked to Jesus, and the people of her village became excited. Then the word spread to the surrounding villages, and more people became excited. Finally the word reached the cardinal's palace in Manila and a monsignor was appointed to investigate the phenomenon. So the girl was summoned to the palace for a series of interviews. At the end of the third interview the monsignor felt ready to throw up his hands. "I don't know whether you're for real or not," he exclaimed in frustration. "But there is one acid test. This next week when you talk to Jesus, I want you to ask Jesus what I confessed to at my last confession."

The little girl agreed. So when she returned the next week, the monsignor immediately asked, "Well, my dear, did you talk to Jesus this past week?"

"Yes, your holiness," the little girl replied.

"And when you talked to him this past week, did you remember to ask Jesus what I confessed to at my last confession?"

"Yes, your holiness, I did."

"Well," inquired the monsignor with barely concealed eagerness, "when you asked Jesus what I confessed to at my last confession, what did Jesus answer?"

The little girl immediately responded, "Jesus said, 'I've forgotten.'"

You might want to think that the little girl was just a smart fabricator, but her answer was pure and perfect Christian theology. It is possible to acknowledge sin without contrition. But if we are genuinely repentant, then our sins are completely forgotten by God. It is as if they never existed. The slate is wiped completely clean. Every day can be a totally new one. ◆

Philip Graham Ryken

JESUS ONCE TOLD a story about a young man who fell into debt. He was sick of home, tired of living under the authority of his father, and he decided to ask for his share of the inheritance before the old man died. Then he took the money and ran away from home. When he got to a far country, he squandered his wealth on wild living. Soon the young man's entire inheritance was spent, and he fell into bankruptcy....

Then one day, as he was slopping pigs, his thoughts suddenly turned to his father's house. Jesus told the story like this: "When he came to his senses, he said, 'How many of my father's hired men have food to spare, and here I am starving to death! I will set out and go back to my father and say to him:

Father, I have sinned against heaven and against you. I am no longer worthy to be called your son; make me like one of your hired men'" (Luke 15:17–19).

So the young man set off for home, hoping his dad would give him a job in the family business. There was only one flaw in his thinking: he underestimated his father's capacity for forgiveness. He was still thinking like a debtor, expecting to have to work off his debts. Then to the son's amazement, "While he was still a long way off, his father saw him and was filled with compassion for him; he ran to his son, threw his arms around him and kissed him" (Luke 15:20).

Then the son made his little speech: "Father, I have sinned against heaven and against you. I am no longer worthy to be called your son" (Luke 15:21). But there was no talk then of becoming a hired hand. It was all robes and sandals, golden rings and fatted calves. There was no need for the son to slave away in his father's fields; he had been welcomed into the embrace of his father's forgiveness. For this is what forgiveness means: to let go without a sense of guilt, obligation, or punishment.

This is precisely what we ask God to do in the fifth petition of the Lord's Prayer. We ask our Father to forgive our debts. We declare our moral bankruptcy, freely admitting that we owe God more than everything we have. Then we do the only thing we can do, which is ask him to forgive us outright. Because he is our loving Father, God does what we ask. When we go to him, weighed down with the debt of all our guilt and sin, he does not sit down with us to work out a payment plan. Instead, he offers forgiveness full and free. ✦

Frederica Mathewes-Green

WHEN WE CONTINUE to be distraught over a forgiven sin in the past, it's linked to our pride. It's that we can't believe we would ever *do* such a thing. It doesn't fit our sense of the "kind of person" we are. So we can never quite assimilate it; we keep being startled by it, and regard it as strange and appalling. We think of it as something inexplicable that "happened," rather than something we did.

Yet it stares back at us steadily, reminding us that we *did* do it. Apparently, we *are* the kind of person who would do that. Maybe only that one time, maybe only under extreme circumstances, only when exhausted or under terrible stress. But there it is.

People usually say that such a person "won't accept forgiveness," but I think what we won't accept is that we did it in the first place.

Speaking very precisely, God is never disappointed in us. He's never disappointed. That's because his expectations weren't that high to begin with. We're the ones with an artificially-inflated idea of our innate goodness, and groundless certainty about the things we'd never do. But God knows what combination of temptations would be able to overthrow us. He knows us, even if we don't know ourselves.

My spiritual father, Father George Calciu (1925–2006) was tortured in communist prison, and compelled to renounce his faith. And he did. When out of your mind with pain, you don't even know what you are saying. The torturers added outrage to outrage, and compelled the prisoners to do things they never would otherwise have done. Their aim was to create in the prisoners a horror of themselves, breaking them down psychologically, in order to rebuild them into the "ideal communist man."

But, Father George said, when he was taken back to his cell at night, and could pray and weep, the mercy and forgiveness he sensed streaming from God was profoundly sweet. He had learned he was capable of doing things he thought it would be impossible for him to do. But God had known his limits, all along; God knew him better than he knew himself.

Broken down in repentance, Father George could receive mercy more deeply than he ever had. The expert brainwashers never did make Father George into the "ideal communist man." He became instead a man of faith and courage, who spent his life as a valiant witness for Christ.

Deep repentance can do that for you. But first you have to accept that you really did do the things you want God to forgive. ◆

As We Forgive

◆ ◆ ◆ ◆ ◆

And forgive us our debts, as we also have forgiven our debtors. . . .
For if you forgive other people when they sin against you, your
heavenly Father will also forgive you. But if you do not forgive
others their sins, your Father will not forgive your sins.
Matthew 6:12, 14–15

Horace Bushnell

IN THE GOSPELS, it is given us in Christ's own
words – "forgive, and ye shall be forgiven" – "for if ye
forgive men their trespasses, your heavenly Father will also
forgive you; but if ye forgive not men their trespasses, neither
will your heavenly Father forgive your trespasses." He will
not even allow us to pray for forgiveness, save as we ourselves
forgive – "Forgive us our trespasses, even as we forgive those
who trespass against us." All this on the ground that there
is such an analogy between the forgiveness of Christ to us,
and ours to our brethren and our fellow men, as makes them

virtually alike in spirit and kind, though not equal of course in degree. The quality of the virtue, the greatness of feeling, and height of meaning, will be so far correspondent, at least, that the smaller will represent the larger, and, according to its measure, reveal the same properties.

I state the point thus distinctly, because, in the matter of forgiveness among people, a kind of lapse, or sinking of grade, appears to have somehow occurred; so that, holding still the duty of forgiveness, we have it in a form so cheap and low, as to signify little when it is practiced. "O, yes," says the brother, finally worn out by much expostulation, on account of the grudge he is holding against another who has greatly injured him, "I will forgive him, but I hope never to see him again." Christ does not say that to the man whom he forgives, and I suppose it would commonly be regarded among brethren as a rather scant mode of forgiveness – such a mode of it as scarcely fulfills the idea. Another degree of it, which would probably pass, says – "Yes, let him come to me and ask to be forgiven, and it will be time for me to answer him." Probably a quotation is made, in this connection, of the scripture text which says – "If thy brother repent forgive him." And most certainly he should be thus forgiven, when the repentance appears to be an actual and present fact; but suppose that no such repentance has yet appeared. Is it then enough to say, "Let him come and ask to be forgiven?" Many think so, and the argument appears to be conclusive, when they demand – "How can I be expected to forgive, where there is no repentance, and the wrong is just as stubbornly adhered to as ever? What but a mockery is it for me to forgive, when there is no forgiveness wanted, and my adversary has not even come into the right?"

Well then, suppose that Christ had stopped just there. Nobody is asking to be forgiven, all are in their sins and mean to be there. They love their sins. They have asked no release or forgiveness. They are not repentant in the least degree. What then is there for him to do? Is he not absolved from any such matter as the preparing and publishing of forgiveness, by the simple fact that nobody wants it, or asks for it? "If they were penitent," he might say, "it would lay a heavy charge upon me. But they are not, and what is forgiveness thrust upon souls that do not even so much as care for it?"

Why, my friends, it is just here that Christ and his gospel begin – just here, in fact, that his forgiveness begins; viz., in forgiving, giving himself for, and to, the blinded and dead heart of unrepentant people, to make them penitent, and regain them to God. The real gist of his forgiveness antedates their penitence; it is what he does, shows, suffers, in a way of gaining his enemy – bringing him off and away, that is, from his wrongs, to seek, and, in a true sorrow, find, the forgiveness that has been searching beforehand so tenderly after him. . . .

You have seen what this forgiveness means, what a volunteering there is in it, how the true Christian works in it, long before the forgiveness is wanted, works in sacrifice and patience, even as all love must. What I want therefore to know, my brethren, is whether you find this forgiveness in you? Can you give yourself for your brother, or do you hold off in the stiff pretense, that he must come to you first and right himself? Can you be the Christian towards him, or can you more easily hug your injury, as a wound bleeding internally, and hold yourself aloof? . . .

Have then Christian brethren, under Christ's own gospel, nothing better left, than to take themselves out of sight of each other? – going apart just to get rid of forgiveness; going to carry the rankling with them, live in the bitterness, die in the grudges of their untamable passion? What is our gospel

but a reconciling power even for sin itself, and what is it good
for – cross, and love, and patience, and all – if it cannot reconcile? No, there is a better way; Christ lays it on them, by his
own dear passion where he gave himself for them, by his
bloody sweat, by his pierced hands, and by his open side, to
go about the matter of forgiving one another even as he went
about forgiving them. O, it is a short method, and how beautiful, and one that never failed. When they are ready to go
before all relentings, and above all grudges, and be weary, and
sick, and sad, and sorrowful, and so to give themselves for their
adversaries, weeping on their necks in tender and true confession, they will not be adversaries long, but they will be turning
all together to the cross, and joining in the prayer – forgive us
our trespasses, as we forgive those who trespass against us. ◆

Dorothy L. Sayers

FORGIVENESS IS a very difficult matter. Many vari-
eties of behavior go by that name, and not all of them
are admirable. There is the kind that says: "I forgive
her as a Christian, but I shall never speak to her again." This
is adequately dealt with by the caustic definition: "Christian
forgiveness, which is no forgiveness at all," and need not be
discussed, any more than the self-interest of those who

> Drink the champagne that she sends them,
> But they never can forget.

There is also the priggish variety, which greets persecution
with the ostentatious announcement, "I forgive you, Jones,
and I will pray for you." This, though it can base itself strongly
on ethical and Scriptural sanction, shares with pacifism the

serious practical disadvantage of so inflaming the evil passions
of Jones that if the injured party had malignantly determined
to drive Jones to the devil he could scarcely have hit upon
a surer way. There is the conditional: "I will forgive you on
condition you say you are sorry and never do it again." That
has about it something which smacks too much of a legal
bargain, and we are forced to remember that no man is so free
from trespass himself that he can afford to insist on conditions.
Only God is in a position to do that; and we recall the Catholic
teaching that confession, contrition and amendment are the
necessary conditions of absolution. But if we assert that divine
forgiveness is of this bargaining kind, we meet with a thun-
dering denial from poet and prophet and from God himself:

> *Doth Jehovah forgive a debt only on condition that it shall*
> *Be payed? Doth he forgive pollution only on conditions of*
> *purity?*
> *That debt is not forgiven! That pollution is not forgiven!*
> *Such is the forgiveness of the gods, the moral virtues of the*
> *Heathen, whose tender mercies are cruelty. But Jehovah's*
> *salvation*
> *Is without money and without price, in the continual forgive-*
> *ness of sins,*
> *In the perpetual mutual sacrifice in great eternity. For behold!*
> *There is none that liveth and sinneth not! And this is the*
> *covenant*
> *Of Jehovah. "If you forgive one another, so shall Jehovah forgive*
> *you;*
> *That He Himself may dwell among you."*
> (William Blake, *Jerusalem*)

God's conditions, it appears, are of another kind. There is
nothing about demanding repentance and restitution or

promises not to offend again: we must forgive unconditionally if we hope to be forgiven ourselves: "as we forgive our
debtors" – "unto seventy times seven."

It may be easier to understand what forgiveness is, if we first
clear away misconceptions about what it does. It does not wipe
out the consequences of the sin. The words and images used
for forgiveness in the New Testament frequently have to do
with the cancellation of a debt: and it is scarcely necessary to
point out that when a debt is cancelled, this does not mean that
the money is miraculously restored from nowhere. It means
only that the obligation originally due from the borrower is
voluntarily discharged by the lender. If I injure you and you
mulct me in damages, then I bear the consequences; if you
forbear to prosecute, then you bear the consequences. If the
injury is irreparable, and you are vindictive, injury is added to
injury; if you are forgiving and I am repentant, then we share
the consequences and gain a friendship. But in every case
the consequences are borne by somebody. The Parable of the
Unmerciful Servant adds a further illuminating suggestion:
that forgiveness is not merely a mutual act, but a social act. If
injuries are not forgiven all round, the grace of pardon is made
ineffective, and the inexorable judgment of the Law is forced
into operation.

One thing emerges from all this: that forgiveness is not a
doing-away of consequences; nor is it primarily a remission
of punishment. A child may be forgiven and "let off" punishment, or punished and then forgiven; either way may bring
good results. But no good will come of leaving him unpunished
and unforgiven.

Forgiveness is the re-establishment of a right relationship, in
which the parties can genuinely feel and behave as freely with
one another as though the unhappy incident had never taken

place. But it is impossible to enjoy a right relationship with an offender who, when pardoned, continues to behave in an obdurate and unsocial manner to the injured party and to those whom he has injured, because there is something in him that obstructs the relationship. So that, while God does not, and man dare not, demand repentance as a condition for *bestowing* pardon, repentance remains an essential condition for *receiving* it. Hence the church's twofold insistence – first that repentance is necessary, and secondly that all sin is pardoned instantly in the mere fact of the sinner's repentance. Nobody has to sit about being humiliated in the outer office while God dispatches important business, before condescending to issue a stamped official discharge accompanied by an improving lecture. Like the father of the prodigal son, God can see repentance coming a great way off and is there to meet it, and the repentance *is* the reconciliation. ◆

C. S. Lewis

I REALLY MUST DIGRESS to tell you a bit of good news. Last week, while at prayer, I suddenly discovered – or felt as if I did – that I had really forgiven someone I have been trying to forgive for over thirty years. Trying, and praying that I might. When the thing actually happened – sudden as the longed-for cessation of one's neighbor's radio – my feeling was "But it's so easy. Why didn't you do it ages ago?" So many thing are done easily the moment you can do them at all. But till then, sheerly impossible, like learning to swim. There are months during which no efforts will keep you up; then comes the day and hour and minute after which, and ever after, it becomes almost impossible to sink. It also seemed to me that forgiving (that man's cruelty) and being forgiven (my resentment) were the very same thing. "Forgive and you shall be forgiven" sounds like a bargain. But perhaps it is something much more. By heavenly standards, that is, for pure intelligence, it is perhaps a tautology – forgiving and being forgiven are two names for the same thing. The important thing is that a discord has been resolved, and it is certainly the great Resolver who has done it. Finally, and perhaps best of all, I believed anew what is taught us in the Parable of the Unjust Judge (Luke 18:1–8). No evil habit is so ingrained nor so long prayed against (as it seemed) in vain, that it cannot, even in dry old age, be whisked away. ◆

Temptation

• • • • •

And lead us not into temptation ...
Matthew 6:13

Charles H. Spurgeon

YOU ARE AFRAID that God may lead you into temptation; but he will not do so; or should he see fit to try you, he will also afford you strength to hold out to the end. He will be pleased in his infinite mercy to preserve you. Where he leads it will be perfectly safe for you to follow, for his presence will make the deadliest air to become healthful. But since instinctively you have a dread lest you should be conducted where the fight will be too stern and the way too rough, tell it to your heavenly Father without reserve. That is the way to keep up love and confidence. So if you have a suspicion in your soul that perhaps your Father might put you into temptation too strong for you, tell it to him. Tell it to him, though it seems taking a great liberty. Though the fear may be the fruit of unbelief yet make it known to your Lord, and do not harbor it sullenly. Remember the Lord's prayer was not made for him but for you, and therefore it reads matters from your standpoint and not from his. . . .

Weakness is our strength: and our strength is weakness. Cry unto God that he try you not beyond your strength; and in the shrinking tenderness of your conscious weakness breathe out the prayer, "Lead us not into temptation." Then if he does lead you into the conflict, his Holy Spirit will strengthen you, and you will be brave as a lion before the adversary. Though trembling and shrinking within yourself before the throne of God, you would confront the very devil and all the hosts of hell without one touch of fear. It may seem strange, but so the case is. ◆

Thomas à Kempis

MANY PEOPLE TRY to escape temptations, only to fall more deeply. We cannot conquer simply by fleeing, but by patience and true humility we become stronger than all our enemies. The man who only shuns temptations outwardly and does not uproot them will make little progress; indeed they will quickly return, more violent than before.

Little by little, in patience and long-suffering you will overcome them, by the help of God rather than by severity and your own rash ways. Often take counsel when tempted; and do not be harsh with others who are tempted, but console them as you yourself would wish to be consoled.

The beginning of all temptation lies in a wavering mind and little trust in God, for as a rudderless ship is driven hither and yon by waves, so a careless and irresolute man is tempted in many ways. Fire tempers iron and temptation steels the just. Often we do not know what we can stand, but temptation shows us what we are.

Above all, we must be especially alert against the beginnings of temptation, for the enemy is more easily conquered if he is refused admittance to the mind and is met beyond the threshold when he knocks.

Someone has said very aptly: "Resist the beginnings; remedies come too late, when by long delay the evil has gained strength." First, a mere thought comes to mind, then strong imagination, followed by pleasure, evil delight, and consent. Thus, because he is not resisted in the beginning, Satan gains full entry. And the longer a man delays in resisting, so much the weaker does he become each day, while the strength of the enemy grows against him.

Some suffer great temptations in the beginning of their conversion, others toward the end, while some are troubled almost constantly throughout their life. Others, again, are tempted but lightly according to the wisdom and justice of Divine Providence, who weighs the status and merit of each and prepares all for the salvation of his elect.

We should not despair, therefore, when we are tempted, but pray to God the more fervently that he may see fit to help us, for according to the word of Paul, God will make issue with temptation that we may be able to bear it. Let us humble our souls under the hand of God in every trial and temptation for he will save and exalt the humble in spirit. ◆

N. T. Wright

GETHSEMANE SUGGESTS the deepest meanings of the prayer: "Do not let us be led into the testing, but deliver us from evil." Again and again Jesus says to his followers: Watch and pray, that you may not enter into temptation. Now it would be absurd to suppose, at that moment of all moments, that Jesus was telling his followers to say their prayers in case they might be tempted to commit some trivial personal sin. No. Jesus has seen that the moment all his life has pointed towards – the moment all Israel's history has been driving towards – is rushing upon him. The word "temptation" here means "testing" or "tribulation." The great tribulation, the birth pangs of the new age, the moment of horror and deep darkness, is coming swiftly towards him. And in his own moment of agony he fears, with good reason, that the whirlpool of evil which is to engulf him will suck down his close followers as well. Jesus knows that he must go, solo and unaided, into the whirlpool, so that it may exhaust its force on him and let the rest of the world go free. And his followers must therefore pray: Let us not be brought into the testing, into the great tribulation. . . .

To say "lead us not into temptation" does not, of course, mean that God himself causes people to be tempted. It has, rather, three levels of meaning. First, it means "let us escape the great tribulation, the great testing, that is coming on all the world." Second, it means "do not let us be led into temptation that we will be unable to bear" (compare 1 Cor. 10:12–13). Finally, it means "Enable us to pass safely through the testing of our faith." Enable us, in other words, to hear the words of Annunciation and, though trembling, to say: Behold, the handmaid of the Lord. Thy will be done; deliver us from evil. We are thus to become people in whose lives the joy and pain of the whole world meet together once more, so that God's new world may at length come to birth.

This will mean different things for each of us, as we each grapple with our own testing and temptation. But, as we do so, we are caught up into something bigger than ourselves. We are part of that great movement whereby the hopes and fears of all the years are brought together and addressed by the living God. And, as we hear the gentle and powerful address to our own hopes and fears, we are called to become, in our turn, the means whereby that same address goes out to the wider world. . . .

We are called to look out on the world from that viewpoint and to pray, to pray earnestly, *Do not let us be led to the test! Deliver us from evil!* This is part of the prayer for the kingdom: it is the prayer that the forces of destruction, of dehumanization, of anti-creation, of anti-redemption, may be bound and gagged, and that God's good world may escape from being sucked down into their morass. It is our responsibility, as we pray this prayer, to hold God's precious and precarious world before our gaze, to sum up its often inarticulate cries for help, for rescue, for deliverance. Deliver us from the horror of war! Deliver us from human folly and the appalling accidents it can produce! Let us not become a society of rich fortresses and cardboard cities! Let us not be engulfed by social violence, or by self-righteous reaction! Save us from arrogance and pride and the awful things they make people do! Save us – from ourselves . . . and deliver us from the evil one.

And you can't pray these prayers from a safe distance. You can only pray them when you are saying yes to God's kingdom coming to birth within you, as Mary was called to do; when you are saying yes to the call to follow Jesus to Gethsemane, even when you don't understand why; when you are saying yes to the vocation to go to the place of pain, to share it in the name of Jesus, and to hold that pain prayerfully in the presence of the God who wept in Gethsemane and died on Calvary. Paul speaks, in a dramatic and daring passage (Col. 1:24), of "completing in my flesh that which is lacking in the afflictions of Christ"; and, in one of his greatest pieces of writing and of theology (Rom. 8:18–27), he explains prayer in terms of the Spirit groaning within the church as the church groans within the world. The call to pray this clause of prayer is therefore the call to be Annunciation-people; Gethsemane-people; and, yes, Calvary-people. We are called to live and pray at the place where the world is in pain, so that the hopes and fears, the joy and the pain of the whole world may become, by the Spirit and in our own experience, the hope and fear, the joy and pain of God. ◆

Deliver Us

• • • • •

. . . but deliver us from the evil one.
  Matthew 6:13

Earl F. Palmer

J ESUS CHRIST, the one who endured temptation, is the
one who now in his sermon teaches us to pray, "lead us not
into temptation." But the good news is that we now know
that Jesus himself stands with us in the face of the danger of
temptation; he has taken hold of temptation and has recognized
its threat. But more than that, Jesus has invited his disciples to
bring this danger before our Father and seek his help. . . .

[Saint John] Chrysostom tells us that by this prayer – "deliver
us from the evil one" – we signal once and for all that we are
engaged as Christians in a battle against all forms of evil, a
battle that knows no truce. It is a battle in which we need God's
resources because behind all evil at its source is the evil one.
This means that there are many different kinds of evil; there are

bad choices made by individual human beings, there is also the wider crisis of dehumanization that makes up evil in the social whole, and there is evil at the cosmic level of creation too. . . .

The seventeenth-century Puritan Thomas Watson put it very well in his commentary on the Lord's Prayer – "Satan envies man's happiness. To see a clod of dust so near to God, and himself, once a glorious angel, cast out of heavenly paradise, makes him pursue mankind with inveterate hatred."

But the prayer that Jesus teaches now has intervened in our behalf. The devil, and for that matter all forms of evil, have power but they do not have final power. There is a boundary beyond the boundary of their terror, and this prayer recognizes that greater boundary. . . .

The power of this brief and crystal-clear petition in the Lord's Prayer rests in its ability to set us free from the need to fear the evil one. This is the only sentence we need to make use of in order to exorcise demons and all of the evil charades of our generation. We must in fact beware of any exaggeration of the power of evil. . . . It is never correct either theologically or practically to say "the devil made me do it." The devil only tempts; we are the ones who decide and act. Therefore we are the ones that must ask for forgiveness and we are the ones who must seek God's help and then thank him for his goodness and faithfulness.

There is a larger battle before us than simply the contest between our own selfishness and the good will of God. Against such evil therefore there must be a warrior who fully understands the total scale of the battle. There is such a warrior, and only one. He who teaches this prayer is the one who must make the prayer possible, and this forms the profoundly Messianic element in the prayer. Jesus Christ, and he alone, will win the battle against the evil one. The cross and the empty grave are the battlefields of that greater warfare. His victory fulfills this prayer. Therefore, our strength in the face of evil is the knowledge that Jesus Christ has the upper hand in that great struggle. ◆

Pope Benedict XVI

WHEN WE PRAY [the Lord's Prayer] we are saying to God: "I know that I need trials so that my nature can be purified. When you decide to send me these trials, when you give evil some room to maneuver, as you did with Job, then please remember that my strength goes only so far. Don't overestimate my capacity. Don't set too wide the boundaries within which I may be tempted, and be close to me with your protecting hand when it becomes too much for me." . . . We make this prayer in the trustful certainty that Saint Paul has articulated for us: "God is faithful, and he will not let you be tempted beyond your strength, but with the temptation will also provide the way of escape, that you may be able to endure it" (1 Cor. 10:13). ◆

Romano Guardini

AN EVIL THAT IS oppressing me now does not come out of the blue. It comes from words that were spoken before; from ineptitude, negligence, and evil deeds of the past. The wickedness of the heart takes tangible shape in the world. It becomes distilled into evil, and emerges to confront someone somewhere else in the form of scandal, hindrance, or an oppressive atmosphere. The evil I have to contend with is a distillation from past evil that comes from others or myself. This evil, then, enkindles further evil, which bears new seed of evil; one arises continually out of the other, and so the evil chain is unending.

As with our personal history, so it is with history in the large sense. Wars are not started by the force of nature, but by selfishness everywhere: by hardness that thought only of its own advantage; by indifference to the fate of others; by greed for power; by vainglory; by inordinate ambition; by greed for possessions; by the mysterious urge to oppress others, to torture, to destroy. When the last war started, its force had been accumulated from the wickedness of millions of hearts, from the evil in the depths of the human race. The suffering that oppresses humankind everywhere confronts the individual as a universal evil; it does not originate from the earth or from the necessities of nature, but from humanity.

When we ask ourselves whether the earth has room and bread for all, there can be only one answer. Nevertheless, many have neither room nor bread, because the real evil does not stem from nature, but from the coldness and hardness of self-ishness, the negligence of the indolent, the thoughtlessness of the superficial and pleasure-loving. Therefore, the petition "Deliver us from evil" means: Grant that the rightful chain reaction may be broken by which evil continually arises out of wickedness and, in turn, engenders new evil. But it can be broken only in each heart that gives itself to God and under-takes to care that his will be done.

True, a tangled skein of evil exists, but to be entangled in it is not blind fate. Redemption has come to all and can be real-ized in each one. The freedom of the children of God can be awakened in us from God, and the power of the Redemption, emanating from liberated hearts, can penetrate the chain of universal evil.

Paul tells us that all evil comes from sin. This is the one great sin of all: the sin that happened when the first man – and in him, all humankind – broke away from loving union with the will of God, and so humanity fell into abandonment, desolation, ruin, and death. This sin lives in every heart. It continues to operate in the personal sins of us all, and engenders new sin. For there are not so many separate and independent sins; rather, the sin of the individual is embedded, as it were, in sin itself; in that frightful, mysterious unity, that bondage and power of which the letter to the Romans speaks.

On each individual, the sin of all weighs, and all are somehow or other affected by the sin each commits. Hence, the plea for deliverance from evil becomes a petition on behalf of all humanity. In it, the individual brings before God the guilt of humanity from which the evils of our life come; each individual brings the guilt and the misery of all, his own included. It is a petition for deliverance from evil as a whole. . . .

At the end of Revelation, the cry "Come, Lord Jesus!" arises out of the company of those awaiting the Lord. Out of the depths of the petition "Deliver us from evil," the selfsame cry resounds. Ceaselessly, from countless hearts, there rises up to God a petition of which many do not know the inmost meaning. But the depth is there all the same, heaving up its darkness. It is the inmost core of the created world, which sighs for God, and "groans and travails in pain" (Rom. 8:22) for the coming of the last things. It is this depth that calls to God in the petition.

It is the deepest layer of Christian consciousness that calls out here – the layer that knows that the world cannot be patched up, that it cannot by positive thinking be turned to the good. Too much of unthinkable magnitude has happened. What God has staked against it is the full measure of his love. The immeasurable catastrophe of sin, the frightful chain of wickedness and evil that runs through history: after we, individually and generically, have done our utmost to defeat it, the realization breaks through that only God can truly do something about it. And the longing swells for the coming of that which not only can turn all things to the good, but also leads into the new: the end of time, which is the breakthrough of the eternal. ◆

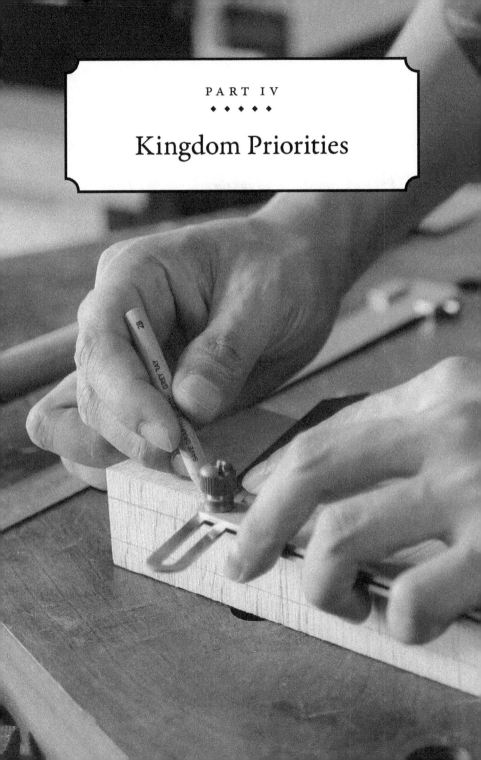

PART IV

· · · · ·

Kingdom Priorities

The good fruit of the deed and the new love for all that flows from the heart is what marks the new life spoken of in the Sermon on the Mount. Where these words of Jesus become life and action, there is God's firm building, which cannot be overthrown even in the final catastrophe.

EBERHARD ARNOLD, *Salt and Light*

JESUS HAS SHOWN US that his kingdom is a community that lives in stark contrast to the world's expectations and established religious systems. That doesn't mean his followers have arrived at a utopia or escaped temptation, sin, or the idols of their age. There are still dangers to those who follow the way of Jesus, which he addresses next.

For instance, Jesus warns against wealth and storing up earthly treasures. We cannot serve both God and money. Only when we are free of the cares and comforts of this world are we completely free to serve God. Matthew's Gospel doesn't specify what storing up treasure in heaven entails. Luke's account, however, makes it clear: eternal treasure consists of deeds, especially those that meet the needs of the poor. Jesus then warns against judging others. Instead, we should do for them what we would have them do for us. We must be humble yet discerning when it comes to those who reject what is holy.

All this requires prayer. We should confidently and persistently turn to God with our requests. The Father in heaven will give the Holy Spirit to all who ask him. He hears us, cares for us, and provides for us.

At the end of the Sermon, Jesus leaves us with a choice. Following him demands that we embark on a narrow way. This way is unconditional and absolute. "Not everyone who says to me, 'Lord, Lord,' will enter the kingdom of heaven, but only the one who does the will of my Father who is in heaven." We must put Christ's words into practice with all we have and are; otherwise, we are like a house built on sand and will not withstand the storms of life. When it comes to following Jesus, there can be no exceptions, no excuses, no compromises, and no complacency. ◆

39

Lasting Treasures

· · · · ·

*Do not store up for yourselves treasures on earth, where moths
and vermin destroy, and where thieves break in and steal. But
store up for yourselves treasures in heaven, where moths and
vermin do not destroy, and where thieves do not break in and
steal. For where your treasure is, there your heart will be also.*
Matthew 6:19–21

John Wesley

"LAY NOT UP for yourselves treasures upon earth..."
This is a flat, positive command; full as clear as "Thou
shalt not commit adultery." How then is it possible for a
rich man to grow richer without denying the Lord that bought
him? Yea, how can any man who has already the necessaries of
life gain or aim at more, and be guiltless? "Lay not up," saith
our Lord, "treasures upon earth." If, in spite of this, you do and
will lay up money or goods, which "moth or rust may corrupt,
or thieves break through and steal"; if you will add house to

house, or field to field – why do you call yourself a Christian? You do not obey Jesus Christ. . . . Why do you name yourself by his name? "Why call ye me, Lord, Lord," saith he himself, "and do not the things which I say?"

If you ask, "But what must we do with our goods, seeing we have more than we have occasion to use, if we must not lay them up?" . . . The true way of employing what you do not want yourselves you may learn from those words of our Lord which are the counterpart of what went before: "Lay up for yourselves treasures in heaven; where neither moth nor rust doth corrupt, and where thieves do not break through and steal." Put out whatever thou canst spare upon better security than this world can afford. Lay up thy treasures in the bank of heaven; and God shall restore them in that day. "He that hath pity upon the poor lendeth unto the Lord, and look, what he layeth out, it shall be paid him again." "Place that," saith he, "unto my account. Howbeit, thou owest me thine own self besides!"

Give to the poor with a single eye, with an upright heart, and write, "So much given to God." For "Inasmuch as ye did it unto one of the least of these my brethren, ye have done it unto me."

This is the part of a "faithful and wise steward": not to sell either his houses or lands, or principal stock, be it more or less, unless some peculiar circumstance should require it; and not to desire or endeavor to increase it, any more than to squander it away in vanity; but to employ it wholly to those wise and reasonable purposes for which his Lord has lodged it in his hands. The wise steward, after having provided his own household with what is needful for life and godliness, makes himself friends with all that remains from time to time of the "mammon of unrighteousness; that when he fails they may receive him into everlasting habitations" – that whensoever his earthly tabernacle is dissolved, they who were before carried into Abraham's bosom, after having eaten his bread, and worn the fleece of his flock, and praised God for the consolation, may welcome him into paradise, and to "the house of God, eternal in the heavens."

We "charge" you, therefore, "who are rich in this world," as having authority from our great Lord and Master, to be habitually doing good, to live in a course of good works. "Be ye merciful as your Father which is in heaven is merciful," who doth good, and ceaseth not. "Be ye merciful" – how far? After your power, with all the ability which God giveth. Make this your only measure of doing good, not any beggarly maxims or customs of the world. We charge you to "be rich in good works"; as you have much, to give plenteously. "Freely ye have received; freely give"; so as to lay up no treasure but in heaven. Be ye "ready to distribute" to everyone according to his necessity. Disperse abroad, give to the poor: deal your bread to the hungry. Cover the naked with a garment, entertain the stranger, carry or send relief to them that are in prison. Heal the sick; not by miracle, but through the blessing of God upon your seasonable support. Let the blessing of him that was ready to perish through pining want come upon thee. Defend the oppressed, plead the cause of the fatherless, and make the widow's heart sing for joy. ❖

Basil the Great

THE WEALTH YOU HANDLE belongs to others; think of it accordingly. Not for long will it delight you; soon it will slip from you and be gone, and you will be asked to give strict account of it. Yet you keep it all locked away behind doors and sealed up; then you are sleepless at night

worrying about it. You take counsel about it inwardly but your
only counsel is yourself, like the rich fool in the gospel. You ask:
What can I do? How easy it would be to say: I will fill the souls
of the hungry, open my barns, invite all the poor. . . .

"I am wronging no one," you say, "I am merely holding on
to what is mine." What is yours! Who gave it to you so that
you could bring it into life with you? Why, you are like a man
who pinches a seat at the theater at the expense of latecomers,
claiming ownership of what was for common use. That's what
the rich are like; having seized what belongs to all, they claim
it as their own on the basis of having got there first. Whereas if
everyone took for himself enough to meet his immediate needs
and released the rest for those in need of it, there would be no
rich and no poor. Did you not come naked out of the womb?
Will you not go naked back into the earth? (Job 1) So whence
came the wealth you now enjoy? If you say: from nowhere, you
deny God, ignore the Creator, are ungrateful to the Giver. If
you say: from God, then explain why it was given to you.

Is God unjust when he distributes unequally? Explain
why you are rich when others are poor. Surely it is so that
you can win the reward of being generous, of being a faithful
steward. . . . And yet you purse up everything in pockets of
unsatisfied covetousness, thinking that you defraud no one
when in fact you defraud so many. Who is the covetous man?
Is it not the one for whom enough is not enough? And who is
the defrauder? Is it not he who takes what belongs to everyone?
And are you not both covetous and defrauding when you keep
for private use what you were given for sharing?

When a man strips another of his clothes, he is called a
thief. Should not a man who has the power to clothe the naked
but does not do so be called the same? The bread in your larder
belongs to the hungry. The cloak in your wardrobe belongs

to the naked. The shoes you allow to rot belong to the barefoot. The money in your vaults belongs to the destitute. You do injustice to every man whom you could help but do not. ◆

Clement of Alexandria

THOSE WHO ARE in earnest about salvation must settle the following beforehand in their mind. All we possess is given to us for the sake of meeting our needs, and one may attain that with only a few things. They are silly who greedily take delight in what they have hoarded up. "He that gathers wages," it is said, "gathers into a bag with holes" (Haggai 1:6). Such is the one who gathers grain and shuts it up; by giving to no one, he becomes poorer. ◆

GOD BROUGHT OUR RACE into communion by first imparting what was his own, when he gave his own Word, common to all, and made all things for all. All things therefore are common, and not for the rich to appropriate an undue share. The expression, therefore "I possess, and possess in abundance: why then should I not enjoy?" is suitable neither to individuals nor societies. Much better is this: "I have: why would I not give to those who need?" Such a one – who fulfills the command, "You shall love your neighbor as yourself" – is perfect. For this is the true luxury – the treasured wealth. But that which is squandered on foolish desires should be considered waste, not investment.

God has given to us, I know well, the liberty of using things – but only so far as necessary; and he has determined that our use of them should be shared. It is monstrous for one to live well-off, while many are in want. How much more glorious is it to serve many, than to live sumptuously! How much wiser to spend money on human beings, than on jewels and gold! How much more valuable to acquire friends than lifeless things! ◆

THE FOLLOWING ought to be repeated again and again: The good man, being temperate and just, treasures up his wealth in heaven; he who has sold his worldly goods, and given them to the poor, and finds the imperishable treasure, "where is neither moth nor robber." Blessed truly is he, though he be insignificant, and without strength, and unnoticed. It is he who is truly rich with the greatest of all riches. Wealth is like a serpent, which will twist round the hand and bite, unless one knows how to lay hold of it without danger by the point of the tail. Riches, wriggling either in an experienced or inexperienced grasp, are dexterous at adhering and biting; unless one, despising them, uses them skillfully, so as to crush the creature by the charm of God's Word, and so escape unscathed.

In the end it is not the one who keeps, but the one who gives away, who is rich; and it is giving away, not possession, which renders a person happy. The fruit of the Spirit is generosity. It is in the soul, then, that riches are found. . . . For righteousness is true riches; and the Word is more valuable than all treasure, not accruing from cattle and fields, but given by God – riches which cannot be taken away. ◆

A. W. Tozer

THERE IS WITHIN the human heart a tough fibrous root of fallen life whose nature is to possess, always to possess. It covets "things" with a deep and fierce passion. The pronouns "my" and "mine" look innocent

enough in print, but their constant and universal use is significant. They express the real nature of the old Adamic man
better than a thousand volumes of theology could do. They
are verbal symptoms of our deep disease. The roots of our
hearts have grown down into *things*, and we dare not pull up
one rootlet lest we die. Things have become necessary to us, a
development never originally intended. God's gifts now take
the place of God, and the whole course of nature is upset by the
monstrous substitution. . . .

Now, what should he do? . . . No careless or casual deal-
ings will suffice. Let him come to God in full determination to
be heard. Let him insist that God accept his all, that He take
things out of his heart and Himself reign there in power. It may
be he will need to become specific, to name things and people
by their names one by one. . . . The ancient curse will not go
out painlessly; the tough old miser within us will not lie down
and die obedient to our command. He must be torn out of our
heart like a plant from the soil; he must be extracted in agony
and blood like a tooth from the jaw. He must be expelled from
our soul by violence as Christ expelled the money changers
from the temple. And we shall need to steel ourselves against
his piteous begging, and to recognize it as springing out of self-
pity, one of the most reprehensible sins of the human heart. ◆

40

The Good Eye

✦ ✦ ✦ ✦ ✦

The eye is the lamp of the body. If your eyes are healthy, your whole body will be full of light. But if your eyes are unhealthy, your whole body will be full of darkness. If then the light within you is darkness, how great is that darkness!
Matthew 6:22–23

Timothy Keller

O NE OF THE CURIOUS THINGS for anybody trying to understand the passage is this illustration about the eye. It says, "The eye is the lamp of the body. If your eyes are good, your whole body will be full of light. But if your eyes are bad, your whole body will be full of darkness." Now what that means is simple. There's light in this room, and if your eye works, if it takes the light in, you will by the light be able to move your body through the room. You'll see where the aisle is, and you won't stumble or fall. All this is saying is if your eye isn't working, even though there's light around the rest of your body, your whole body is, in a sense, in the darkness. If your eye is not working, there's a sense in which no other part of your body can see or take the light in. So if your eye is not working, your whole body is in darkness, whether or not the whole room is flooded with light.

In Luke 11 Jesus uses the same illustration, that the eye is the lamp of the body, that if your eye is dark, your whole body is dark. He also talks about money again. It's connected. When you get into Luke 12, after he talks about the eye and the lamp, he says: so watch out for greed.

He's saying that materialism is an inordinate desire or dependence on money and material things has the peculiar effect of blinding you spiritually, of distorting the way you see things. It has power over the way you see everything. Let me give you some examples. First of all, materialism has the power to blind you to materialism.

Some years ago, my wife, Kathy, noticed I was doing a series of monthly morning breakfasts on the seven deadly sins. The seven deadly sins include lust, pride, envy, anger, and so forth. And, of course, one of the seven deadly sins is greed. Kathy asked, "Are they advertising these things?" I said, "Yes, they're advertising." She said, "So they'll know the month you're speaking on greed?" I said, "Right." She said, "Watch, the attendance is going to drop. They're not going to come out to hear about greed." And she was right. It was the least attended of all of them.

Why? It's not that they were hostile. It's not that people said, "That's a terrible idea. I don't want to hear about greed." No. Everybody was just so sure it wasn't true of them.

Greed is different than other sins. This is why Jesus says this is an eye sin. This darkens your eye spiritually. Jesus did not say to anybody, "Watch out, you might be committing adultery."

If you're committing adultery; you know you're committing adultery. You don't say, "Oh, you're not my wife!" It doesn't happen. But Jesus has to say, Watch out, you might be greedy. Greed hides itself. It blinds you in a way that adultery doesn't. Over the years as a pastor, I've had people come in to talk to me about sins, but I don't remember anybody coming to me to confess the sin of greed.

Jesus is saying: You don't ask. You don't consider the possibility that you're greedy. You don't think you are. You say, "Me? Greedy?" You think of rich people. You think of people that spend tons. Most of you even have a relative who's more extravagant with money than you are. That's all it takes. All you have to do is know somebody who's really greedy, and you won't think you're greedy. You wouldn't even consider the possibility that you're materialistic.

If you say, "This is not a problem of mine," that's a very bad sign. A symptom of this sin is thinking, *I'm sure it's not true of me.* Jesus is saying watch out. This is a sin of the eye. It darkens your eye.

For example, materialism has the power to get you to choose a job, not one that you love, not one that you're good at, not one that helps people, but one that makes you money. You do it because it will get you to a certain status in life. You choose the job on the basis of that. For five to ten years the adrenaline can keep you going, but after a while you find yourself empty inside. Why did you choose the job? Your eye was dark.

Not only can materialism blind you as you choose your job, but it can blind you in the conduct of your job. For example, many companies are making money, but they're hurting neighborhoods. They're hurting towns. They're hurting people. There are all sorts of people in the company, and what are they doing? Are they saying, "Aha! In order to make money

I will ruin the environment of that little town"? No, they're not doing that. They're not asking. They don't want to go there. They don't want to ask hard questions: Are the things my company is doing helping people or hurting people? Is it helping the town or is it hurting the town? Is it helping the neighborhood or is it hurting? You don't want to know. That's the blindness. That's what Jesus is talking about. Greed doesn't go, "Aha! I am gouging the poor!" No, but are you asking whether your company is? You need to ask that.

Materialism also keeps you from asking hard questions about your lifestyle. One of the problems is the kinds of people you come into contact with. Sometimes your friends are making ten times the money you are. You might have a good job, but here's a person making ten times, fifty times what you're making. Don't forget, the person you think is rich is hanging out with people who make ten times more than they do every year. Therefore, nobody ever feels rich.

You don't ask these questions: Do I really need to spend as much money on this? Do I need to be putting this much money into my apartment? Do I need to be spending this much money on clothes? Immediately you think of people who spend much more, so you don't ask the questions. You don't say: Aren't there ways I could be giving more of my money to the church, to the poor, to my friends, to the neighbors? Aren't there ways I could be more radically generous if I made this and that and that change? You don't want to ask. You don't want to think.

In 1635, a guy named Robert Cain was a member of the First Congregational Church of Boston. He was doing well as a businessman, but his elders disciplined him for the sin of greed. Now how did they do that? It was because he was selling his product at a six percent profit, and the church had decided three or four years before that Christians were only allowed to sell their wares at a four percent profit. So when they found out he was doing six percent, they disciplined him for the sin of greed.

Some of you are saying, "Where does it say in the Bible four percent? What are you talking about?" These church elders knew that when you're committing adultery you know you're committing adultery, but when you're being greedy you never know. So they sat down as Christians and said: Jesus talks about money all the time. He's constantly saying watch out for greed. He's always saying give your money away. He's always saying don't spend all your money on yourself. So some business practices must be greedy. Some lifestyles have to be greedy. How are we going to know? As a Christian community, let's sit down and decide, at our time in our place in this spot, what is a greedy lifestyle and what are greedy business practices. So by consensus they decided on some rules and decided to hold each other accountable. It was consensual. And of course Robert Cain knew about it, but he tried to move past it.

I am not saying by any means that today, in our economy, you could come up with a nice, simple rule of thumb. But here's the point: Who are you accountable to? What Christians have you gotten together with and said, "Let's talk about how we're spending our money on each other, on ourselves, how much we're giving away, how much we're keeping, what we're doing"? You have to talk about this with somebody. You've got to have some standards. And you can't trust yourself. That's the principle. You cannot trust yourself to decide this. ◆

God or Mammon

♦ ♦ ♦ ♦ ♦

No one can serve two masters. Either you will hate the one and
love the other, or you will be devoted to the one and despise the
other. You cannot serve both God and money.
  Matthew 6:24

Eberhard Arnold

NOBODY CAN SERVE two masters. "You cannot
serve God and mammon." Jesus defined with
utmost sharpness the nature of this mammon spirit.
He unmasked the piety of the wealthy classes, exposing their
worship of the spirit of death. This mammon spirit leads to
war. It causes impurity to become business. Murder and lying
become part of daily life because of this urge to possess.

Jesus called Satan the murderer from the beginning, the
leader of unclean spirits. Murder is the nature of mammon.
Wars are not the only sign of the mammon spirit. We have
become used to countless people being crushed to death
because of our affluence, as if they were vermin to be squashed.

Even the blind can see that the development of the mammon spirit means the incessant murder of hundreds and thousands of people. Mammon and big business rule through the power of the lying spirit. It is impossible to wage war without a basic inner deception. In the same way, only by lying and by duping the public can a capitalistic society be maintained.

This lie cannot be described, nor can we discuss it in detail here. It is up to each individual to examine the economic problems and to inquire into the murderous effects of the rule of mammon. If we were really concerned with the problem, if we saw how much injustice prevails without the world's conscience being aroused to action, we would realize the true situation very quickly. If people recognized that capitalism involves injustice, it would mean total revolt against the greatest deception in the history of mankind.

But we are a long way from revolting. Most pious circles and even working-class people think, "Rich and poor have to be. When a rich person can give work and livelihood to others, we have to be glad that such a one exists." This ignores the fact that it is impossible to amass this kind of fortune without cheating, without depriving and hurting others and destroying their lives. People fail to realize that big business, concentrated in a few hands, can push hundreds of thousands into certain ruin through unemployment. This is happening today.

Why do these facts remain hidden from us? How is it possible to be cheated of justice and be blind to it? It is because we ourselves are also under the rule of this god, mammon.

Mammon is the rule of money over people. Because we ourselves are dominated by the money spirit, we lack the strength to rebel. Dependence on material affluence and financial security – that is mammon. We recognize that money is the real enemy of God, but even so we are not in a position to apply the lever that lifts the slave rule of mammon off its hinges, because we are dependent on our income and our personal lives are broken by our own mammonism.

Spirit or money. God or mammon. Spirit is the deepest relationship, the innermost fellowship of everything that is alive. . . . God gives us the richest relationships of love between people, from spirit to spirit, heart to heart, that lead to a growing, organic, constructive fellowship. But there is a devilish means that seeks to rob all relationships of heart and spirit, of God. This means is money. Money reduces human relationships to a materialistic association, until the only value left is money itself. Satan uses property and money to destroy the highest goals. Eventually money becomes a commodity in itself instead of a means of barter, and this results in money as power. Many relationships are founded solely on finances, and people give up heart-to-heart relationships and let money transactions take their place. In the end, money destroys all true fellowship.

Money and love are mutually exclusive. Money is the opposite of love, just as sexual defilement of bodies is the opposite of love and respect; just as the killing in war is the radical opposite of life and of love that helps others; just as lying is the opposite of love and truth.

It would be impossible for capitalism to have such power to enslave and murder if the mammon spirit did not dominate. Where mammon rules, the possessive will is stronger than the will to community; the struggle to survive by mutual killing is stronger than the urge to love, stronger than the spirit of mutual help; destructive powers are stronger than constructive powers, matter is stronger than spirit, things and circumstances are stronger than God, self-assertion stronger than the spirit of love and solidarity that brings fellowship. The spirit of mammon has never motivated people to work in a creative way for the life of fellowship. Instead it has engendered an enslavement of the soul and a scorn of it that has made us more subject to circumstances than religious people are to God. In truth, this spirit of mammon – the spirit of lying, impurity, and murder – is the spirit of weakness and death. ◆

Jacques Ellul

THE PROBLEM of the ownership of money is not at the heart of the question. Jesus raises the question in its fullness when he calls money mammon, an Aramaic word that usually means "money" and also can mean "wealth." Here Jesus personifies money and considers it a sort of god. . . .

What Jesus is revealing is that money is a power. This term should be understood not in its vague meaning, "force," but in the specific sense in which it is used in the New Testament. Power is something that acts by itself, is capable of moving other things, is autonomous (or claims to be), is a law unto itself, and presents itself as an active agent. This is its first characteristic. Its second is that power has a spiritual value. It is not only of the material world, although this is where it acts. It has spiritual meaning and direction. Power is never neutral. It is oriented; it also orients people. Finally, power is more or less personal. And just as death often appears in the Bible as a personal force, so here with money. Money is not a power because humans use it, because it is the means of wealth or because accumulating money makes things possible. It is a power *before* all that, and those exterior signs are only the manifestations of this power which has, or claims to have, a reality of its own.

We absolutely must not minimize the parallel Jesus draws between God and mammon. He is not using a rhetorical figure but pointing out a reality. God as a person and mammon as a person find themselves in conflict. Jesus describes the relation between us and one or the other the same way: it is the relationship between servant and master. Mammon can be a master the same way God is; that is, mammon can be a personal master.

Jesus is not describing the particular situation of the miser, whose master is money because his soul is perverted. Jesus is not describing a relationship between us and an object, but between us and an active agent. He is not suggesting that we use money wisely or earn it honestly. He is speaking of a power which tries to be like God, which makes itself our master and which has specific goals.

Thus when we claim to use money, we make a gross error. We can, if we must, use money, but it is really money that uses us and makes us servants by bringing us under its law and subordinating us to its aims. We are not talking only about our inner life; we are observing our total situation. We are not free to direct the use of money one way or another, for we are in the hands of this controlling power. . . .

Love, in the Bible, . . . comes from the entire person; it involves the whole person and binds the whole person without distinction. Love reaches down into the roots of human beings and does not leave them intact. It leads to identification and assimilation between the lover and the beloved. Jesus Christ teaches us in great detail that our love binds us to the spiritual future of our beloved. This is how we must understand the connection between Christians and Christ, which is a love relationship. Love led Christ to follow us in our entire condition, but inversely, today it joins us to Christ in everything – his life, his death, his resurrection, and his glory. Where Christ is, there also is the one who loves Christ. Such is the force, the vigor, of this bond.

Love for money is not a lesser relationship. By this love, we join ourselves to money's fate. "For where your treasure is, there will your heart be also" (Matt. 6:21). Ultimately, we follow what we have loved most intensely either into eternity or into death. To love money is to be condemned to follow it in its destruction, its disappearance, its annihilation, and its death. . . .

Because love makes us follow the beloved and nothing else, we cannot love two things at the same time. Jesus firmly points out the necessity of choosing. "He will hate the one, and love the other." To love one is not simply to be unacquainted with or indifferent to the other; it is *to hate the other*. Do we really believe that if money were only an object with no spiritual significance Jesus would have gone that far? ✦

David Bentley Hart

IT IS UNDENIABLY TRUE that there are texts that condemn an idolatrous obsession with wealth, and that might be taken as saying nothing more than that. At least, 1 Timothy 6:17–19 is often cited as an example of this – though it probably should not be. Perhaps, to avoid trying to serve both God and mammon, one need only have the right *attitude* toward riches. But if this were all the New Testament had to say on the matter, then one would expect those texts to be balanced out by others affirming the essential benignity of riches honestly procured and well-used. Yet this is precisely what we do not find. Instead, they are balanced out by still more uncompromising comminations of wealth *in and of itself*.

Certainly Christ condemned not only an unhealthy preoccupation with riches, but the getting and keeping of riches as such. The most obvious citation from all three synoptic Gospels would be the story of the rich young ruler who could not bring himself to part with his fortune for the sake of the kingdom, and of Christ's astonishing remark about camels passing through needles' eyes more easily than rich men through the kingdom's gate. As for the question the disciples then put to Christ, it should probably be translated not as "Who then can be saved?" or "Can anyone be saved?" but rather "Then can any [of them, the rich] be saved?" To which the sobering reply is that it is humanly impossible, but that by divine power *even* a rich man might be spared.

But one can look everywhere in the Gospels for confirmation of the message. Christ clearly means what he says when quoting the prophet: he has been anointed by God's Spirit to preach good tidings *to the poor* (Luke 4:18). To the prosperous, the tidings he bears are decidedly grim. "Woe to you who are rich, for you are receiving your comfort in full; woe to you who are full fed, for you shall hunger; woe to you who are now laughing, for you shall mourn and weep" (Luke 6:24–25). Again, perhaps many of the practices Christ condemns in the rulers of his time are merely misuses of power and property; but that does not begin to exhaust the rhetorical force of his teachings as a whole. He not only demands that we give freely to all who ask from us (Matt. 5:42), and to do so with such prodigality that one hand is ignorant of the other's largesse (Matt. 6:3); he explicitly *forbids* storing up earthly wealth – not merely storing it up too obsessively – and allows instead only the hoarding of the treasures of heaven (Matt. 6:19–20). It is truly amazing how rarely Christians seem to notice that these counsels are stated, quite decidedly, as commands. After all, as Mary says, part of the saving promise of the gospel is that the Lord "has filled the hungry with good things and sent the rich away starving" (Luke 1:53). ◆

Beyond Worry

• • • • •

Therefore I tell you, do not worry about your life, what you will eat or drink; or about your body, what you will wear. Is not life more than food, and the body more than clothes? Look at the birds of the air; they do not sow or reap or store away in barns, and yet your heavenly Father feeds them. Are you not much more valuable than they? Can any one of you by worrying add a single hour to your life?

And why do you worry about clothes? See how the flowers of the field grow. They do not labor or spin. Yet I tell you that not even Solomon in all his splendor was dressed like one of these. If that is how God clothes the grass of the field, which is here today and tomorrow is thrown into the fire, will he not much more clothe you – you of little faith? So do not worry, saying, 'What shall we eat?' or 'What shall we drink?' or 'What shall we wear?' For the pagans run after all these things, and your heavenly Father knows that you need them.

Matthew 6:25–32

Madame Guyon

A BANDONMENT is the casting off of all selfish care, that we may be altogether at the divine disposal. All Christians are exhorted to this resignation: for it is said to all, "Be not anxious for tomorrow, for your Heavenly Father knoweth all that is necessary for you" (Matt. 6:34). "In all thy ways acknowledge him, and he shall direct thy paths" (Prov. 3:6). "Commit thy ways unto the Lord, and thy thoughts shall be established" (Prov. 16:3). "Commit thy ways unto the Lord, and he himself will bring it to pass" (Ps. 37:5).

Our abandonment . . . is practiced by continually losing our own will in the will of God; by renouncing every particular inclination as soon as it arises, however good it may appear, that we may stand in indifference with respect to ourselves, and only will that which God from eternity hath willed; by being resigned in all things, whether for soul or body, whether for time or eternity; by leaving what is past in oblivion, what is to come to Providence, and devoting the present moment to God, which brings with itself God's eternal order, and is as infallible a declaration to us of his will as it is inevitable and common to all; by attributing nothing that befalls us to the creature, but regarding all things in God, and looking upon all, excepting only our sins, as infallibly proceeding from him. Surrender yourselves, then, to be led and disposed of just as God pleaseth, with respect both to your outward and inward state. ◆

Christoph Friedrich Blumhardt

AT PRESENT the whole world lies deep in worries and cares, including the wealthiest of nations. But within the society and organism that proceeds from Christ, worries can and should cease. There we should care for one another. When the apostle Paul says, "Do not worry," he takes it for granted that these are people who are united by a bond of solidarity so that no one says anymore, "This is mine," but all say, "Our solidarity, our bond, must take away our worries. All that we share together must help each one of us and so rid us of anxiety."

In this way the kingdom of heaven comes. First it comes in a small flock free from anxiety. Thus Jesus teaches: "I tell you, do not worry about your life, what you will eat or drink; or about your body, what you will wear. . . . But seek first God's kingdom and his righteousness, and all these things will be given to you as well" (Matt. 6:32–33). From the beginning, ever since Christ was born, people have sought such a society, a fellowship of the kingdom, free from cares and worries. There is an enormous strength when people stand together, when they unite together in a communal way. The idea of private property falls away, and they are so bound together in the Spirit that each one says, "What I have belongs to the others, and if I should ever be in need, they will help me" (2 Cor. 8:13–15). This firm and absolute standing together in a shared life where each is responsible for the other is the kind of life in which you can indeed say, "Don't worry!" ✦

Clarence Jordan

OW DOES GOD "add all these things" (Matt.
6:33) to kingdom citizens? Does he rain them from
the skies or provide them miraculously merely "in
answer to prayer"? Certainly not. That isn't the way he does it
for the birds and lilies. They are nourished *from the system to
which they have committed themselves*. The needs of kingdom
citizens are supplied *through the kingdom*. It is God's distrib-
uting agency.

Let's be more specific and turn to an actual illustration. In
the Book of Acts we are told that the Holy Spirit came upon
120 people on the day of Pentecost. This powerful, indwelling
Spirit brought them, and three thousand more shortly there-
after, into the kingdom, into the love relationship with God
and their brothers and sisters. One result of this tremendous inward change was a radically different attitude toward
possessions. Luke was so amazed at it that he described it
twice (Acts 2:44–45; 4:32–35). He said, "Now the heart and
soul of the multitude of believers was one, and not a one of
them claimed any of his possessions for himself, but all things
were shared by them. And with great power the apostles were
exhibiting the evidence of the Lord Jesus' resurrection, and
everybody was greatly delighted. *For there wasn't among them
anyone in need*. Those who were owners of lands and houses
sold them and brought the proceeds of the sale and turned
them over to the apostles." . . .

How did it happen that there wasn't a needy person among
these people? Had more food, clothing, and shelter been miraculously created? No, but a new way of life had been adopted.
Need, not greed, became the principle by which they lived. By

partaking of the spirit of Jesus, they became new citizens of the kingdom of God. Sharing completely with one another in love and unity and making distribution according to the new standard of measurement, they took the assets *which God had already given them* and cared for those in need. . . .

When God first made humankind, he made provision for all our needs. This has been true ever since. God has already "added all these things." There is enough in the world today to meet all our needs. The problem is not in supply but in distribution, not with God but with us. Poverty and riches are the result of man's rebellion against the will of God. When his kingdom comes, when his will is done on earth, both poverty and riches will go! ◆

Christina Rossetti

CONSIDER THE LILIES OF THE FIELD

Flowers preach to us if we will hear:—
The rose saith in the dewy morn:
I am most fair;
Yet all my loveliness is born
Upon a thorn.
The poppy saith amid the corn:
Let but my scarlet head appear
And I am held in scorn;
Yet juice of subtle virtue lies
Within my cup of curious dyes.
The lilies say: Behold how we
Preach without words of purity.
The violets whisper from the shade

Which their own leaves have made:
Men scent our fragrance on the air,
Yet take no heed
Of humble lessons we would read.
But not alone the fairest flowers:
The merest grass
Along the roadside where we pass,
Lichen and moss and sturdy weed,
Tell of His love who sends the dew,
The rain and sunshine too,
To nourish one small seed. ◆

Howard Thurman

W E SPREAD BEFORE THEE, our Father, all of the mounting concerns of our lives and even as we do so we are not sure of what thou canst do about them. But there is within us the great necessity to expose the heights and the depths of our concerns to thee, whose wisdom transcends our little wisdoms, whose caring contains all the reaches of our own love, and whose mind holds all our little minds in their place.

We are concerned as we hear the tidings of the destruction and the suffering from the raging storms and winds and the snows of winter, as in combination they beat down upon thy children in other lands. The suffering, the desolation, the panic, the fear – these reach us even in the quietness. . . . We try to encompass in the sweep of our awareness the intimate overtones of colossal misery and frustration and hurt and pain and hate and love. One by one we might speak of our various desires. But thou knowest how far these reach and where they are limited and bounded by our ignorance or our indifference or by the intensity of the personal struggle with which we ourselves are faced.

We lay bare the personal concerns of our private lives: the decisions we must make and do not know how to make; the anxiety which we feel because of what is going on within our minds or our bodies, the outcome of which we cannot even guess. The little awareness of the little problems of our little lives mounts to overwhelming proportions when we still ourselves in thy waiting presence. We ask nothing. We wait. We wait, our Father, until at last something of thy strength becomes our strength, something of thy heart becomes our heart, something of thy forgiveness becomes our forgiveness. We wait, O God, we wait. ◆

God's Kingdom First

• • • • •

But seek first his kingdom and his righteousness, and all these
things will be given to you as well. Therefore do not worry about
tomorrow, for tomorrow will worry about itself. Each day has
enough trouble of its own.
Matthew 6:33–34

Leonhard Ragaz

THE KINGDOM OF GOD is no religion but rather
the abolishment of all religion. For many people this
must be the most shocking thing that can be said,
for from time immemorial people have embraced in the word
religion everything that their souls conceive as most holy. Is it
not the word that brings sunshine to our souls? No matter how
often it is misused, it nevertheless represents for the pious soul
the highest possession: communion of the soul with God. Do
we want to impugn this treasure of the soul, this absolutely
holiest possession, by speaking out against religion? Is it not

just a question of a word, and would it not be better to let a word that is so precious to so many people stand rather than create terrible misunderstandings through questioning it? In questioning it we run the risk of appearing to be atheists, blasphemers, destroyers of all that is holy.

And yet, we cannot do otherwise. For here two worlds separate. We are dealing with one of the basic truths, one of the basic decisions.

What do we usually understand by the word *religion*? Certainly not the communion of the soul with God, but something else. More often than not, a person sees in the word *religion* a certain spiritual structure that can easily be described. Included in it is a doctrine – a doctrine about God and divine things, a holy doctrine. Included in it are also certain practices and customs, exercises and institutions. Above all, included in it is what is called "worship," or "cult," and also some kind of community that gathers around this doctrine and worship. In addition, there is some kind of organization that arranges this worship, regulates this community, transmits the professed truth to the coming generations and to those outside the community. There has to be some kind of formulated confession of faith, even if it takes the freest form. And there will be a certain separation from other religions.

In general, it is a characteristic of religion that in this fashion it creates its own image. It becomes a kingdom for itself. It separates itself from morality, art, science, politics. Naturally, it will try to come into contact with these areas of life to dominate or penetrate them, but basically it remains something that has an identity of its own, and it is often believed that the more it guards itself against mixing with the world, the more genuine and sincere it is.

Let us add that vital religion is not just a dogma or a ritual or an organization but above all a matter of feeling, disposition, and sentiment. It is a whole world of dispositions, an unending symphony of sentiments. The scale of religious feelings reaches from the deepest hell to the highest heaven. All jubilation and all agony, all light and all darkness that inhabit the infinite reaches of the human soul find their strongest and fullest expression in religion. A large part of religious life has to do with the cultivation of these feelings. . . .

What Jesus wants is something quite different, virtually the opposite. We would have to say that already about Israel. What is called the religion of Israel is in fact no religion. At any rate, this is true of the kernel and basic purpose of Old Testament faith. To call it a religion is to misjudge and distort it. It is precisely the uniqueness of Israel that it seeks to do something unlike what the heathen religions do. Moses wanted no religion, and the battle of the prophets was a battle *against* religion. What did they want then? Not a religion, but rather a kingdom – the kingdom of God and people, a world of justice and goodness. In the name of God they stood against the temple and the priests for the lordship of God himself.

Jesus also stands in this line: he follows it to the end. Not only does he not bring a new religion, he does not bring any religion at all. One can't make this fact clear enough. He does not want a religion, but rather a kingdom, a new creation, a new world. He wants God, the people, the brother, a new justice, the liberation of the world from fear and sensuality, from mammonism, from despair, from death – and from religion. The old era is to pass and a new one is to come. . . .

One doesn't need a religion to serve this God. One serves him by serving people. Let us consider certain obvious truths that are nonetheless of enormous importance. Nowhere does Jesus give instruction regarding any special practices or works. With a smile he rejects fasting as a religious law, though on the other hand he does not forbid or condemn it. Nor does he urge people to pray – or at any rate not in the way that we usually understand it. On the contrary, he recommends moderation; only a few great petitions should fill the hearts of the disciples (and these should be as natural as breathing), and should all pertain to the coming of the kingdom. One shouldn't pray just for prayer's sake, in order to be pious and pleasing to God, or for the sake of religious practices or mood, but rather as a co-worker and fellow combatant with God.

In this sense alone Jesus urges one to make courageous, even impudent petitions. Likewise, he does not establish a worship service – there is no trace of it. He does go to the synagogue on the Sabbath day, but not to "build up" the synagogue. Rather, the synagogue is the place where Israel's hopes are still represented; it is a community gathering, a place where the kingdom of God is discussed in some way, even though it is done under the cloak of religion. The Sabbath he views in the same way, in that he basically stands above it. Nor do we find anywhere any instructions on how to cultivate a pious disposition or religious sincerity. There is no mysticism, no forced talk about God. One can say, using Gottfried Keller's words, that his God beams with worldliness. As he reveals himself in everyday life, so he is served in everyday life.

In short, it is a plain truth and yet a great paradox: Jesus does not have the slightest interest in making people pious. He does not want any religious people. His sphere is not religion. What he wants is not some mystical power cut off from the rest of life; he does not want any separation at all. He does not draw lines of demarcation among religions, but rather the opposite: he tears down religious barriers. . . . There is nowhere a temple atmosphere, a church atmosphere, be it ever so sacred, or a mystical twilight; instead, everywhere there is God's free sky and God's fresh air. There is nowhere anything artistic, extravagant, or man-made, but rather something simple, natural, genuine, healthy, clear as daylight, very human and very divine.

So very human and so very divine! We had better say so very human *because* so very divine – for this is actually the remarkable thing: here, where religion stops, we have the deep awareness of being with God. Religion ends *because* God is present. Everything is earthly *because* God has been seen in stark reality. Wherever one needs that holy, secluded, special world that is called religion, there one cannot be sure that God is near, there one needs a substitute – namely, religion. Where God is a self-evident, supremely clear, all-penetrating reality, there he can be seen in all things, can be felt in all things, can be honored in all things, can be served in all things. The world is truly his temple; therefore the special temple falls by the wayside. All people automatically become priests; therefore a special priesthood is not needed. All days become holy; therefore special holy days are not needed. Every deed becomes an act of worship; therefore worship services are no longer needed. Everything becomes holy; therefore nothing remains that is specially holy or unholy. Religion tumbles before God.

That is the revolution of Jesus, the immeasurable, still little-understood revolution. To be sure, the religion of his time understood it, and the result was the cross. Many more crosses will be raised before it is clearly understood. But precisely here lies the endless drawing power of Jesus for all human souls, pious and "godless." ◆

Christoph Friedrich Blumhardt

GOD'S KINGDOM works in strange ways. Where is there a church, congregation, or even a single person manifesting the kingdom of God today? Yet the kingdom of God is astir under the surface and spreads in new ways. Now, more than ever, we must proclaim, "The Lord is at hand!" We are part of this, quietly and actively, through our faith and expectation. It is enough for us to know that God is weaving his design in the warp and weft of the world. His goal will be reached, not just for this or that person, but for everyone. ❖

IN SEEKING GOD'S KINGDOM you must also seek his righteousness, his justice, and build on an economic foundation, not just a spiritual one. For it is on the material plane that Jesus is victorious on earth. The devil laughs up his sleeve at all our religious meetings and theology. Spiritual communities that fail to be a corrective in everyday life and practical work will soon end in a fiasco, be they Buddhist or Christian. There must be absolutely no Christian pretense, however religious it may appear, for lots of religious activity deprives people of their true life. People need to be guided properly through practical work, not through the might of weapons or proselytizing or religious fervor.

Someday, when God's kingdom conquers the earth, true piety will infuse hands-on activity and work. For unity between people can only come about on the foundation of communal life. Think more deeply about this. In God's kingdom, Christian churches are done for, since they have become little more than egotistical worlds consisting of personal concerns that keep people apart. The misery of the masses can only be alleviated by forming associations of people who live by the Holy Spirit and freely lend practical help to one another. This, in the end, is the surest way to influence those in power. A people's community that accomplishes something on the practical level will gain respect and authority among those who don't believe.

This may shock you, but we must preach that religious knowledge by itself is of no value. People should learn how to be truly active, especially with their neighbors, and to see to it that all have what they need to live a fruitful life. We need to keep the true goal in mind: the need of the world and the benefit of the people. That is the mind and spirit of Christ who reconciles all things. This is what we mean by seeking first the kingdom of God. ◆

Judging Others

• • • • •

Do not judge, or you too will be judged. For in the same way you judge others, you will be judged, and with the measure you use, it will be measured to you.

Why do you look at the speck of sawdust in your brother's eye and pay no attention to the plank in your own eye? How can you say to your brother, "Let me take the speck out of your eye," when all the time there is a plank in your own eye? You hypocrite, first take the plank out of your own eye, and then you will see clearly to remove the speck from your brother's eye.

Matthew 7:1–5

Fyodor Dostoyevsky

LET NOT THE SIN OF MEN disturb you in your actions. Fear not that it will wear away your work and hinder you from accomplishing it. Do not say, "Sin is mighty, wickedness is mighty, evil environment is mighty; we are lonely and helpless, and evil environment is wearing us away and hindering our good work from being done." Fly from that dejection, children! There is only one means of salvation: take yourself and make yourself responsible for all men's sins – friends, that is the truth, you know, for as soon as you sincerely make yourself responsible for everything and for all people, you will see at once that it is really so and that you are to blame for everyone and for all things. But by throwing your own indolence and impotence on others you will end up sharing the pride of Satan and murmuring against God. . . .

Remember particularly that you cannot be a judge of anyone. For no one can judge a criminal until he recognizes that he is just such a criminal as the man standing before him and that he, perhaps more than all people, is to blame for that crime. When he understands that, he will be able to be a judge. Though that sounds absurd, it is true. If I had been righteous myself, perhaps there would have been no criminal standing before me. If you can take upon yourself the crime of the criminal whom your heart is judging, take it at once, suffer for him yourself, and let him go without reproach. And even if the law itself makes you his judge, act in the same spirit so far as possible, for he will go away and condemn himself more bitterly than you have done. . . .

If the evildoing of men moves you to indignation and overwhelming distress, even to a desire for vengeance on the evildoers, shun above all things that feeling. Go at once and seek suffering for yourself, as though you were yourself guilty of that wrong. Accept that suffering and bear it, and your heart will find comfort, and you will understand that you too are guilty, for you might have been a light to the evil-doers even as the one man sinless, and you were not a light to them. If you had been a light, you would have lightened the path for others too, and the evil-doer might perhaps have been saved by your light from his sin. ◆

Anthony de Mello

HOW COULD YOU go about creating a happy, loving, peaceful world? By learning a simple, beautiful, but painful art called the art of looking. This is how you do it: Every time you find yourself irritated or angry with someone, the one to look at is not that person but yourself. The question to ask is not, "What's wrong with this person?" but "What does this irritation tell me about myself?" Do this right now. Think of some irritating person you know and say this painful but liberating sentence to yourself. "The cause of my irritation is not in this person but in me."

Having said that, begin the task of finding out how you are causing the irritation. First look into the very real possibility that the reason why this person's defects or so-called defects annoy you is that you have them yourself. But you have repressed them and so are projecting them unconsciously into the other. This is almost always true but hardly anyone recognizes it. So search for this person's defects in your own heart and in your unconscious mind, and your annoyance will turn to gratitude that his or her behavior has led you to self-discovery....

And here is a final truth for you to consider: Given the background, the life experience, and the unawareness of this person, he cannot help behaving the way he does. It has been so well said that to understand all is to forgive all. If you really understood this person you would see him as crippled and not blameworthy, and your irritation would instantly cease. And the next thing you know you will be treating him or her with love, and he or she is responding with love and you find yourself living in a loving world which you have yourself created. ◆

Christena Cleveland

I WAS TAKING A BUS RIDE through the snow-capped Rockies in Colorado, complaining to myself about this guy at my church who drove me crazy. Ben and I were pretty much the only unmarried adults in our small church community, so we were often paired together during social events. As if this weren't annoying enough, Ben happened to be quite possibly the most offensive person I knew.

I wish I could say this wasn't the case, but everything about Ben bugged me – from his inflexible and preachy conservatism to his career as an engineer who designs nuclear warheads. . . .

When I first began walking with Christ, I felt an immediate and authentic connection with any other Christian who crossed my path. Orthodox, Catholic, charismatic, Lutheran, evangelical, black, white, Asian, Ben – didn't matter. We were family.

But as I walked with Jesus, somehow my "growth" had been coupled with increasingly stronger opinions about the "right" way to be a follower. I started keeping people I didn't enjoy or agree with at arm's length. I managed to avoid most of the Bens in my life by locating them, categorizing them and gracefully shunning them, all while appearing to be both spiritual and community oriented. Further, I could do all of this without wasting any of my precious brainpower. I was quite good.

I chose to build community with people with whom I could pretty much agree on everything. . . . Over time, when I met other Christians, I found myself asking them what church they attended. Some answers were more acceptable than others. The way I saw it, there were two types of Christians: the wrong kind of Christian and the right kind of Christian. . . .

So it all began with two labels: Right Christian and Wrong Christian. The funny thing is, the more I talk with people about these labels, the more I realize that many of us carry our own descriptions of Right Christian and Wrong Christian. Perhaps in your opinion, my Right Christian is your Wrong Christian and my Wrong Christian is your Right Christian. . . .

Maybe to you, Wrong Christian attends a church that allows female leadership. Or maybe Wrong Christian attends a church that *doesn't* allow female leadership. Maybe Wrong Christian went to a Christian college. Maybe Wrong Christian doesn't speak English. Maybe Wrong Christian is in a college fraternity. Maybe Wrong Christian drives a Hummer. Maybe Wrong Christian promotes Reformed theology. Maybe Wrong Christian dresses like she's in a music video. Maybe Wrong Christian is pro-choice. Maybe Wrong Christian takes the bus. Maybe Wrong Christian is just annoying. Maybe Wrong Christian is unequivocally pro-Israel. Maybe Wrong Christian is a Yankees fan.

You get the picture. . . .

For the most part, I was happy to keep Wrong Christian at bay. There was just one cosmic problem. As I got to know Jesus, I began to realize that this was not exactly what he had in mind when he invited us to participate in his kingdom on earth.

I discovered that Jesus apparently didn't get the memo concerning the colossal importance of my distinction between Right Christian and Wrong Christian. In fact, he doesn't seem to care much for this distinction at all. I think this is what God meant when he said, "So are my ways higher than your ways and my thoughts than your thoughts" in Isaiah 55:9.

There I was, convinced that I was defending Jesus by condemning Wrong Christian, when I saw that Jesus was beckoning both Right Christian *and* Wrong Christian and inviting all of us to know more of his heart. As I read through the Gospels, I noticed that he had a habit of connecting with everybody: conservative theologians, liberal theologians, prostitutes, divorcées, children, politicians, people who party hard, military servicemen, women, lepers, ethnic minorities, celebrities, you name it. He was pretty serious about connecting, in spite of natural and ideological differences. And it doesn't end in the Gospels. He repeatedly disregards my Right Christian and Wrong Christian labels and continues to beckon me, even though I still tend to cling to such earthly distinctions. He's relentless. ◆

Roy Hession

THAT FRIEND OF OURS has got something in his eye! Though it is only something tiny – what Jesus called a speck of sawdust – how painful it is and how helpless he is until it is removed! It is surely our part as a friend to do all we can to remove it, and how grateful he is to us when we have succeeded in doing so. We should be equally grateful to him, if he does the same service for us.

In the light of that, it seems clear that the real point of the well-known passage in Matthew 7:3–5 about the plank and the speck is not the forbidding of our trying to remove the fault in the other person, but rather the reverse. It is the injunction that at all costs we should do this service for one another. True, its first emphasis seems to be a condemnation of censoriousness, but when the censoriousness in us is removed, the passage ends by saying, "Then you will see clearly to remove the speck from your brother's eye." ◆

Casting Pearls

· · · · ·

Do not give dogs what is sacred; do not throw your pearls to pigs.
If you do, they may trample them under their feet, and turn and
tear you to pieces.
　Matthew 7:6

Dallas Willard

THE LONG-STANDARD USE of this verse is
directly opposed to the spirit of Jesus and his teachings. That use suggests that we may have certain
wonderful treasures, of truth and of service perhaps, that we
could give to others. Perhaps the "treasure" is the very gospel
itself. But there are some who are not *worthy* of those treasures.
We have to watch for such people. Normally they are thought
of as people who will not accept our "treasure" or would not
use it rightly. They are the "pigs" or the "dogs" in question.
And we are not to waste our good things on these worthless or
evil people. So goes the standard reading of verse 6.

But it is hard to imagine anything more opposed to the spirit of Jesus than this. Indeed, the very coming of Christ, the pearl of God, into the world, would be a case of pearls before pigs thus understood.

So let us be clear once and for all that Jesus is not suggesting that certain classes of people are to be viewed as pigs or dogs. Nor is he saying that we should not give good things and do good deeds to people who might reject or misuse them. In fact, his teaching is precisely the opposite. We are to be like the Father in the heavens, "who is kind to the unthankful and the evil" (Luke 6:35).

The problem with pearls for pigs is not that the pigs are not worthy. It is not worthiness that is in question here at all, but helpfulness. Pigs cannot digest pearls, cannot nourish themselves upon them. Likewise for a dog with a Bible or a crucifix. The dog cannot eat it. The reason these animals will finally "turn and rend you," when you one day step up to them with another load of Bibles or pearls, is that *you* at least are edible. Anyone who has ever had serious responsibilities of caring for animals will understand immediately what Jesus is saying.

And what a picture this is of our efforts to correct and control others by pouring our good things, often truly precious things, upon them – things that they nevertheless simply cannot ingest and use to nourish themselves. Often we do not even listen to them. We "know" without listening. Jesus saw it going on around him all the time, as we do today. And the outcome is usually exactly the same as with the pig and the dog. Our good intentions make little difference. The needy person will finally become angry and attack us. The point is not the waste of the "pearl" but that the person given the pearl is not helped.

How often this happens between child and parent! Along with condemnation – they usually go hand in hand – the counterattack is the number one cause of alienation between the generations. Our children or others do not know what else to do with us pearl-pushers. And even though they love us – as parent or friend, for example – they simply cannot take any more of our "pushy irrelevance," as they see it, or possibly our stubborn blindness.

Forcing religion upon the young even though it makes no sense to them is a major reason why they "graduate" from church about the same time they graduate from high school and do not return for twenty years, if ever. The gap is only widened when the elders are in turn condemned for not responding to the newfound wisdom of the young.

Frankly, our "pearls" often are offered with a certain superiority of bearing that keeps us from paying attention to those we are trying to help. *We* have solutions. That should be enough, shouldn't it? And very quickly some contempt, impatience, anger, and even condemnation slips into our offer.

And the very goodness of our "pearl" may make us think that we couldn't possibly have the wrong attitude toward the intended recipient. Would we be offering them such pearls if our heart were not right? Unfortunately, we just might. It has been done. And how we honestly feel when our "pearl" is left there on the ground to be walked on by the unenthusiastic recipient will be a pretty good sign of where our heart was in the first place. ✦

Jacques Ellul

TO PROCLAIM the word of God in the abstract, to people who are in a situation which prevents them from understanding it, means that we are tempting God. Let us meditate once more on this incisive saying of our Lord. This is a striking description of the relation between the church and the world at the present time. The church, which has received the "pearls" of the gospel, throws them with pious indifference as food to the "swine," who are human beings (and this includes ourselves, "good Christians") embedded in the clay of this world which is so exclusively material-istic, submerged by economic and political problems, by their personal fears and their financial worries, by their anxieties and their daily troubles, absolutely dominated by the spirit of the present age.

And these people turn against the church, saying: "We find no nourishment in your pearls, no satisfaction in their beauty. What are we to do with them? They are no good to us in our present situation!" (And this is true!) And they attack the church which has only given them fair words and illu-sions – they want to tear it down. These people are wrong, for the Word of God is always valid, and if they do not get anything from it today, it is because they are in a false posi-tion: it is not the Word that needs to be changed, and to bring them something; it is their own position that needs to be changed. But they are right in their feeling about the church, because it is the church that ought to initiate this changed situation, in order that the Word of God may be heard in human life as a whole.

And the church has no right to confine itself to "casting pearls before swine." First of all, the church should do some preparatory work, in order that "the swine" may be able to receive "the pearls." It is not for the church to separate human beings into two categories – first of all the "swine" (Communists, non-conformists, people who have "mistaken ideas," workingmen, and so on) to whom we cannot proclaim the gospel, and, secondly, those who are not "swine," those dull, good "sheep," which our world creates in such numbers!

What the church ought to do is to try to place all people in an economic, intellectual – yes, and also in a psychological and physical – situation, which is such that they can actually *hear* this gospel – that they can be sufficiently responsible to say yes or no, that they can be sufficiently alive for these words to have some meaning for them. The secret of their choice belongs to God, but they should be able to make a decision; it is up to the church to see to it that they are not placed in such conditions that they cannot react otherwise than as swine, to whom pearls have been thrown. ✦

Ask, Seek, Knock

• • • • •

Ask and it will be given to you; seek and you will find; knock and the door will be opened to you. For everyone who asks receives; the one who seeks finds; and to the one who knocks, the door will be opened.

Which of you, if your son asks for bread, will give him a stone? Or if he asks for a fish, will give him a snake? If you, then, though you are evil, know how to give good gifts to your children, how much more will your Father in heaven give good gifts to those who ask him!

Matthew 7:7–11

Andrew Murray

NEXT TO THE REVELATION of the Father's love, there is, in the whole course of the school of prayer, not a more important lesson than this: Every one that asketh, receiveth. In the three words the Lord uses, *ask, seek, knock*, a difference in meaning has been sought. If such was indeed his purpose, then the first, ask, refers to the gifts we pray for. But I may ask and receive the gift without the giver. Seek is the word scripture uses of God himself; Christ assures me that I can find himself. But it is not enough to find God in time of need, without coming to abiding fellowship: knock speaks of admission to dwell with him and in him. Asking and receiving the gift would thus lead to seeking and finding the giver, and this again to the knocking and opening of the door of the Father's home and love. One thing is sure: the Lord does want us to count most certainly on it that asking, seeking, knocking cannot be in vain: receiving an answer, finding God, the opened heart and home of God, are the certain fruit of prayer.

That the Lord should have thought it needful in so many forms to repeat the truth, is a lesson of deep import. It proves that he knows our heart, how doubt and distrust toward God are natural to us, and how easily we are inclined to rest in prayer as a religious work without an answer. He knows too how, even when we believe that God is the hearer of prayer, believing prayer that lays hold of the promise is something spiritual, too high and difficult for the half-hearted disciple. He therefore, at the very outset of his instruction to those who would learn to pray, seeks to lodge this truth deep into their hearts: prayer does avail much; ask and ye *shall* receive; *every one* that asketh, receiveth. This is the fixed eternal law of the kingdom: if you ask and receive not, it must be because there is something amiss or wanting in the prayer. Hold on; let the Word and the Spirit teach you to pray aright, but do not let go the confidence he seeks to waken: Every one that asketh, receiveth.

"Ask, and it shall be given you." Christ has no mightier stimulus to persevering prayer in his school than this. As a child has to prove a sum to be correct, so the proof that we have prayed aright is *the answer*. If we ask and receive not, it is because we have not learned to pray aright. Let every learner in the school of Christ therefore take the Master's word in all simplicity: every one that asketh, receiveth. He had good reasons for speaking so unconditionally. Let us beware of weakening the Word with our human wisdom. When he tells us heavenly things, let us believe him: his Word will explain itself to him who believes it fully. If questions and difficulties arise, let us not seek to have them settled before we accept the Word. No, let us entrust them all to him; it is his to solve them; our work is first and fully to accept and hold fast his promise. Let in our inner chamber, in the inner chamber of our heart too, the Word be inscribed in letters of light: every one that asketh, receiveth.

According to this teaching of the Master, prayer consists of two parts, has two sides, a human and a divine. The human is the asking, the divine is the giving. Or, to look at both from the human side, there is the asking and the receiving – the two halves that make up a whole. It is as if he would tell us that we are not to rest without an answer, because it is the will of God, the rule in the Father's family: every childlike believing petition is granted. If no answer comes, we are not to sit down in the sloth that calls itself resignation, and suppose that it is not God's will to give an answer. No, there must be something in the prayer that is not as God would have it, childlike and believing; we must seek for grace to pray so that the answer may come. It is far easier to the flesh to submit without the answer than to yield itself to be searched and purified by the Spirit, until it has learnt to pray the prayer of faith.

It is one of the terrible marks of the diseased state of Christian life in these days, that there are so many who rest content without the distinct experience of answer to prayer. They pray daily, they ask many things, and trust that some of them will be heard, but know little of direct definite answer to prayer as the rule of daily life. And it is this the Father wills: he seeks daily intercourse with his children in listening to and granting their petitions. He wills that I should come to him day by day with distinct requests; he wills day by day to do for me what I ask. It was in his answer to prayer that the saints of old learned to know God as the Living One, and were stirred to praise and love (Ps. 34). Our Teacher waits to imprint this upon our minds: prayer and its answer, the child asking and the father giving, belong to each other. There may be cases in which the answer is a refusal, because the request is not according to God's Word, as when Moses asked to enter Canaan. But still, there was an answer: God did not leave his servant in uncertainty as to his will. The gods of the heathen are dumb and cannot speak. Our Father lets his child know when he cannot give him what he asks, and he withdraws his petition, even as the Son did in Gethsemane. Both Moses the servant and Christ the Son knew that what they asked was not according to what the Lord had spoken: their prayer was the humble supplication whether it was not possible for the decision to be changed. God will teach those who are teachable and give him time, by his Word and Spirit, whether their request be according to his will or not. Let us withdraw the request, if it be not according to God's mind, or persevere till the answer come. Prayer is appointed to obtain the answer. It is in prayer and its answer that the interchange of love between the Father and his child takes place.

How deep the estrangement of our heart from God must be, that we find it so difficult to grasp such promises. Even while we accept the words and believe their truth, the faith of the heart, that fully has them and rejoices in them, comes so slowly. It is because our spiritual life is still so weak, and the capacity for taking God's thoughts is so feeble. But let us look to Jesus to teach us as none but he can teach. If we take his words in simplicity, and trust him by his Spirit to make them within us life and power, they will so enter into our inner being, that the spiritual divine reality of the truth they contain will indeed take possession of us, and we shall not rest content until every petition we offer is borne heavenward on Jesus' own words: "Ask, and it shall be given you."

Beloved fellow disciples in the school of Jesus, let us set ourselves to learn this lesson well. Let us take these words just as they were spoken. Let us not suffer human reason to weaken their force. Let us take them as Jesus gives them, and believe them. He will teach us in due time how to understand them fully: let us begin by implicitly believing them. Let us take time, as often as we pray, to listen to his voice: every one that asketh, receiveth. Let us not make the feeble experiences of our unbelief the measure of what our faith may expect. Let us seek, not only just in our seasons of prayer, but at all times, to hold fast the joyful assurance: man's prayer on earth and God's answer in heaven are meant for each other. Let us trust Jesus to teach us so to pray that the answer can come. He will do it, if we hold fast the word he gives today: "Ask, and ye shall receive." ◆

The Golden Rule

◆ ◆ ◆ ◆ ◆

So in everything, do to others what you would have them do to you, for this sums up the Law and the Prophets.
Matthew 7:12

Roger L. Shinn

O NE REASON the Golden Rule is so popular is that it seems to require no specific faith and no specific religious beliefs. People may argue over many questions, but often they can agree on the Golden Rule. Religious teachers all over the world, many of them long before Jesus, taught one form or another of the Golden Rule. Look at a few examples.

1. The Hindu Mahabharata teaches: "People gifted with intelligence and purified souls should always treat others as they themselves wish to be treated."

2. A Jainist writing, also from India, says: "A man should wander about treating all creatures in the world as he himself would be treated."

3. When Confucius was asked for a single word to sum up the rules of life, he answered: "Is not reciprocity such a word? What you do not want done to yourself, do not do to others."

4. The Taoists taught: "Regard your neighbor's gain as your own gain, and regard your neighbor's loss as your own loss."

5. In the generation before Jesus a man asked the great Rabbi Hillel to teach him the Law while standing on one foot. Hillel answered: "What thou thyself hatest, do not to thy neighbor. This is the whole Law. The rest is commentary. Go and learn it."

Not only the great religions have framed this rule. Some philosophers, unwilling to accept the Christian belief in God's revelation in Christ, have worked out principles of conduct much like the Golden Rule. Thus Immanuel Kant tried to base his ethics simply on the principle of logical consistency. He decided that rationality demands that he act on principles that he could will all other people to act upon. . . .

But the Golden Rule is not enough. . . . For example, suppose you are someone with plenty of ability, well able to look out for yourself. You may say: "I am tough. I believe life is a dog-eat-dog struggle, with everyone out for himself. I ask no mercy and I give none." You can still live by the letter of the Golden Rule. You want no love or forgiveness; you do not extend it to others. The chances are that someday you will awaken to realize your dependence on others; but for years you can live by cheap standards, all the while quoting the Golden Rule.

Or take the case of Thomas Hobbes in the seventeenth century. He may have been a better man than his theory; but if we take him at his word, we find a crude theory of morality. He believed that all people are moved by the restless desire for power. This makes us bitter competitors, each endangering the other. Without some political power controlling us, life would be "solitary, poor, nasty, brutish, and short." Every person naturally has the right to anything he can grab, including the lives of others. But to save our own skins we decide to limit our grasping. We make agreements with our fellowmen. We'll not kill them if they'll not kill us. So Hobbes comes around to quoting the Golden Rule from Jesus. And all for frankly selfish reasons.

Or say that you find in business that the Golden Rule "pays off." So, again selfishly, you may live up to it as strictly as the businessman next door who honestly loves his fellowman.

Or, to take a last example, a moral pervert might use the letter of the Golden Rule to justify involving others in his evil ways. He would gladly have others encourage him in his vice, and he will so encourage them.

All this is simply saying what the Sermon on the Mount has been saying to us week after week: No external form of action, no rule is enough.

The Golden Rule cannot be applied legalistically anyway. The child cannot do for the parent what he wants the parent to do for him. The patient doesn't do for the doctor what the doctor does for the patient. The Golden Rule requires the imagination to put oneself in the place of another and see his needs. It requires love.

The Golden Rule can be a source of frustration. Even though, as we have seen, it is not always a very high ethic, it often rises above our normal conduct. Frequently we praise the

Golden Rule, then live by some lower code. Someone says, "I'll treat him the way he treated me – tit for tat." (It reminds us of "an eye for an eye, a tooth for a tooth.") Or someone tries the popular slogan, "Do unto others what they would like to do to you, but do it first."

Someone has said, "The Golden Rule works like gravitation." But it doesn't. Gravitation is natural, independent of us. We can't argue with it or disobey it. We do disobey the Golden Rule. History records countless acts of disobedience to it. Our inclinations are to make exceptions of ourselves, to claim privileges – maybe "just this once" – which we do not give. The person of insight knows that often he does not live up to the Golden Rule. Any rule hanging over us, especially a rule that we disobey, is frustrating. To try to obey it and not succeed is even more frustrating.

The Christian gospel is not a set of rules. It is God's gift to us, a gift that awakens a new spirit in us. The spirit takes the frustration away. With the spirit we want to guide our conduct by the Golden Rule. "The written code kills, but the Spirit gives life" (2 Cor. 3:6).

Within the gospel the Golden Rule can become a pathway of life. When the words convey the spirit of the Sermon on the Mount, they become a helpful guide in many a situation. In Luke's Gospel the Golden Rule concludes the paragraph which starts, "Love your enemies." Love, mercy, forgiveness, the spirit of the Beatitudes – here we find the spirit in which Jesus meant the Golden Rule. ◆

John Wesley

HERE IS A PLAIN RULE, always ready at hand, always to be applied. In all cases relating to your neighbor, make his case your own. Suppose the circumstances were changed. Suppose yourself to be just as he is now. Then beware that you indulge neither temper nor thought, that no word gets out of your lips, that you take no step, which you would have condemned in him upon the reverse of the circumstances. If understood in a direct and positive sense, the meaning is plain. "Whatever you could reasonably desire of him, supposing you were in his circumstances, do that to the uttermost of your power, to every person on earth."

We can apply this in one or two obvious instances. It is clear to every person's conscience that we would not want others to judge us. We would not want anyone to think evil of us, either lightly or without cause. We would not have anyone speak evil of us, or publish our real faults or failings. Apply this to yourself. . . .

We would have all people love and esteem us. We would have them behave toward us according to justice, mercy, and truth. We would have them do all of the good for us that they can without injuring themselves. In all outward things, according to the known rule, their luxury should give way to our conveniences. Their conveniences should give way to our necessities. Their necessities should give way to our extreme needs. Now, let us walk by the same rule. Let us do to all as we would have them do unto us. Let us love and honor all people. Let justice, mercy and truth govern all of our minds and actions. . . .

Believe in Jesus Christ and your faith will work by love. You will love the Lord your God because he has loved you. You will love your neighbor as yourself. Then, it will be your glory to exert and increase this love; not merely by abstaining from what is contrary to it, every unkind thought, word, and action, but by showing all that kindness to every man which you would have him show to you. ◆

Leo Tolstoy

W E ARE ALL BROTHERS – and yet every morning a brother or a sister must empty the bedroom slops for me. We are all brothers, but every morning I must have a cigar, a sweetmeat, an ice, and such things, which my brothers and sisters have been wasting their health in manufacturing, and I enjoy these things and demand them. We are all brothers, yet I live by working in a bank, or mercantile house, or shop at making all goods dearer for my brothers. We are all brothers, but I live on a salary paid me for prosecuting, judging, and condemning the thief or the prostitute whose existence the whole tenor of my life tends to bring about, and who I know ought not to be punished but reformed. We are all brothers, but I live on the salary I gain by collecting taxes from needy laborers to be spent on the luxuries of the rich and idle. We are all brothers, but I take a stipend for preaching a false Christian religion, which I do not myself believe in, and which only serves to hinder people from understanding true Christianity. I take a stipend as priest or bishop for deceiving people in the matter of the greatest importance to them. We are all brothers, but I will not give the poor the benefit of my educational, medical, or literary labors except for money. We are all brothers, yet I take a salary for being ready to commit murder, for teaching people to murder, or making firearms, gunpowder, or fortifications. . . .

A man of sensitive conscience cannot but suffer if he lives such a life. The only means by which he can escape from this suffering is by blunting his conscience, but even if some people succeed in dulling their conscience they cannot dull their fears. ◆

Two Ways

* * * * *

Enter through the narrow gate. For wide is the gate and broad is the road that leads to destruction, and many enter through it. But small is the gate and narrow the road that leads to life, and only a few find it.

  Matthew 7:13–14

The Didache

THERE ARE TWO WAYS, one of life and one of death, and there is a great difference between these two ways.

Now this is the way of life: First, you shall love God, who made you. Second, you shall love your neighbor as yourself; but whatever you do not wish to happen to you, do not do to another. The teaching of these words is this: Bless those who curse you, and pray for your enemies, and fast for those who persecute you. For what credit is it if you love those who love you? Do not even the Gentiles do the same? But you must love those who hate you, and you will not have an enemy. Abstain from fleshly and bodily cravings. If someone gives you a blow on your right cheek, turn to him the other as well and you will be perfect. If someone forces you to go one mile, go with him two miles; if someone takes your cloak, give him your tunic also; if someone takes from you what belongs to you, do not demand it back, for you cannot do so. . . .

Be humble, for the humble shall inherit the earth. Be patient and merciful and innocent and quiet and good, and revere always the words that you have heard. Do not exalt yourself or permit your soul to become arrogant. Your soul shall not associate with the lofty, but live with the righteous and the humble. Accept as good the things that happen to you, knowing that nothing transpires apart from God.

My child, remember night and day the one who preaches God's word to you, and honor him as though he were the Lord. For wherever the Lord's nature is preached, there the Lord is. Moreover, you shall seek out daily the presence of the saints, so that you may find support in their words. You shall not cause division, but shall make peace between those who quarrel. You shall judge righteously; you shall not show partiality when reproving transgressions. You shall not waver with regard to your decisions. . . .

You shall hate all hypocrisy and everything that is not pleasing to the Lord. You must not forsake the Lord's commandments but must guard what you have received, neither adding nor subtracting anything. In church you shall confess your transgressions, and you shall not approach your prayer with an evil conscience. This is the way of life.

But the way of death is this: first of all, it is evil and completely cursed; murders, adulteries, lusts, sexual immoralities, thefts, idolatries, magic arts, sorceries, robberies, false testimonies, hypocrisies, duplicity, deceit, pride, malice, stubbornness, greed, abusive language, jealousy, audacity, arrogance, boastfulness. It is the way of persecutors of good people, of those who hate truth, love a lie, do not know the reward of righteousness, do not adhere to what is good or to righteous judgment, who are vigilant not for what is good but for what is evil, from whom gentleness and patience are far removed, who love worthless things, pursue a reward, have no mercy for the poor, do not work on behalf of the oppressed, do not know the one who made them, are murderers of children, corrupters of God's creation, who turn away from someone in need, who oppress the afflicted, are advocates of the wealthy, lawless judges of the poor, utterly sinful. May you be delivered, children, from all these things!

See that no one leads you astray from this way of the teaching, for such a person teaches you without regard for God. For if you are able to bear the whole yoke of the Lord, you will be perfect. But if you are not able, then do what you can. ❖

C. S. Lewis

THE ORDINARY IDEA which we all have before we become Christians is this. We take as starting point our ordinary self with its various desires and interests. We then admit that something else – call it "morality" or "decent behavior," or "the good of society" – has claims on this self: claims which interfere with its own desires. What we mean by "being good" is giving in to those claims. Some of the things the ordinary self wanted to do turn out to be what we call "wrong": well, we must give them up. Other things, which the self did not want to do, turn out to be what we call "right":

well, we shall have to do them. But we are hoping all the time that when all the demands have been met, the poor natural self will still have some chance, and some time, to get on with its own life and do what it likes. In fact, we are very like an honest man paying his taxes. He pays them all right, but he does hope that there will be enough left over for him to live on. Because we are still taking our natural self as the starting point.

As long as we are thinking that way, one or other of two results is likely to follow. Either we give up trying to be good, or else we become very unhappy indeed. For, make no mistake: if you are really going to try to meet all the demands made on the natural self, it will not have enough left over to live on. The more you obey your conscience, the more your conscience will demand of you. And your natural self, which is thus being starved and hampered and worried at every turn, will get angrier and angrier. In the end, you will either give up trying to be good, or else become one of those people who, as they say, "live for others" but always in a discontented, grumbling way – always wondering why the others do not notice it more and always making a martyr of yourself. And once you become that you will be a far greater pest to anyone who has to live with you then you would have been if you had remained frankly selfish.

The Christian way is different: harder, and easier. Christ says, "Give me All. I don't want so much of your time and so much of your money and so much of your work: I want You. I have not come to torment your natural self, but to kill it. No half-measures are any good. I don't want to cut off a branch here and a branch there, I want to have the whole tree down. I don't want to drill the tooth, or crown it, or stop it, but to have it out. Hand over the whole natural self, all the desires which you think innocent as well as the ones you think wicked – the whole outfit. I will give you a new self instead. In fact, I will give you myself: my own will shall become yours."

Both harder and easier than what we are all trying to do. You have noticed, I expect, that Christ himself sometimes describes the Christian way as very hard, sometimes as very easy. He says, "Take up your cross" – in other words, it is like going to be beaten to death in a concentration camp. Next minute he says, "My yoke is easy and my burden light." He means both. And one can just see why both are true.

Teachers will tell you that the laziest student in the class is the one who works hardest in the end. . . . Laziness means more work in the long run. Or look at it this way. In a battle, or in mountain climbing, there is often one thing which it takes a lot of pluck to do; but it is also, in the long run, the safest thing to do. If you funk it, you will find yourself, hours later, in far worse danger. The cowardly thing is also the most dangerous thing.

It is like that here. The terrible thing, the almost impossible thing, is to hand over your whole self – all your wishes and precautions – to Christ. But it is far easier than what we are all trying to do instead. For what we are trying to do is to remain what we call "ourselves," to keep personal happiness as our great aim in life, and yet at the same time be "good." We are all trying to let our mind and heart go their own way – centered on money or pleasure or ambition – and hoping, in spite of this, to behave honestly and chastely and humbly. And that is exactly what Christ warned us you could not do. . . .

That is why the real problem of the Christian life comes where people do not usually look for it. It comes the very moment you wake up each morning. All your wishes and hopes for the day rush at you like wild animals. And the first job each morning consists simply in shoving them all back; in listening to that other voice, taking that other point of view, letting that other larger, stronger, quieter life come flowing in. And so on, all day. Standing back from all your natural fussings and frettings; coming in out of the wind.

We can only do it for moments at first. But from those moments the new sort of life will be spreading through our system: because now we are letting Christ work at the right part of us. It is the difference between paint, which is merely laid on the surface, and a dye or stain which soaks right through. He never talked vague, idealistic gas. When he said, "Be perfect," he meant it. He meant that we must go in for the full treatment. It is hard; but the sort of compromise we are all hankering after is harder – in fact, it is impossible. ◆

Dietrich Bonhoeffer

I F WE FOLLOW this way as one we follow in obedience to an external command, if we are afraid of ourselves all the time, it is indeed an impossible way. But if we behold Jesus Christ going on before us step by step, we shall not go astray. But if we worry about the dangers that beset us, if we gaze at the road instead of at him who goes before, we are already straying from the path. For he is himself the way, the narrow way and the strait gate. He, and he alone, is our journey's end. When we know that, we are able to proceed along the narrow way through the strait gate of the cross, and on to eternal life, and the very narrowness of the road will increase our certainty. The way which the Son of God trod on earth, and the way which we too must tread as citizens of two worlds on the razor edge between this world and the kingdom of heaven, could hardly be a broad way. The narrow way is bound to be right. ◆

The Shepherd of Hermas

I SAID TO HIM, "Sir, these commandments are great and good and glorious, and are able to gladden the heart of the one who is able to keep them. But I do not know if these commandments can be kept by a human, for they are very hard."

He answered and said to me, "If you propose to yourself that they can be kept, you will keep them easily and they will not be hard. But if the idea that they cannot be kept by a human has already entered your heart, you will not keep them. . . ."

. . . "Those who have the Lord in their heart," he said, "can master everything, including all these commandments. But to those who have the Lord on their lips but whose heart is hardened and who are far from the Lord, these commandments are hard and difficult. You, therefore, who are empty and fickle in the faith, put the Lord in your heart and you will realize that nothing is easier or sweeter or more gentle than these commandments." ◆

49

False Prophets

♦ ♦ ♦ ♦ ♦

Watch out for false prophets. They come to you in sheep's clothing, but inwardly they are ferocious wolves. By their fruit you will recognize them. Do people pick grapes from thorn bushes, or figs from thistles? Likewise, every good tree bears good fruit, but a bad tree bears bad fruit. A good tree cannot bear bad fruit, and a bad tree cannot bear good fruit. Every tree that does not bear good fruit is cut down and thrown into the fire. Thus, by their fruit you will recognize them.
Matthew 7:15–20

Scot McKnight

I WOULD URGE YOU to turn the text into a mirror to let it ask you a simple question: Am I the false prophet of this text? Am I the person who exercises gifts well, who does things as a leader that many admire, but who is also the person who in my private life, in my home, in the quiet hours of the day, is not following what Jesus has taught in this Sermon? If that is the case, then I would urge you to fall to your knees, confess your sins, wait on the Spirit of God to cleanse your heart, and ask God to quicken in you the way of Jesus – the way of doing what he calls us to do.

Sensitive theologians are sometimes nervous about the way Jesus talks, and sometimes we need to exercise a special caution, but we need to trust that Jesus said what he wanted. No one is saved *by* works, of course; but everyone is *judged* by works because works are the inevitable life of the one who surrenders to, trusts in, and follows Jesus. Thus, you can tell the true charismatically gifted leader from the false *by their fruit* (obedience to Jesus).

This leads to a fundamental question: What kind of good works? . . . Do we show mercy to those who are in need? Do we care for the marginalized, unlike the rich man who did not concern himself with the poor man at his gate (Luke 16:19-31)? Do our neighbors think we are gracious and loving or obstinate and judgmental? Do we nurture love and patience in our own children? Do we serve our spouse as Christ serves the church? Is our charismatic gift so important that menial tasks have to be done by others? Or, put differently, do we expect our spouse to do all the dirty work around the home so we can carry on our holy business? . . .

What Jesus is getting at is this: leaders are first of all followers of Jesus before they are leaders. If they forget that, they will hear these words of Jesus as a searching judgment. ◆

John R. W. Stott

IT IS SURELY not an accident that Jesus' warning about false prophets immediately follows his teaching about the two gates, ways, crowds and destinations. For false prophets are adept at blurring the issue of salvation. Some so muddle or distort the gospel that they make it hard for seekers to find the narrow gate. Others try to make out that the narrow way is in reality much broader than Jesus implied, and that to walk it requires little if any restriction on one's belief or behavior. Yet others, perhaps the most pernicious of all, dare to contradict Jesus and to assert that the broad road does not lead to destruction, but that as a matter of fact all roads lead to God, and that even the broad and the narrow roads, although they lead off in opposite directions, ultimately both end in life. No wonder Jesus likened such false teachers to ravenous wolves, not so much because they are greedy for gain, prestige or power (though they often are), but because they are "ferocious" (NIV), that is, extremely dangerous. They are responsible for leading some people to the very destruction which they say does not exist. ✦

Gene L. Davenport

FALSE PROPHETS are frequently quite sincere. Usually, they truly believe themselves to be God's messengers, called into service to do battle with the forces of evil. Usually, also, they assume that every problem has a simple solution, a single solution given them by God himself. Missing altogether in the false prophets is any sense of the mystery of God, any hint of the incomprehensibility of God. Taking the Bible as a combination almanac and moral rule book, they have a quotation for every occasion. If a disease such as AIDS sweeps the world, it is said to be God's way of getting at some unpopular group or some deviant nation. If someone dies in a horrible accident, it is said to be the will of God. Movie stars say they have become prominent because God blessed them; politicians say they have been elected because God gave them the victory; a business prospers, the owner says, because God has blessed it; a congregation or denomination suddenly grows by leaps and bounds, because it says God has given it growth; and so on. Whatever is, we are told, would not be were it not for God. So much knowledge! So much certainty! So little mystery! Such a trivial god!

A god who blesses our self-centeredness, who cherishes our vulgarity, who pulls our strings – a god whose thoughts are our thoughts, whose ways are our ways; it is a god all right: the god of darkness! Such a god has an answer for everything – even for the Holocaust.

The God of Jesus Christ has no such easy answers. . . . The God of Jesus Christ upsets all our answers and forces us to ask the most disturbing of questions. The God of Jesus Christ chooses when to speak, but he also chooses when to remain aloof, when to abandon us, when to leave us to struggle with the experience of his silence.

For the phony prophets, God is never silent. He constantly speaks to them in confidential revelations or points them to a simplistic text that can be quoted with a silly grin or a grotesque snarl. Their god is ever ready to accede to their most frivolous, most self-serving whims. How easy to serve such a god! How easy to gain a following from the masses who thrive

on ego-building, simple answers! How easy to enter the wide
gate and walk the spacious way! For the way of destruction, the
way of death, is not only easy; it is alluring.

The way of the God of Jesus Christ, however, is found
through the narrow gate. The way is difficult to find, because
the wide gate has all the best public relations experts. It is
difficult to walk because it is the way of mystery, the way of
the cross. ◆

Basilea Schlink

MANY CHRISTIANS SPEND themselves in
service for the Lord. They offer one sacrifice after
another. And still they will bear no fruit. There
is no blessing in their work, although they may be praised by
many. God sees their hearts, but people only see what is before
their eyes. Because of their work in the kingdom of God others
might praise them "to highest heaven," but in reality their
place may be very far away from God. For their sacrifices were
self-chosen; they were offered in disobedience to God.

There may have been a missionary who was sent home from
the field, because she was sick. At the mission she had been
admired for her dedication, love, and willingness to sacrifice.
Back home she suddenly became unbearable, rebelling against
everything, because she had to do administrative work. Why?
She said, "I cannot live without serving people." But then God
will pronounce this verdict over her: "To obey is better than
sacrifice" (1 Sam. 15:22). She could not humble herself in obedience to God's will – leaving her former work because of illness.
Her ministry was not done out of love for God nor out of pure
love for people. She had lived for herself; she performed this

ministry to satisfy her own ego. She was missing the true love for Jesus, for Jesus said, "If a man loves me, he will keep my word" (John 14:23); he will do God's will.

We see how cleverly the enemy deals with us so-called "pious" Christians. He knows that we will not consciously commit an obvious sin, because we know that disobedience is a sin and will be punished severely. That is why he uses a different method to catch us in his trap. He tells us that we should sacrifice something special for God and his service, or for our neighbor in his need. But in face of the serious consequences that disobedience has for time and eternity, we should stop and ask God, "Place me in the light of your truth. Let me see the true motives for my actions and repent when you unmask them and show me that my decisions and actions stemmed from disobedience!" ◆

50

Lord, Lord

◆ ◆ ◆ ◆ ◆

*Not everyone who says to me, "Lord, Lord," will enter the
kingdom of heaven, but only the one who does the will of my
Father who is in heaven. Many will say to me on that day, "Lord,
Lord, did we not prophesy in your name and in your name drive
out demons and in your name perform many miracles?" Then
I will tell them plainly, "I never knew you. Away from me, you
evildoers!"*

Matthew 7:21–23

George MacDonald

D O YOU ASK, "What is faith in him?" I answer,
The leaving of your way, your objects, your self, and
the taking of his and him; the leaving of your trust
in men, in money, in opinion, in character, in atonement itself,
and doing as he tells you. I can find no words strong enough
to serve for the weight of this necessity – this obedience. It is
the one terrible heresy of the church, that it has always been
presenting something else than obedience as faith in Christ. . . .

Get up, and do something the master tells you; so make
yourself his disciple at once. Instead of asking yourself whether
you believe or not, ask yourself whether you have this day done
one thing because he said, Do it, or once abstained because he
said, Do not do it. It is simply absurd to say you believe, or even
want to believe in him, if you do not anything he tells you. . . .

We must learn to obey him in everything, and so must begin
somewhere: let it be at once, and in the very next thing that
lies at the door of our conscience! Oh fools and slow of heart,
if you think of nothing but Christ, and do not set yourselves
to do his words, you but build your houses on the sand. What
have such teachers not to answer for who have turned your
regard away from the direct words of the Lord himself, which
are spirit and life, to contemplate plans of salvation tortured
out of the words of his apostles, even were those plans as true
as they are false! There is but one plan of salvation, and that is
to believe in the Lord Jesus Christ; that is, to take him for what
he is – our Master, and his words as if he meant them, which
assuredly he did. To do his words is to enter into vital relation
with him, to obey him is the only way to be one with him. The
relation between him and us is an absolute one; it can nohow
begin to live but in obedience: it is obedience. There can be
no truth, no reality, in any initiation of at-one-ment with him,
that is not obedience.

What? Have I the poorest notion of a God, and dare think
of entering into relations with him, the very first of which
is not that what he saith, I will do? The thing is eternally
absurd, and comes of the father of lies. I know what he whis-
pers to those to whom such teaching as this is distasteful: "It
is the doctrine of works!" But one word of the Lord humbly
heard and received will suffice to send all the demons of false
theology into the abyss. He says the man that does not do

the things he tells him, builds his house to fall in utter ruin. He instructs his messengers to go and baptize all nations, "teaching them to observe all things whatsoever I have commanded you." Tell me it is faith he requires: Do I not know it? And is not faith the highest act of which the human mind is capable? But faith in what? Faith in what he is, in what he says – a faith which can have no existence except in obedience – a faith which is obedience. To do what he wishes is to put forth faith in him. . . .

What have you done this day because it was the will of Christ? Have you dismissed, once dismissed, an anxious thought for the morrow? Have you ministered to any needy soul or body, and kept your right hand from knowing what your left hand did? Have you begun to leave all and follow him? Did you set yourself to judge righteous judgment? Are you being ware of covetousness? Have you forgiven your enemy? Are you seeking the kingdom of God and his righteousness before all other things? Are you hungering and thirsting after righteousness? Have you given to some one that asked of you? Tell me something that you have done, are doing, or are trying to do because he told you. ◆

Wendell Berry

I WILL BEGIN by dealing with the embarrassing questions that the Gospels impose, I imagine, upon any serious reader. There are two of these, and the first is this: If you had been living in Jesus' time and had heard him teaching, would you have been one of his followers? To be an honest taker of this test, I think you have to try to forget that you have read the Gospels and that Jesus has been a "big name" for two thousand years. You have to imagine instead that you are walking past the local courthouse and you come upon a crowd listening to a man named Joe Green or Green Joe, depending on judgments whispered among the listeners on the fringe. You too stop to listen, and you soon realize that Joe Green is saying something utterly scandalous, utterly unexpectable from the premises of modern society. He is saying: "Don't resist evil. If somebody slaps your right cheek, let him slap your left cheek too. . . ." Well, you know how happily *that* would be received, not only in the White House and the Capitol, but among most of your neighbors. And then suppose this Joe Green looks at you over the heads of the crowd, calls you by name, and says, "I want to come to dinner at your house."

I suppose that you, like me, hope very much that you would say, "Come ahead." But I suppose also that you, like me, had better not be too sure. You will remember that in Jesus' lifetime even his most intimate friends could hardly be described as overconfident.

The second question is this – it comes right after the verse in which Jesus says, "If you love me, keep my commandments." Can you be sure that you would keep his commandments if it became excruciatingly painful to do so? And here I need to tell another story, this time one that actually happened.

In 1569, in Holland, a Mennonite name Dirk Willems, under threat of capital sentence as a heretic, was fleeing from arrest, pursued by a "thief catcher." As they ran across a frozen body of water, the thief-catcher broke through the ice. Without help, he would have drowned. What did Dirk Willems do then?

Was the thief-catcher an enemy merely to be hated, or was he a neighbor to be loved as one loves oneself? Was he an enemy whom one must love in order to be a child of God? Was he "one of the least of these my brethren"?

What Dirk Willems did was turn back, put out his hands to his pursuer, and save his life. The thief-catcher, who then of course wanted to let his rescuer go, was forced to arrest him. Dirk Willems was brought to trial, sentenced, and burned to death by a "lingering fire."

I, and I suppose you, would like to be a child of God even at the cost of so much pain. But would we, in similar circumstances, turn back to offer the charity of Christ to an enemy? Again, I don't think we ought to be too sure. We should remember that "Christian" generals and heads of state have routinely thanked God for the deaths of their enemies, and that the persecutors of 1569 undoubtedly thanked God for the capture and death of the "heretic" Dirk Willems.

Those are peculiar questions. I don't think we can escape them, if we are honest. And if we are honest, I don't think we can answer them. We humans, as we well know, have repeatedly been surprised by what we will or won't do under pressure. A person may come to be, as many have been, heroically faithful in great adversity, but as long as that person is alive we can only say that he or she did well but remains under the requirement to *do* well. As long as we are alive, there is always a next time, and so the questions remain. These are questions we must live with, regarding them as unanswerable and yet profoundly influential. ◆

51

Building on Rock

• • • • •

Therefore everyone who hears these words of mine and puts them into practice is like a wise man who built his house on the rock. The rain came down, the streams rose, and the winds blew and beat against that house; yet it did not fall, because it had its foundation on the rock. But everyone who hears these words of mine and does not put them into practice is like a foolish man who built his house on sand. The rain came down, the streams rose, and the winds blew and beat against that house, and it fell with a great crash.

Matthew 7:24–27

Jarrett Banks

THE SERMON ON THE MOUNT contains some of the most difficult passages to preach in the entire Bible. . . . So, to avoid offending too many people, we preachers use a little trickery, a little flimflam, a little smoke and mirrors. We pull this off by talking less about what the passages are saying, and more about what they are not saying.

It's a technique that we preachers often employ to basically ignore what they are actually saying. For example:

"But if anyone strikes you on one cheek, turn the other also."

Now, this is not saying that we should be pushovers.

"Someone forces you to go one mile, go also the second mile. Give to everyone who begs from you, and do not refuse anyone who wants to borrow from you!"

This is not saying that we should help those who are perfectly capable of helping themselves.

"Love your enemies."

Now this is not saying we have to like them!

See how that is done? Preachers get by with this all the time, and their congregations let them, because they are only preaching what we all wished the Sermon on the Mount actually said.

And then, to put the finishing touch on this chicanery, we quickly skip to the end of the passage and point out the last verse: "Be perfect, as your heavenly Father is perfect."

It is then we say: "You see. None of us can be perfect. Therefore, Jesus really does not expect us to do any of these things. He is just laying out some high ideals – ideals that we can never live up to."

That's when we preachers leave the Sermon on the Mount and go off on a tangent about grace and the need to accept Christ as our personal savior because none of us are perfect, and we all fall short of the glory of God.

Now, I believe in grace. I need grace. I am by no means close to being perfect, so grace is my friend. Grace is my hope. Grace is amazing. But here's the problem with using grace as an excuse to not act on the offensive countercultural commands of the Sermon on the Mount, and it is a huge problem – at the end of the sermon, Jesus (as if he knows we will try to use grace as some get-out-of-doing-what-I-say card) says: "Everyone who hears these words of mine and *does not act* on them will be like a foolish man who built his house on sand. The rain fell, and the floods came, and the winds blew and beat against that house, and it fell – and great was its fall!"

So, what are we to do with these passages? "Do not resist the evil doer?" Really? Someone slaps us in the face, Jesus *really* wants us to turn and give them the other cheek to slap? And are we *really* supposed to give people the very shirts off our backs? Give to everyone who begs of us? Go the second mile? Really? . . .

When was the last time that you have taken a stand against an evil, an injustice, and because of that stand, because you stood up and spoke out, the supporters of that evil not only sent you a nasty email, defriended you on Facebook, personally confronted you, but physically attacked you by slapping you in the face? What I am asking is: when was the last time that you even had an opportunity to turn the other cheek?

When was the last time someone who was very cold approached you and knew you well enough to ask you to give them the very coat that you were wearing? Asked you to sacrifice warmth so they could be warm? When was the last time that you even had the opportunity to offer someone in need the shirt off your back?

When was the last time that someone with limited mobility or perhaps a disability, whether that disability be physical, mental or spiritual, asked you to walk just one mile on their behalf? When was the last time that you even had the opportunity to go an extra mile? For mile two is impossible without mile one.

When was the last time that someone in great need came to you and begged for you to help them? I am not talking about the person you see holding a sign at an intersection, "Help. Homeless Vet." I am talking about someone whose name you knew, someone who knew your name, who felt like they could trust you, coming to you personally, swallowing their pride, and asking you for help?

When was the last time that you even made an enemy? After all, isn't confrontation something we all like to avoid? Isn't it better, especially in this day and time, to mind our own business, keep our thoughts to ourselves?

Our problem is not that we are unwilling to turn the other cheek. Our problem is that we are so private, so unconcerned about anyone other than ourselves, that we never cause any confrontations.

Our problem is not that we are unwilling to give someone the shirt off our back. Our problem is that we are never around anyone who needs our coat.

Our problem is not that we are unwilling to go the second mile. Our problem is that we lack the empathy to put ourselves in the shoes of another and go one mile.

Our problem is not that we are unwilling to give to the needy who personally approach us and beg of us. Our problem is that we do not personally know anyone in need.

Our problem is not that we are unwilling to love our enemies. Our problem is that most of us have never created any. We are so self-absorbed, so afraid of any controversy that might cause us a little pain, we simply never put ourselves out there to make any enemies. . . .

The good news is that before you go the second mile, you have to go the first mile, and because you are here, in this place, in this community, listening to the difficult words of Jesus, you are well on your way to going that first mile!

The good news is: You are here, and together, as a church, we are going to go places where we will encounter people who are in such need that they may ask for our coats. And we will have opportunities to sacrificially offer them our shirts.

We will get to know people who are so desperate that they may beg of us. And we will have opportunities to selflessly give.

Together, we will speak up, speak out, and stand firm for the gospel of Jesus Christ, for prophetic justice, for the unconditional love of all people. And sadly, because of this, we will make some enemies. We are apt to stir up so much anger in some people that they will not only defriend us on Facebook, send us ugly emails, but they may want to slap us in the face! But together, because it is impossible to do it alone, together, as part of the household of God, we will not ignore them. We will pray for them. We will learn to love them.

And no we are not perfect, far from it. But we are at least on our way to becoming like the wise who built a house on rock. The rain fell, the floods came, and the winds blew and beat on that house, but it did not fall, because it had been founded on rock. ◆

Oswald Chambers

E SPEAK OF BUILDING castles in the air; that is where a castle should be – whoever heard of a castle underground! The problem is how to get the foundation under your castle in the air so that it can stand upon the earth.

The way to put foundations under our castles is by paying attention to the words of Jesus Christ. We may read and listen and not make much of it at the time, but by and by we come into circumstances when the Holy Spirit will bring back to us what Jesus said – are we going to obey? Jesus says that the way to put foundations under spiritual castles is by hearing and doing "these sayings of mine." Pay attention to his words, and give time to doing it. Try five minutes a day with your Bible. The thing that influences us most is not the thing we give most time to, but the thing that springs from our own personal relationship; that is the prime motive that dominates us.

"You call me Teacher and Lord, and you say well, for so I am" – but is he? Think of the way we back out of what he says! "I have given you an example, that you should do as I have done to you" (John 13:13, 15). We say it is all very well up to a certain point, and then we abandon it. If we do obey the words of Jesus Christ we are sure to be called fanatics. The New Testament associates shame with the gospel (see Rom. 1:16; 1 Pet. 4:12–13).

Our spiritual castles must be conspicuous, and the test of a building is not its fair beauty but its foundations. There are beautiful spiritual fabrics raised in the shape of books and of lives, full of the finest diction and activities, but when the test comes, down they go. They have not been built on the sayings of Jesus Christ, but built altogether in the air with no foundations under them.

Build up your character bit by bit by attention to my words, says Jesus, then when the supreme crisis comes, you will stand like a rock. The crisis does not come always, but when it does come, it is all up in about two seconds; there is no possibility of pretense, you are unearthed immediately. ◆

Our Final Authority

• • • • •

*When Jesus had finished saying these things, the crowds were
amazed at his teaching, because he taught as one who had
authority, and not as their teachers of the law.*
Matthew 7:28–29

Søren Kierkegaard

NOW, IT IS of course well known that Christ
continually uses the expression "imitators." He
never says that he asks for admirers, adoring
admirers, adherents; and when he uses the expression
"follower" he always explains it in such a way that one
perceives that "imitators" is meant by it, that it is not adherents of a teaching but imitators of a life, who do not, because
of some accidental loftiness, make wanting to resemble it
into presumptuousness or madness. It is also well known,
as I have repeated elsewhere again and again, that it is the
abased Christ who is speaking, that every word we have from

Christ is from him, the abased one. Now it certainly may be assumed that Christ himself was fully aware of why he chose this particular expression, which solely and unconditionally is in innermost and deepest harmony with what he continually said about himself or claimed himself to be: namely, the Truth and the Way and the Life. [He was fully aware] that he was not a teacher in the sense that he only had a teaching to present, so that he could be satisfied with adherents who accepted the teaching – but in their lives ignored or let things take their course. One must also certainly assume that he himself was fully aware of why his whole life on earth, from first to last, was designed solely to be able to have imitators and designed to make admirers impossible.

Christ came to the world with the purpose of saving the world, also with the purpose – this in turn is implicit in his first purpose – of being the prototype, of leaving footprints for the person who wanted to join him, who then might become an imitator; this indeed corresponds to "footprints." That is why he let himself be born in lowliness and thereupon lived poor, abandoned, despised, abased – yes, no human being has lived so abased as he. By comparing the conditions of his life with Christ's, even the otherwise lowliest person would have to come to the conclusion that his own life, humanly speaking, is far preferable in comparison with the conditions of Christ's life. . . .

In that sense, to admire Christ is the untrue invention of a later age, aided by "loftiness." Understood in that way, there was unconditionally nothing to admire, unless one wanted to admire poverty, misery, contempt, etc. He was not even exempted from the worst – being pitied, a pitiable object of sympathy. No, there was truly not the least thing to admire. . . .

What, then, is the difference between an admirer and an imitator? An imitator is or strives to be what he admires, and an admirer keeps himself personally detached, consciously or unconsciously does not discover that what is admired involves a claim upon him, to be or at least to strive to be what is admired. . . .

When it comes to the moral, to want to admire instead of to imitate is not an invention by bad people – no, it is the spineless invention by those who must be called the better but also weak people, whereby they seek to keep themselves detached. They are related to the admired one only through the imagination; to them he is like a theatrical play, except that he, since this is in actuality, has a somewhat stronger effect. But for their part, they make the same demands that are made in the theater: to sit safe and calm oneself, detached from any actual relation to danger, while they still put it down in their favor that they admire him, whereby they presumably think to share in his merits of truth and right – in a rather convenient, cheap way that is also almost sensual.

Therefore, if he is willing to accept their admiration, they are at his service; then to them his life is an occasion for celebration, that is, celebration with proper caution lest one personally come in contact with danger. But they refuse to understand that his life should be a demand, and if they as much as perceive that he himself understands that it ought to be so, it is already half over with the admiration – they are offended at him; his bizarre nature so offends them that they are unable to have the tranquility for spineless admiration; they perceive that to associate with him amounts almost to being up for examination, because even though he says nothing his life tacitly examines theirs. . . .

And Christ's life has indeed made it manifest, terrifyingly manifest, what dreadful untruth it is to admire in relation to the truth instead of imitating, something that ought to be

called to people's attention, if possible, every Sunday in the
calm and easy days of Christendom, where peace and security
favor the misunderstanding. When there is no danger, when
there is a dead calm, when everything is favorable to Christianity, it is all too easy to confuse an admirer with a follower,
and this can happen very quietly; the admirer can die in the
delusion that the position he took was the true one. . . .

[In Nicodemus] one sees what an admirer is, for Nicodemus
did not become an imitator. It is as if Nicodemus might have
said to Christ, "If we are able to reach a compromise, then I
will accept your teaching in eternity – but here in this world,
no, that I cannot do. Could you not make an exception of me;
could it not be enough if once in a while I came to you during
the night – but during the day (yes, I confess it, I myself feel
how humiliating this is for me and how disgraceful, indeed
also how very insulting it is toward you), during the day, I
do not know you, during the day I say: "I do not know this
man!" See in what a web of untruth an admirer entangles
himself – and do not forget that in established Christendom
there is no danger of actuality that can make manifest the
extent to which someone is really only an admirer.

Nicodemus certainly was willing to assure and reassure in
the strongest expressions, words, and phrases that he accepted
the truth of the teaching – it perhaps escaped him that there
is a limit to this ascending scale of assurances and reassur-
ances, that it veers around, that the assurance becomes just
the opposite, counterevidence against the one who more and
more zealously gives assurances; it perhaps escaped him that
the more strongly someone makes such assurances while his
life still remains unchanged, the more he is only making a
fool of himself, informs on himself as being either a fool or
a deceiver. There is congruity and meaning if someone says

that there perhaps is something to a teaching and yet his life is unchanged. But it is both a most dubious and a ludicrous self-contradiction if someone is so convinced as to give assurances and, in addition, if the slightest doubt is expressed about his conviction, is ready to give assurances even more strongly – and then this conviction has no power whatsoever over his life. If Christ had permitted a cheaper edition of being a follower – an admirer who swears by all that is high and holy that he is convinced – then Nicodemus would have been acceptable. . . .

Let us now completely forget this danger connected with confessing Christ and think rather of the danger of actuality that is inescapably bound up with being Christian. Does not Christian teaching about ethics and obligation, Christianity's requirement to die to the world, to surrender the earthly, its requirement of self-denial, does this not contain enough requirements – if they were to be obeyed – to produce the danger of actuality that makes manifest the difference between an admirer and an imitator, makes it manifest precisely in this way, that the imitator has his life in these dangers and the admirer personally remains detached although they both are nevertheless united in acknowledging in words the truth of Christianity? Thus the difference still remains. The admirer will make no sacrifices, renounce nothing, give up nothing earthly, will not transform his life, will not be what is admired, will not let his life express it – but in words, phrases, assurances he is inexhaustible about how highly he prizes Christianity. The imitator, however, aspires to be what is admired – and then, remarkably enough, even though he is living in "established Christendom," the same danger results for him as once was bound up with confessing Christ. By means of the imitator's life, it will once again become manifest who the admirers are, for the admirers will become very exasperated with this imitator. And even that this is presented as it is presented here will exasperate many – but they must belong to the admirers. ◆

Dietrich Bonhoeffer

WE HAVE LISTENED to the Sermon on the Mount and perhaps have understood it. But who has heard it aright? Jesus gives the answer at the end. He does not allow his hearers to go away and make of his sayings what they will, picking and choosing from them whatever they find helpful, and testing them to see if they work. He does not give them free rein to misuse his word with their mercenary hands, but gives it to them on condition that it retains exclusive power over them. Humanly speaking, we could understand and interpret the Sermon on the Mount in a thousand different ways. Jesus knows only one possibility: simple surrender and obedience, not interpreting it or applying it, but doing and obeying it. That is the only way to hear his word. But again he does not mean that it is to be discussed as an ideal, he really means us to get on with it.

This word, whose claim we recognize, this word which issues from his saying "I have known thee," this word which sets us at once to work and obedience, is the rock on which to build our house. The only proper response to this word which Jesus brings with him from eternity is simply to do it. Jesus has spoken: his is the word, ours the obedience. Only in the doing of it does the word of Jesus retain its honor, might, and power among us. Now the storm can rage over the house, but it cannot shatter that union with him, which his word has created.

There is only one other possibility, that of failing to do it. It is impossible to want to do it and yet not do it. To deal with the word of Jesus otherwise than by doing it is to give him the lie. It is to deny the Sermon on the Mount and to say No to his word. If we start asking questions, posing problems, and offering interpretations, we are not doing his word. Once again the shades of the rich young man and the lawyer of Luke 10 are raising their heads. However vehemently we assert our faith, and our fundamental recognition of his word, Jesus still calls it "not-doing." But the word which we fail to do is no rock to build a house on. There can then be no union with Jesus. He has never known us. That is why as soon as the hurricane begins we lose the word, and find that we have never really believed it. The word we had was not Christ's, but a word we had wrested from him and made our own by reflecting on it instead of doing it. So our house crashes in ruins, because it is not founded on the word of Jesus Christ. ♦

• • • • •

Discussion Guide

The aim of the following reflection questions is to help readers live out the implications of Jesus' teachings. How do we need to change? As you discuss the Sermon on the Mount, keep this question front and center.

PART I

Kingdom Character

1. Master Teacher

- Think of examples of how Jesus lived out the Sermon on the Mount.

- Why is it important to not separate Jesus' teachings from who he is and why he came? How is following a teaching different from following a teacher?

- Do you see Jesus' teachings, by and large, as "good news" or "hard commands"? Why?

Related Scripture: Philippians 2:1–11; 3:7–11; 1 Peter 2:21–25; 1 John 2:3–6

2. Good News

- What difference does it make to see the Sermon on the Mount in the light of God's coming kingdom?

- Blumhardt says, "Today God wants to rule, and he is already making a beginning." Where do you see God's kingdom breaking into our world today?

- What influences on the church today might keep us from experiencing more of the kingdom?

Related Scripture: Matthew 10:1–8; Acts 19:8; 28:23–31;
1 Corinthians 4:20

3. Foolish Wisdom

- The first time you heard or read the Sermon on the Mount, did you find it shocking? Did it ever have such an effect on you?

- Of the teachings in the Sermon on the Mount, which ones do you think today's Christians ignore or fail to implement the most? Why?

- Have you ever found yourself trying to be a "spiritual hero"? How might we help each other avoid that?

Related Scripture: Mark 8:31–38; 1 Corinthians 1:18–31; 2:1–5;
James 3:13–18

4. Blessedness

- What is the difference between being "blessed" and being "happy"? Have you ever experienced the blessing of any of these Beatitudes?

- Why is it a mistake to see the Beatitudes as commands?

- In what ways can we practice what Kathy Escobar calls "downward mobility"?

- Wherein lies the *blessing* in the Beatitudes? Does it lie in some reward or in something else, or in both?

Related Scripture: Psalm 1; James 1:12, 25; 5:11; 1 Peter 3:14; 4:14

5. Poverty of Spirit

- Matthew refers to the "poor in spirit" whereas Luke (6:20–26) refers simply to the "poor." Is the difference very important?

- Why do you think Jesus starts with this Beatitude in particular?

- Why do you think the promise in this verse is in the present tense?

Related Scripture: Luke 18:9–14; 2 Corinthians 12:1–10; James 1:9–11; 2:1–7

6. Mourning

- Think of all the reasons why people grieve or mourn. What pains your heart the most?
- How does Tagore's piece illustrate the meaning of this Beatitude?
- How might mourning over one's own sin lead to blessing?

Related Scripture: Luke 7:36–50; 19:41–44; John 11:17–44; 20:10–18; 2 Corinthians 1:3–11; 7:8–13

7. The Meek

- When you hear the word "meek" what comes to mind? Why does "meekness" have a negative connotation today?
- Besides Jesus, can you think of others who exhibit meekness?
- What factors in our world today make it hard for you to exhibit meekness?

Related Scripture: Matthew 11:25–30; Luke 1:26–28; 14:1–11; 1 Corinthians 6:1–8

8. Hungry and Thirsty

- What, exactly, is righteousness? What other words can you use to describe its meaning?
- What do you hunger and thirst for in life?
- In what ways do we satiate ourselves with things other than righteousness?

Related Scripture: Matthew 4:1–11; Luke 13:34–35; John 2:12–25

9. The Merciful

- ◆ Why is "tit-for-tat" justice so alluring? Why is it not enough?

- ◆ When have you extended or received mercy? Is there anyone in particular you need to be more merciful toward?

- ◆ Is it possible to forgive or show mercy too much?

Related Scripture: Matthew 9:35–38; Luke 10:25–37; John 8:1–11; 2 Corinthians 2:5–11; Jude 20–23

10. Purity of Heart

- ◆ Why is the notion of "purity" scorned today?

- ◆ What does it mean to "will one thing?" Is this even possible?

- ◆ What are ways you can help foster a pure heart – in yourself and in others?

Related Scripture: John 1:43–51; 2:21–40; 1 John 3:1–3

11. Peacemaking

- ◆ When you think of a peacemaker, who comes to your mind? What qualities does a peacemaker exhibit?

- ◆ If Christ's way of peacemaking is not political or military, does this mean he is only interested in spiritual peace?

- ◆ Notice Jesus said, "Blessed are the peace*makers.*" How can we actively make peace today?

Related Scripture: 2 Corinthians 5:18–21; Ephesians 2:11–18; Hebrews 12:14; 1 Peter 3:8–12

12. Persecution

- ◆ Have you ever experienced opposition for your faith?

- ◆ Can you think of a time when you missed an opportunity to stick your neck out?

◆ Is there a difference between being persecuted and being persecuted *for the sake of Christ?* Does it matter?

◆ How might persecution itself be a blessing?

Related Scripture: John 15:18–25; 2 Timothy 3:10–12; James 1:2–8; 1 Peter 4:1–7

13. Salt and Light

◆ What do you think Jesus was driving at with the metaphors of salt and light?

◆ How might the church today have lost its effectiveness as salt and light?

◆ Jesus refers to a city on a hill. In what ways should the church be distinct from the world? Can this separation be carried too far?

Related Scripture: 2 Corinthians 4:1–6; Ephesians 5:8–15; 1 Thessalonians 4:1–12; 1 Peter 2:11–12

Kingdom Commands

14. The Law

- If the Law was God's gift to the Jews, why does it receive such a bad rap, especially among Christians?

- Taylor and Wilkin both suggest that many Christians misunderstand God's grace. How did Jesus view the Law and keeping God's commandments?

- According to Jesus, the Law is not the problem. Something else is. What?

Related Scripture: Matthew 15:1–20; Galatians 3:15–4:7; James 1:19–27; 2 Corinthians 1:20

15. The Greater Righteousness

- Think of ways in which Jesus' righteousness surpassed that of the Pharisees.

- Why are "external rules" so enticing? Why do we gravitate to them and yet resist them at the same time? Why are they so dangerous?

- Can you think of any Christian teachings or practices that have become more important than Christ's original will?

Related Scripture: Romans 6:1–23; 13:8–14; Galatians 5:13–26

16. Anger

- What kind of anger is Jesus referring to in this passage?

- Is anger a big problem today? Can you name ways in which you've allowed too much anger into your life?

- What have you found to be helpful in dealing with anger? What's not helpful?

Related Scripture: Genesis 4:1–12; Ephesians 4:26–31; Hebrews 12:14–15

17. Right Worship

- Nouwen argues that "so much of our energy, our time, and money goes into maintaining distance from one another." Does this apply to you in any way?

- Where might there exist a wall between you and someone else? What can you do to bring about reconciliation? What keeps you from making the first move?

- The need to be right can be a curse. What are ways to overcome it?

Related Scripture: 1 Corinthians 1:10–17; 11:17–34; Philippians 4:2–7; 1 Timothy 2:8

18. Sexual Purity

- What factors cause you to give in to temptation?

- What environments or situations make your struggle against lust especially difficult? Are there contexts you should remove yourself from to lessen temptation?

- Sin isolates us, but all of us struggle with sin and temptation. Is there someone you can turn to for help? What hinders you from doing so?

Related Scripture: 1 Corinthians 10: 12–13; 1 Timothy 4:7–8; 5:1–2; 2 Timothy 2:22; Philippians 4:8–9; 1 Peter 5:5–11

19. Marriage

- Why do you think Jesus refers to remarriage as adultery? What is he really getting at here?

- In what ways have you been affected by divorce and remarriage?

- How have churches today compromised Jesus' teaching when it comes to divorce and remarriage?

- What factors in society contribute to the erosion of marriage? How might the church better support faithfulness in marriage?

Related Scripture: Matthew 19:1–12; Romans 7:1–3; 1 Corinthians 7:1–24

20. Truthfulness

- Does Jesus' teaching against swearing oaths apply to Christians today?

- When you speak, do you always mean what you say and say what you mean? Is it ever OK not to?

- Can people trust you? What establishes and builds trust?

Related Scripture: Ecclesiastes 5:4–7; Matthew 23:16–22; Ephesians 4:25; James 5:12

21. Nonresistance

- Does Jesus literally mean we're not to resist an evil person? If not, what *does* he mean?

- Papini says: "Only by accepting this command of Christ can we solve the problem of violence." Do you agree or disagree?

- Some people argue that Jesus only forbids personal retaliation, not the use of force in the defense of others. Is this a valid distinction?

Related Scripture: Matthew 26:47–56; John 18:33–36; 2 Corinthians 10:1–6; Hebrews 10:30–39

22. Overcoming Evil

- What's the difference between "passive resistance" and "active resistance"?

- What do you think about Bonhoeffer's critique of the distinction between personal duty and official duty?

- In Matthew 5:39–41, Jesus illustrates what nonresistance means with three examples. If he were living today, what kind of examples do you think he would use?

Related Scripture: 1 Samuel 24, 26; Luke 22:49–53; Romans 12:17–21

23. Love of Enemy

- What enemy do you find most difficult to love?

- What, if anything, in this chapter helps you to see "enemies" in a different light?

- In what ways does our culture exacerbate an "us vs. them" mentality? What can you do to reverse it?

Related Scripture: Genesis 50:15–21; Exodus 23:4–5; John 13:1–30; Matthew 26:47–56

24. Perfect Love

- What kind of perfection is Jesus referring to in this passage?

- Why does God shower love on good and evil alike?

- How can we pass on this perfect love to others without discrimination?

Related Scripture: Luke 6:36; Romans 5:6–11; 1 Corinthians 13

PART III

Kingdom Devotion

25. From the Heart

- What problem is Jesus addressing in this passage?

- In what ways do you like to be seen or noticed by others?

- Ferguson says *why* we do something is as important as *what* we do. Consider why you engage in particular acts of devotion. Are they genuinely motivated, or mostly just habit?

Related Scripture: Matthew 23; Acts 5:1–11; 8:9–25; 1 Corinthians 4

26. When You Give

- Tolstoy confronts a particular kind of hypocrisy. What implications follow from what he says?

- What is Mother Teresa getting at? What kind of giver are you?

- Is almsgiving enough, or does Jesus expect more from his disciples?

Related Scripture: Isaiah 58:1–10; Mark 10:17–31; Luke 21:1–4; 2 Corinthians 8:1–15

27. When You Pray

- Are your own prayers too wordy? Why might that be?

- Why, Heschel asks, do our collective prayers lack soul? What is the answer?
- If prayer is about God, and not about us, how might this change the way you pray?

Related Scripture: Luke 5:16; 9:18; Romans 8:26–27; 1 Thessalonians 5:16–18

28. The Father Knows

- Why do we come to God with our requests if he already knows what we need?
- If God knows our needs better than we do, what should we pray for?
- What is the purpose of prayer anyway?

Related Scripture: John 11:38–44; 1 Thessalonians 1:2; Philippians 1:3–11, 18–20

29. Teach Us to Pray

- Why do we need to be *taught* to pray?
- Are formulaic prayers good or bad? What do you think of Trueblood's perspective?
- What role should prayer play in our common life? In our personal life?

Related Scripture: Matthew 26:36–46; John 17:1–26; Ephesians 5:18–20; Colossians 3:16–17

30. Our Father

- When you think of the word "father," what comes to your mind?
- Scripture also uses other names and metaphors for God. If Jesus addresses God as "Father," shouldn't we?

◆ With fatherhood in crisis today, many people find it hard to relate to God as "Father." How does Jesus himself relate to his heavenly Father? How might this be helpful in our understanding of God's fatherliness?

Related Scripture: John 1:18; Romans 8:15–17; Galatians 4:1–7; 1 John 3:1–2

31. God's Name

◆ In your opinion, what is the opposite of hallowing or sanctifying God's name?

◆ In what ways is God's name misused today?

◆ In the Bible, there is power in the "name." What does this mean for us today?

Related Scripture: Leviticus 22:31–32; Romans 2:17–24; James 3:9–12

32. God's Kingdom

◆ Arnold claims that unless we actively work for God's kingdom, praying "your kingdom come" is "a lie on our lips." How can one work for God's kingdom?

◆ Is Blumhardt right not to trust those who console "with hopes of eternity"? Is he expecting too much here and now?

◆ What do you think about the kind of Christianity that overemphasizes heaven and everlasting life? What about the kind that equates the kingdom with social justice?

Related Scripture: Matthew 13; Romans 14:17; Colossians 1:3–14; 4:10–11

33. God's Will

◆ Do you find it hard to surrender to God? How so?

◆ Have you ever had trouble discerning God's will for your life?

◆ What kinds of things does God will? Are you living in the light of that will?

Related Scripture: Luke 22:39–46; John 6:35–40; Romans 12:1–2; Hebrews 4:7; James 4:13–17

34. Daily Bread

◆ When we ask for our daily bread, what all are we asking for?

◆ What does this prayer mean for those who already have more than enough?

◆ Does this prayer help you worry less about things you really need?

Related Scripture: Philippians 4:10–20; 1 Timothy 6:6–10; Hebrews 13:5–6

35. Forgive Us

◆ Do you find it difficult to ask God for forgiveness? If so, why?

◆ Have you taken God's forgiveness for granted? Does this prayer remind you of specific things for which you need to be forgiven?

◆ When we ask for God's forgiveness we usually think in individual terms. What collective sins might we also need to ask God's forgiveness for?

Related Scripture: Psalm 51; Hebrews 3; James 5:16; 1 John 1:8–10

36. As We Forgive

◆ Why do you think Jesus ties God's forgiveness to our forgiving others? What is the relationship between the two?

◆ Does this prayer remind you of anyone you need to forgive?

◆ Does Jesus expect us to forgive as unconditionally and generously as God does?

Related Scripture: Matthew 18:21–35; Luke 17:1–11; Ephesians 4:29–32

37. Temptation

- Are there particular temptations you struggle with most?

- What has helped you to overcome temptation? What hasn't helped?

- How can our weakness be our strength and our strength be our weakness?

Related Scripture: 1 Corinthians 10:12–13; Hebrews 2:14–18; 4:14–16; James 1:13–18

38. Deliver Us

- How is evil manifesting itself today? Are there particular evils that you find especially hideous?

- The evils that are easiest to see are often the result of specific causes. What would it take to address evil at its roots?

- How might asking to be delivered from evil ourselves be related to evil being overcome in the world?

Related Scripture: Matthew 26:40–41; Luke 4:23–30; Acts 23:12–35; 1 Peter 5:6–11

PART IV

Kingdom Priorities

39. Lasting Treasures

- What things do you treasure – what do you invest your money and time and heart in? Are they earthly treasures? How might they have a hold on you?

- The world esteems certain things. How might this affect you and your lifestyle? Where might you spend too much on yourself or live too comfortably?

- What does it mean to store up treasures in heaven?

Related Scripture: Matthew 19:16–30; Luke 12:13–34; 1 Timothy 6:17–19

40. The Good Eye

- What do you think Jesus means by a "good eye"?

- How might this passage relate to Jesus' teachings regarding earthly treasures and mammon?

- How can we keep our spiritual eyes in better shape?

Related Scripture: Hebrews 12:1–3; James 1:19–27; 4:1–10; 1 John 2:15–17

41. God or Mammon

- This chapter argues that money is not just a neutral medium of exchange. Do you agree or disagree?

- What do you think of Arnold's claim that "money and love are mutually exclusive"?

- What changes could you make in your life to demonstrate your allegiance to God and not to mammon?

Related Scripture: Luke 19:1–10; 1 Timothy 6:6–10

42. Beyond Worry

- Jesus commands us not to worry. Is this a realistic expectation?

- What do you worry about? What is the antidote to worry? What has helped you?

- Sharing one's load is often an answer to the worries and cares of life. What might this look like for you?

Related Scripture: Matthew 13:7, 22; Acts 2:42–47; 4:34–35; 2 Corinthians 9:6–15; Philippians 4:8–9; 1 Peter 5:6–7

43. God's Kingdom First

- What does seeking first God's kingdom and his righteousness entail? What needs to take second place?

- Looking at churches today, what would you conclude regarding their highest priorities?

- Does the kingdom of God lead to the abolishment of religion, as Ragaz and Blumhardt suggest?

Related Scripture: 1 Corinthians 10:31; Galatians 5:1–6; 6:12–15; Philippians 3:7–11; Colossians 3:17

44. Judging Others

- What do you think about Dostoyevsky's perspective? Are we really responsible for the sins of others?

- In what sense are we not to judge other people? Does this mean we should never judge? Does not judging mean not confronting sin?

- Do you find yourself dissociating from people you think are wrong? What would Jesus have you do?

Related Scripture: Romans 14:1–15:7; Galatians 6:1–5; James 4:11–12

45. Casting Pearls

- What do you think Jesus is getting at with this metaphor?

- How might this passage apply to the context in which you find yourself?

- Have you ever felt like you have thrown pearls before swine? What would you do differently next time?

Related Scripture: Matthew 10:11–15; 13:10–17; Acts 8:9–25

46. Ask, Seek, Knock

- Have you ever experienced the power of persisting in prayer? Describe what it was like.

- Can we ever become too persistent in prayer? How so?

- What are we to keep on praying and asking God for? What matters are worth persisting in?

Related Scripture: Luke 11:5–13; 18:1–8; Acts 1:12–26; 12:1–11; Ephesians 4:1–3; Colossians 4:12

47. The Golden Rule

- What does Tolstoy mean when he says we can only live the way we do by blunting our consciences?
- What would have to change if we were to truly live by the Golden Rule?
- Is the Golden Rule, in and of itself, enough to guide us in life? If not, what more is needed?

Related Scripture: Matthew 22:34–36; Luke 10:25–37; Romans 13:8–10; James 2:8–13

48. Two Ways

- In what sense is following Jesus the narrow way?
- How would you describe the wide way?
- How can we know we are on the right way?

Related Scripture: Deuteronomy 30:11–20; Joshua 24:14–27; Matthew 10:24–39; Luke 9: 18–27, 57–62; 13:22–30; 18:18–31

49. False Prophets

- What are some of the characteristics of a false prophet?
- When you think of a genuine prophet, what comes to your mind?
- Who are the false prophets today? What false ideas are being promulgated?

Related Scripture: John 15:1–17; Acts 20:22–31; 2 Corinthians 11:13–14; Galatians 5:13–26; 2 Peter 2; 1 John 4:1–6

50. Lord, Lord

- How could it be possible for someone to prophesy, drive out demons, and perform miracles yet still be an evildoer?

- Consider Wendell Berry's question: "If you had been living in Jesus' time and had heard him teaching, would you have been one of his followers?"

- Ask yourself George MacDonald's question: "What have you done this day because it was the will of Christ?"

Related Scripture: 1 Corinthians 13:1–3; James 2:14–26; 1 John 4:7–21

51. Building on Rock

- Have you ever experienced a crisis that tested the foundation of your faith? What happened?

- How can you come closer to others so that you can better live out and apply the Sermon on the Mount?

- Living out the Sermon on the Mount with others takes faith and commitment. Are you ready to move in this direction?

Related Scripture: Matthew 16:13–20; 1 Corinthians 3:10–15; Ephesians 2:19–22

52. Our Final Authority

- Do you feel you've been more an admirer of Christ than a follower?

- Is there a danger of spending too much time interpreting Jesus' words and not enough time doing them?

- What challenge has this book left you with? What is Jesus asking of you now?

Related Scripture: 2 Corinthians 4:5; Colossians 1:15–29; 3:11; Hebrews 2:8–9; 12:1–3

Further Reading

The Beatitudes and the Lord's Prayer for Everyman
William Barclay
> A treatment that sheds light on the original cultural context and significance of Jesus' words.

Christian Counter-Culture: The Message of the Sermon on the Mount
John R. W. Stott
> A modern exposition that gives careful attention to the biblical text while relating it to life today.

The Cost of Discipleship
Dietrich Bonhoeffer
> A classic that calls the Christian to unconditional obedience to Jesus and his word.

Kingdom Citizens
John Driver
> A study of the Sermon the Mount from an Anabaptist perspective that takes the presence of God's kingdom seriously.

Life Can Begin Again: Sermons on the Sermon on the Mount
Helmut Thielicke
> Sermons originally delivered in postwar Germany. Thielicke's *Our Heavenly Father: Sermons on the Lord's Prayer* is equally worthwhile.

Living the Sermon on the Mount
Glen H. Stassen
> A readable work that highlights the social dimensions and practical implications of Jesus' teachings.

Taking Jesus at His Word
Addison Hodges Hart
> Timely and contemporary reflections on the significance of the Sermon on the Mount for Christian life.

Salt and Light: Living the Sermon on the Mount
Eberhard Arnold

A collection of talks by the co-founder of the Bruderhof, an international community movement based on the Sermon on the Mount.

The Sermon on the Mount
Clarence Jordan

A frank and inspiring study of the Sermon on the Mount from a radical perspective.

The Sermon on the Mount: The Character of a Disciple
Daniel M. Doriani

An exposition that focuses on the thoughts and deeds that characterize a disciple of Christ.

The Sermon on the Mount and Human Flourishing
Jonathan T. Pennington

A more scholarly work that highlights the role wisdom plays in Jesus' teachings.

The Sermon on the Mount: Inspiring the Moral Imagination
Dale C. Allison Jr.

A detailed yet accessible treatment that illuminates some of the more difficult and controversial sayings of Jesus.

The Story of God Bible Commentary: Sermon on the Mount
Scot McKnight

A creative commentary that illumines the biblical text while offering relevant insights on how to live out Jesus' commands today.

Sources and Acknowledgments

Plough sincerely thanks each of the authors who contributed to this book, and the publishers and estates that allowed us to include the work of writers who are no longer living. All selections, except those that are in the public domain, are reprinted with the express permission of the author, publisher, or agent in question. Bible quotes at chapter headings are from the Holy Bible, New International Version®, NIV® Copyright © 1973, 1978, 1984, 2011 by Biblica, Inc.® Used by permission. All rights reserved worldwide. Other quotations from scripture follow the translation preferences of the individual writers and translators.

Part I: Kingdom Character

1. **Master Teacher:** E. Stanley Jones, *A Working Philosophy of Life* (Potomac, MD: E. Stanley Jones Foundation, 2017), 35–37. Henri J. M. Nouwen, *Bread for the Journey* (New York: Harper San Francisco, 1997), May 23–31. Used by permission of HarperCollins Publishers.

2. **Good News:** Christoph Friedrich Blumhardt, *Action in Waiting* (Rifton, NY: Plough Publishing House, 2012), 36–43.

3. **Foolish Wisdom:** Virginia Stem Owens, "God and Man at Texas A&M." *Reformed Journal* 37, no. 11 (1987), 3–4. Frederick Buechner, *Whistling in the Dark* (San Francisco: Harper & Row Publishers, 1988), 18–19. Used by permission of HarperCollins Publishers. John Dear, *The Beatitudes of Peace* (New London, CT: Twenty-Third Publications, 2016), 19.

4. **Blessedness:** James C. Howell, *The Beatitudes for Today* (Louisville, KY: Westminster John Knox Press, 2006), 5–6, 28–31. Kathy Escobar, *Down We Go* (Folsom, CA: Civitas Press, 2011), 24–26, 29–30. Francis of Assisi, in Candide Chalippe, *The Life and Legends of Saint Francis of Assisi* (New York: P. J. Kenedy and Sons, 1918) 37–38.

5. **Poverty of Spirit:** Philip Yancey, *The Jesus I Never Knew* (Grand Rapids, MI: Zondervan, 2002), 115–117. Copyright © 1995 by Philip Yancey. Used by permission of Zondervan. Eberhard Arnold, *Eberhard Arnold: A Testimony of Church Communities from His Life and Writings* (Rifton, NY: Plough Publishing House, 1973), 31–33. Dorothy Day, *Dorothy Day: Selected Writings*, ed. Robert Ellsberg (Maryknoll, NY: Orbis Books, 2005), 108.

6. **Mourning:** Nicholas Wolterstorff, *Lament for a Son* (Grand Rapids, MI: Wm. B. Eerdmans Publishing Co., 1987), 85–86. Reprinted by permis-

sion of the publisher. All rights reserved. Rabindranath Tagore, *My Reminiscences* (New York: The Macmillan Co, 1917), 260–264. Frederica Mathewes-Green, *The Illumined Heart* (Brewster, MA: Paraclete Press, 2001), 38–42.

7. **The Meek:** John Chrysostom, *Homilies on Matthew,* 78.4, in *Nicene and Post-Nicene Fathers,* series 1, vol. 10, ed. Philip Schaff (Buffalo, NY: Christian Literature Publishing Co., 1888). Elisabeth Elliot, *Keep A Quiet Heart* (Ann Arbor, MI: Servant Publications, 1995), 106–108. Used by permission of Revell, a division of Baker Publishing Group. Richard Rohr, *Jesus' Plan for a New World* (Cincinnati, OH: St Anthony Messenger Press, 1996), 132-133. St. Teresa of Avila, *The Way of Perfection,* translated by E. Allison Peers (New York: Image Books, 1964), 148–149.

8. **Hungry and Thirsty:** William Barclay, *The Beatitudes and the Lord's Prayer for Everyman* (New York: Harper & Row Publishers, 1975), 49–59. Copyright © 1963, 1964 by William Barclay. Published by Saint Andrew Press. Used by permission.

9. **The Merciful:** Charles E. Moore, written for this collection. Leo Tolstoy, "Help for the Starving" (1892) in *Peace Essays,* ed. Nathan Haskell Dole (New York: Carlton House, 1928).

10. **Purity of Heart:** Irenaeus, *Against Heresies* 4.20.5 in *Catechism of the Catholic Church,* 2nd ed. (Washington, DC: United States Catholic Conference, 2000), 1722. Søren Kierkegaard, *Purity of Heart Is to Will One Thing,* trans. Douglas V. Steere (New York: Harper and Row, 1956), 53–60. Thomas Merton, *No Man Is an Island* (New York: Harcourt Brace Jovanovich, 1955), 70–72. Copyright © 1955 by The Abbey of Our Lady of Gethsemani and renewed 1983 by the Trustees of the Merton Legacy Trust. Reprinted by permission of Houghton Mifflin Harcourt Publishing Company. All rights reserved. Brennan Manning, *Lion and Lamb* (Grand Rapids, MI: Chosen Books, 1986), 181–183. Used by permission of Chosen Books, a division of Baker Publishing Group.

11. **Peacemaking:** John Dear, *The Beatitudes of Peace* (New London, CT: Twenty-Third Publications, 2016), 89–94. Thomas Merton, *New Seeds of Contemplation* (New York: New Directions Publishing Corp., 1961), 122. Copyright © 1961 by The Abbey of Gethsemani, Inc. Reprinted by permission of New Directions Publishing Corp. Peter Kreeft, *Back to Virtue* (San Francisco: Ignatius Press, 1986), 146–151.

12. **Persecution:** Jerome, in *Wisdom of the Saints,* ed. Jill Haak Adels (New York: Oxford University Press, 1987), 75. Gene L. Davenport, *Into the Darkness* (Nashville, TN: Abingdon Press, 1988), 110, 114–117. Copyright © 1988 by Abingdon Press. Used by permission. All rights reserved. Óscar Romero, *A Prophetic Bishop Speaks to His People: The Complete Homilies of*

Archbishop Óscar Arnulfo Romero, vol. 2, trans. Joseph Owens, SJ (Miami: Convivium Press, 2015), 374, 89–90, 203. Jeanne DeCelles, *New Heaven, New Earth*, vol. 7, num. 6 (People of Praise, 1989).

13. **Salt and Light:** Charles E. Moore, written for this collection. Jane Tyson Clement, *No One Can Stem the Tide* (Farmington, PA: Plough Publishing House, 2000) 149. John R. W. Stott, *Christian Counter-Culture: The Message of the Sermon on the Mount* (Downers Grove, IL: InterVarsity Press, 1978), 58–60, 62. Reproduced with permission of Inter-Varsity Press, Ltd. through PLSclear.

Part II: Kingdom Commands

14. **The Law:** Barbara Brown Taylor, "The Grace of Good Works," sermon preached in Duke University Chapel, February 9, 2014. Copyright © 2014 by Barbara Brown Taylor. Jen Wilkin, "Failure Is Not a Virtue," *The Gospel Coalition* (blog), May 1, 2014. Addison Hodges Hart, *Taking Jesus at His Word* (Grand Rapids, MI: Wm. B. Eerdmans Publishing Co., 2012), 37–40. Reprinted by permission of the publisher. Jürgen Moltmann, *The Way of Jesus Christ* (Minneapolis, MN: Fortress Press, 1993), 127.

15. **The Greater Righteousness:** Leo Tolstoy, epilogue to *The Kreutzer Sonata* (1890) trans. Leo Wiener (1904). Oswald Chambers, *Studies in the Sermon on the Mount* (Grand Rapids, MI: Discovery House Publishers, 1995), 22–24. Copyright © 1995 by Oswald Chambers Publications Assn., Ltd. and used by permission of Our Daily Bread Publishing, Grand Rapids MI 49501. All rights reserved.

16. **Anger:** Dallas Willard, *The Divine Conspiracy* (New York: Harper San Francisco, 1998), 149–154. Copyright © 1998 by Dallas Willard. Used by permission of HarperCollins Publishers. Augustine, Letter 38 (AD 397) in *Nicene and Post-Nicene Fathers*, series 1, vol. 1, ed. Philip Schaff (Buffalo, NY: Christian Literature Publishing Co., 1887). Francis de Sales, *Introduction to the Devout Life* (London: Catholic Way Publishing, 2015), 132. William Blake, "A Poison Tree," in *Songs of Experience* (1794).

17. **Right Worship:** F. B. Meyer, *Inherit the Kingdom* (Wheaton, IL: Victor Books), 51–53. Henri J. M. Nouwen, *Bread for the Journey* (New York: Harper San Francisco, 1997), December, 29, 31. Copyright © 1997 by Henri J. M. Nouwen. Used by permission of HarperCollins Publishers. George MacDonald, "The Last Farthing," in *Unspoken Sermons Second Series* (London: Longmans, Green & Co., 1885), 46–53.

18. **Sexual Purity:** J. Heinrich Arnold, *Freedom from Sinful Thoughts* (Farmington, PA: Plough Publishing House, 1997), 13–16, 67–69. Francis Chan, "I Would Rather Die," *Desiring God* (blog), September 2, 2017.

19. **Marriage:** Johann Christoph Arnold, *Sex, God, and Marriage* (Walden, NY: Plough Publishing House, 1996, 2015), 147–157. David Fleer, *Preaching the Sermon on the Mount*, eds. David Fleer and Dave Bland (St. Louis, MO: Chalice Press, 2007), 117-120. Dietrich Bonhoeffer, "Wedding Sermon," in *Letters and Papers from Prison*, ed. Eberhard Bethge, trans. Reginald H. Fuller (New York: Macmillan, 1953), 45–46. Copyright © 1953, 1967, 1971 by SCM Press Ltd. Reprinted by permission of Hymns Ancient and Modern Ltd., and of Touchstone, a division of Simon & Schuster, Inc. All rights reserved.

20. **Truthfulness:** Peter Riedemann, *Peter Riedemann's Hutterite Confession of Faith*, ed. John J. Friesen (Walden, NY: Plough Publishing House, 2019), 204–212. Scot McKnight, *Sermon on the Mount* (Grand Rapids, MI: Zondervan, 2013), 117, 119. Copyright © 2013 by Scot McKnight. Used by permission of Zondervan. Francis de Sales, *Introduction to the Devout Life* (London: Catholic Way Publishing, 2015), 191. Eberhard Arnold, transcript, January 26, 1935, trans. Kathleen Hasenberg (Bruderhof Historical Archive EA 35/16). Thomas Merton, *No Man Is an Island* (New York: Harcourt Brace Jovanovich, 1955), 190–191, 198. Copyright © 1955 by The Abbey of Our Lady of Gethsemani and renewed 1983 by the Trustees of the Merton Legacy Trust. Reprinted by permission of Houghton Mifflin Harcourt Publishing Company. All rights reserved.

21. **Nonresistance:** Giovanni Papini, *Life of Christ*, trans. Dorothy Canfield Fisher (New York: Harcourt, Brace and Company, 1923), 105–109. Fyodor Dostoyevsky, *The Brothers Karamazov*, trans. Constance Garnett (New York: Macmillan, 1912), 340. Harry Emerson Fosdick, *The Man from Nazareth* (New York: Harper and Brothers, 1953), 77. Howard Thurman, *Deep Is the Hunger* (Richmond, IN: Friends United Press, 1973), 10–11. Used by permission of Friends United Press. All rights reserved.

22. **Overcoming Evil:** E. Stanley Jones, *A Working Philosophy of Life* (E. Stanley Jones Foundation, 2017), 158–172. Dietrich Bonhoeffer, *The Cost of Discipleship* trans. Reginald H. Fuller (London: SCM Press, 1959), 128–130. Copyright © 1959 by SCM Press Ltd. All rights reserved. Reprinted with the permission of Scribner, a division of Simon & Schuster, Inc., and of Hymns Ancient and Modern Ltd. Martin Luther King Jr., "Where Do We Go From Here?" speech, Eleventh Annual SCLC Convention, Atlanta, Georgia, August 16, 1967.

23. **Love of Enemy:** Martin Luther King Jr., *A Knock At Midnight*, ed. Clayborne Carson and Peter Holloran (New York: Grand Central Publishing, 1998), 37-57. Copyright © 1998 by The Heirs to the Estate of

Martin Luther King Jr. Helmut Thielicke, *Life Can Begin Again*, trans. John W. Doberstein (Philadelphia, PA: Fortress Press, 1963), 74–79. Nikolai Velimirović, *Prayers by the Lake* (Third Lake, IL: The Serbian Orthodox Metropolitanate of New Gracanica, 1999).

24. **Perfect Love:** Addison Hodges Hart, *Taking Jesus at His Word* (Grand Rapids, MI: Wm. B. Eerdmans, 2012), 66–67, 69. Reprinted by permission of the publisher. Jürgen Moltmann, *The Power of the Powerless* (New York: Harper and Row, Publishers, 1983), 52–53, 60–63. English translation copyright © 1983 by SCM Press Ltd. Used by permission of HarperCollins Publishers and Hymns Ancient and Modern Ltd. Chiara Lubich, Word of Life, February 1992, in *Parole di vita*, ed. Fabio Ciardi, "Opere di Chiara Lubich," Centro Chiara Lubich (Rome: Città Nuova, 2017), 494–495.

Part III: Kingdom Devotion

25. **From the Heart:** Sinclair B. Ferguson, *The Sermon on the Mount: Kingdom Life in a Fallen World* (Edinburgh, UK: Banner of Truth Trust, 2015), 109–113. Abraham Joshua Heschel, *God in Search of Man* (New York: The Noonday Press, 1998), 307–311. Copyright © 1955 by Abraham Joshua Heschel. Copyright renewed 1979 by Sylvia Heschel. Reprinted by permission of Farrar, Straus and Giroux. All rights reserved. John Flavel, *A Saint Indeed* (London: T. Parkhurst, 1689), 27–28.

26. **When You Give:** Leo Tolstoy, *The Kingdom of God Is Within You*, trans. Constance Garnett (London: William Heinemann, 1894), 343–347. John Chrysostom, *On Wealth and Poverty*, trans. Catharine P. Roth (Crestwood, NY: St. Vladimir's Seminary Press, 1981), 49–50. Mother Teresa, *No Greater Love* (Novato, CA: New World Library, 1989), 40–44. Copyright © 1997, 2001 by New World Library. Reprinted with permission of New World Library.

27. **When You Pray:** Karl Barth, *Prayer* (Louisville, KY: Westminster John Knox Press, 2002), 18–20. Daniel M. Doriani, *The Sermon on the Mount: The Character of a Disciple* (Phillipsburg, NJ: P & R Publishing, 2006), 119–120. Abraham Joshua Heschel, *Man's Quest for God* (Santa Fe, NM: Aurora Press, 1998), 51–52. Copyright © 1954 by Abraham Joshua Heschel. Copyright renewed 1982 by Susannah Heschel and Sylvia Heschel. Reprinted by permission of Farrar, Straus and Giroux on behalf of the Heschel Estate. Madeleine L'Engle, *The Weather of the Heart* (Wheaton, IL: Harold Shaw Publishers, 1978), 60. Amy Carmichael, *Gold by Moonlight* (London: SPCK, 1940), 111–112. Mother Teresa, *No Greater Love* (Novato, CA: New World Library, 1989), 8–9, 15–16. Copyright © 1997, 2001 by New World Library. Reprinted with permission of New World Library.

28. **The Father Knows:** Martin Luther, *Commentary on the Sermon on the Mount*, trans. Charles A. Hay (Philadelphia: Lutheran Publication Society, 1892). Helmut Thielicke, *Our Heavenly Father*, trans. John W. Doberstein (New York: Harper and Row, 1960), 34–39. Copyright © 1960 by John W. Doberstein. This book published in Germany under the title *Das Gebet das die Welt umspannt*. Copyright © 1953 by Quell-Verlag, Stuttgart. Used by permission of HarperCollins Publishers. Christoph Friedrich Blumhardt, *The God Who Heals* (Walden, NY: Plough Publishing House, 2016), 65–66.

29. **Teach Us to Pray:** Andrew Murray, *Lord Teach Us to Pray* (Dallas, TX: Gideon House Books, 2016), 10–12. Elton Trueblood, *The Lord's Prayers* (New York: Harper and Row, 1965), 48–49. Copyright © 1965 by Elton Trueblood. Used by permission of HarperCollins Publishers. Pope Benedict XVI, *Jesus of Nazareth* (San Francisco, CA: Ignatius Press, 2007), 130–132.

30. **Our Father:** Cyprian of Carthage, *The Lord's Prayer*, trans. Edmond Bonin (Westminster, MD: Christian Classics, 1983), 33–34. N. T. Wright, *The Lord and His Prayer* (Grand Rapids, MI: Wm B. Eerdmans Publishing Company, 1996), 6–11. Reprinted by permission of the publisher. All rights reserved. Hannah Whitall Smith, *The God of All Comfort* (Chicago, IL: Moody, 1956), 89–90. Teresa of Ávila, *The Way of Perfection*, trans. E. Allison Peers (New York: Image Books, 1964), 109. Dom Hélder Câmara, *Through the Gospel with Dom Hélder Câmara* (Maryknoll, NY: Orbis Books, 1986), 57–59.

31. **God's Name:** William H. Willimon and Stanley Hauerwas, *Lord, Teach Us* (Nashville, TN: Abingdon Press, 1996), 47–49. Copyright © 1996 by Abingdon Press. Used by permission. All rights reserved. Alfred Delp, *Prison Writings* (Maryknoll, NY: Orbis Books, 2004), 104–106. Leonardo Boff, *Praying with Jesus and Mary* (Maryknoll, NY: Orbis Books, 2005), 50–51.

32. **God's Kingdom:** Eberhard Arnold, *The Prayer God Answers* (Walden, NY: Plough Publishing House, 2016), 36–41. Christoph Friedrich Blumhardt, *Action in Waiting* (Rifton, NY: Plough Publishing House, 2012), 129–132, 68–69.

33. **God's Will:** Meister Eckhart, *Meister Eckhart spricht* (Munich: Verlag Ars Sacra/Josef Müller Verlag, 1925), selections translated by Plough editors. Robert McAfee Brown, *Liberation Theology* (Louisville, KY: Westminster John Knox Press, 1993), 67. François Fénelon, "Perfection," in *Spiritual Progress* (New York: M. W. Dodd, 1853). Chiara Lubich, *Essential Writings*, ed. Michel Vandeleene (Hyde Park, NY: New City Press, 2007), 69–70.

34. **Daily Bread:** Gregory of Nyssa, "Fourth Homily," in *Homilies on the Lord's Prayer*, trans. Theodore G. Stylianopoulos (Brookline, MA: Department of Religious Education, Greek Orthodox Archdiocese of America, 2003). Leonardo Boff, *Praying with Jesus and Mary* (Maryknoll, NY: Orbis Books, 2005), 78–80, 86. F. B. Meyer, *Inherit the Kingdom* (Wheaton, IL: Victor Books, 1984), 110–113.

35. **Forgive Us:** M. Scott Peck, *What Return Can I Make?* (London: Arrow Books, 1985), 65–69. Philip Graham Ryken, *The Prayer of Our Lord* (Wheaton, IL: Crossway Books, 2002), 66–68. Used by permission of Crossway, a publishing ministry of Good News Publishers, Wheaton, IL 60187. Frederica Mathewes-Green, "Why It's Hard to Accept God's Forgiveness," *Ancient Faith Ministries* (blog), February 16, 2017.

36. **As We Forgive:** Horace Bushnell, *Christ and His Salvation* (New York: Charles Scribner, 1864), 373–392. Dorothy L. Sayers, "Forgiveness and the Enemy," *Fortnightly* 149 (April 1941), published in *Unpopular Opinions* (London: Victor Gollancz Ltd., 1946). Reproduced by kind permission of David Higham Associates. C. S. Lewis, *Letters to Malcolm* (New York, Harcourt Brace and Company, 1992), 106–107. Copyright © 1963, 1964 by C. S. Lewis Pte. Ltd. Extracts reprinted by permission.

37. **Temptation:** Charles H. Spurgeon, *Spurgeon's Sermons on the Sermon on the Mount*, ed. Al Bryant (Eugene, OR: Wipf & Stock, 2017), 94–95, 102. Thomas à Kempis, *The Imitation of Christ*, trans. Aloysius Croft and Harold Bolton (Mineola, NY: Dover Publications, 2012), 10–11. N. T. Wright, *The Lord and His Prayer* (Grand Rapids, MI: Wm B. Eerdmans Publishing Company, 1996), 50, 54–57. Reprinted by permission of the publisher. All rights reserved.

38. **Deliver Us:** Earl F. Palmer, *The Enormous Exception* (Waco, TX: Word Books, 1986), 92–99. Pope Benedict XVI, *Jesus of Nazareth* (San Francisco, CA: Ignatius Press, 2007), 163–164. Romano Guardini, *The Lord's Prayer* (Manchester, NH: Sophia Institute Press, 1986), 90–93.

Part IV: Kingdom Priorities

39. **Lasting Treasures:** John Wesley, "Sermon 28 – Upon Our Lord's Sermon on the Mount: Discourse Eight" in *The Sermons of John Wesley*, 1872 edition, ed. Thomas Jackson, Wesley Center Online, wesley.nnu.edu. Basil the Great, Homily 6, in *Wealth and Poverty in Early Christianity*, ed. Helen Rhee (Minneapolis, MN: Fortress Press, 2017), 57, 59–60. Clement of Alexandria, *The Instructor*, II.3, II.8, III.6, trans. William Wilson, in *Ante-Nicene Fathers*, vol. 2, ed. Alexander Roberts, James Donaldson, and A. Cleveland Coxe (Buffalo, NY: Christian Literature

Publishing Co., 1885). A. W. Tozer, *The Pursuit of God* (Harrisburg, PA: Christian Publications, 1948), 22, 29–30.

40. **The Good Eye:** Timothy Keller, "Treasure versus Money," sermon preached May 2, 1999, published in *Preaching Today* (August 2005).

41. **God or Mammon:** Eberhard Arnold, *Salt and Light* (Farmington, PA: Plough Publishing House, 2002), 61–67. Jacques Ellul, *Money and Power* (Downers Grove, IL: InterVarsity Press, 1984), 75–76, 83–84. David Bentley Hart, "Christ's Rabble," *Commonweal*, October 7, 2016.

42. **Beyond Worry:** Madame Guyon (Jeanne-Marie Bouvier de La Motte Guyon), *A Short and Easy Method of Prayer* (London: H. R. Allenson, Ltd., 1905), 21–22. Christoph Friedrich Blumhardt, *Action in Waiting* (Rifton, NY: Plough Publishing House, 2012), 141. Clarence Jordan, *Sermon on the Mount* (Valley Forge: Judson Press, 1970), 96–98. Copyright © 1952 by Judson Press. Used by permission of Judson Press. Christina Rossetti, "Consider the Lilies of the Field," from *Goblin Market, The Prince's Progress and Other Poems* (London: Macmillan 1879). Howard Thurman, *The Search for Common Ground* (Richmond, IN: Friends United Press, 1986), 26–28.

43. **God's Kingdom First:** Leonhard Ragaz, *Signs of the Kingdom*, ed. and trans. Paul Bock (Grand Rapids, MI: Wm. B. Eerdmans Publishing Company, 1984), 28–31. Reprinted by permission of the publisher. All rights reserved. Christoph Friedrich Blumhardt, *Everyone Belongs to God* (Walden, NY: Plough Publishing House, 2015), 1–9.

44. **Judging Others:** Fyodor Dostoyevsky, *The Brothers Karamazov*, trans. Constance Garnett (New York: Macmillan, 1912), 342. Anthony de Mello, *The Way to Love* (New York: Image Books, 1995), 118–121. Christena Cleveland, *Disunity in Christ* (Downers Grove, IL: IVP Books, 2013), 11–16. Roy Hession, *The Calvary Road* (London: Christian Literature Crusade, 1950), 21.

45. **Casting Pearls:** Dallas Willard, *The Divine Conspiracy* (New York: Harper San Francisco, 1998), 228–230. Copyright © 1998 by Dallas Willard. Used by permission of HarperCollins Publishers. Jacques Ellul, *Presence of the Kingdom* (Colorado Springs, CO: Helmers & Howard, 1989), 116–118.

46. **Ask, Seek, Knock:** Andrew Murray, *With Christ in the School of Prayer* (New York: Fleming H. Revell, 1895), 33–38.

47. **The Golden Rule:** Roger L. Shinn, *The Sermon on the Mount* (Nashville: Abingdon Press, 1962), ch. 12. John Wesley, *The Sermon on the Mount* (Alachua, FL: Bridge Logos, 2010), 255–256. Leo Tolstoy, *The Kingdom*

of God Is Within You, trans. Constance Garnett. (London: William Heinemann, 1894), 118–119.

48. **Two Ways:** The Didache, *The Apostolic Fathers*, third edition, ed. and trans. Michael W. Holmes (Grand Rapids, MI: Baker Academic, 2007), 345–353. C. S. Lewis, *Mere Christianity* (New York: HarperOne: 2001), 195–201. Copyright © 1942, 1943, 1944, 1952 by C. S. Lewis Pte. Ltd. Extracts reprinted by permission. Dietrich Bonhoeffer, *The Cost of Discipleship*, trans. Reginald H. Fuller (London: SCM Press, 1959), 170. Copyright © 1959 by SCM Press Ltd. All rights reserved. Reprinted with the permission of Scribner, a division of Simon & Schuster, Inc., and of Hymns Ancient and Modern Ltd. The Shepherd of Hermas, *The Apostolic Fathers*, third edition, ed. and trans. Michael W. Holmes (Grand Rapids, MI: Baker Academic, 2007), 549–551.

49. **False Prophets:** Scot McKnight, *Sermon on the Mount* (Grand Rapids, MI: Zondervan, 2013), 268–271. Copyright © 2013 by Scot McKnight. Used by permission of Zondervan. John R. W. Stott, *Christian Counter-Culture* (Downers Grove, IL: InterVarsity Press, 1978), 199. Reproduced with permission of Inter-Varsity Press, Ltd. through PLSclear. Gene L. Davenport, *Into the Darkness* (Nashville, TN: Abingdon Press, 1988), 285–286. Copyright © 1988 by Abingdon Press. Used by permission. All rights reserved. Basilea Schlink, *You Will Never Be the Same* (Minneapolis, MN: Dimension Books, 1972), 72–73.

50. **Lord, Lord:** George MacDonald, "The Truth in Jesus," in *Unspoken Sermons Second Series* (London: Longmans, Green & Co., 1885). Wendell Berry, *Blessed Are the Peacemakers* (Berkeley, CA: Counterpoint, 2005), 51–54.

51. **Building on Rock:** Jarrett Banks, "The First Mile," *A Movement of Selfless Love* (blog), February 19, 2017. Oswald Chambers, *Studies in the Sermon on the Mount* (Grand Rapids, MI: Discovery House Publishers, 1995), 105–106. Copyright © 1995 by Oswald Chambers Publications Assn., Ltd. and used by permission of Our Daily Bread Publishing, Grand Rapids MI 49501. All rights reserved.

52. **Our Final Authority:** Søren Kierkegaard, *Practice in Christianity*, trans. Howard V. Hong and Edna H. Hong (Princeton, NJ: Princeton University Press, 1991), 237–252. Dietrich Bonhoeffer, *The Cost of Discipleship*, trans. Reginald H. Fuller (London: SCM Press, 1959), 175–176. Copyright © 1959 by SCM Press Ltd. All rights reserved. Reprinted with the permission of Scribner, a division of Simon & Schuster, Inc., and of Hymns Ancient and Modern Ltd.

Index of Authors

Lewis, C. S. (1898–1963) 229, 305
British novelist and Christian apologist.

Lubich, Chiara (1920–2008) 152, 209
Italian founder of the Focolare Movement.

Luther, Martin (1483–1546) 175
Seminal leader of the Protestant Reformation.

MacDonald, George (1824–1905) 104, 316
Scottish Congregational minister turned novelist.

Manning, Brennan (1934–2013) 61
American author, laicized priest, and public speaker.

Mathewes-Green, Frederica (1952–) 38, 221
Eastern Orthodox writer.

McKnight, Scot (1953–) 126, 310
New Testament scholar and historian of early Christianity.

Merton, Thomas (1915–1968) 60, 66, 128
Trappist monk, bestselling author, and contemplative.

Meyer, F. B. (1847–1929) 100, 217
English Baptist evangelist involved in inner city mission work.

Moltmann, Jürgen (1926–) 89, 150
German Protestant theologian.

Moore, Charles E. (1956–) . . . . *xiii,* 52, 74
Writer, teacher, and pastor in the Bruderhof community.

Murray, Andrew (1828–1917) 181, 291
South African Dutch Reformed minister and mission organizer.

Nouwen, Henri J. M. (1932–1996) 6, 104
Dutch Catholic priest, spiritual writer, and member of L'Arche.

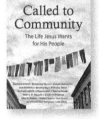

If you liked *Following the Call*
you should have the companion volume . . .

378 pages, softcover,
5.5 x 8 $18.00

Called to Community

The Life Jesus Wants for His People

I am certain that
contained in this book
is the future of
being Christian.

Stanley Hauerwas,
from the foreword

Eberhard Arnold • Benedict • Dietrich Bonhoeffer •
Joan Chittister • Dorothy Day • Richard J. Foster •
Chiara Lubich • Thomas Merton • Mother Teresa •
Henri J. M. Nouwen • John M. Perkins •
Jonathan Wilson-Hartgrove • and others

Edited by Charles E. Moore

Increasingly, Christians want to follow Christ together in
daily life. From every corner of society, they are responding to
Christ's call to share their lives more fully with others. As they
take the plunge, they are discovering the rich, meaningful life
that Jesus has in mind for all people, and pointing the church
back to its original calling: to be a gathered, united community
that demonstrates the transforming love of God.

Of course, community isn't easy. The selections in this volume
are, by and large, written by practitioners – people who have
pioneered life in intentional community and have discovered in
the nitty-gritty of daily life what it takes to establish and sustain a
Christian community over the long haul.

Whether you have just begun thinking about communal
living, are already embarking on a shared life with others, or
have been part of a community for many years, the pieces in this
collection will encourage, challenge, and strengthen you.

**The book's fifty-two chapters can be read weekly
to ignite meaningful group discussion.**

Other Titles from Plough

Salt and Light: Living the Sermon on the Mount
Eberhard Arnold
Thoughts on the "hard teachings" of Jesus and their applicability today

God's Revolution: Justice, Community, and the Coming Kingdom
Eberhard Arnold
Topically arranged excerpts from talks and writings on the church, family, government, world suffering, and more

Watch for the Light: Readings for Advent and Christmas
Dietrich Bonhoeffer, Annie Dillard, Thomas Merton, C. S. Lewis, and others
Selections from some of the world's greatest spiritual writers provide inspiration for the most widely celebrated holiday of the year.

Bread and Wine: Readings for Lent and Easter
Wendell Berry, Dorothy Sayers, Henri J. M. Nouwen, G. K. Chesterton, and others
"Has there ever been a more hard-hitting, beautifully written, theologically inclusive anthology of writings for Lent and Easter? It's doubtful." —*Publishers Weekly*

Evening Prayers: For Every Day of the Year
Christoph Friedrich Blumhardt
These faith-filled prayers will help you turn to God and feel his nearness at the end of every day.

Plough Publishing House
845-572-3455 • info@plough.com • **www.plough.com**

151 Bowne Drive, PO Box 398, Walden, NY 12586, USA
Robertsbridge, East Sussex TN32 5DR, UK
4188 Gwydir Highway, Elsmore, NSW 2360, Australia